The Full Story of the World's Favourite Sportscar

– Brian Long –

VELOCE PUBLISHING
THE PUBLISHER OF FINE AUTOMOTIVE BOOKS

Colour Family Album Series
Alfa Romeo by Andrea & David Sparrow
Bubblecars & Microcars by Andrea & David Sparrow
Bubblecars & Microcars, More by Andrea & David Sparrow
Citroen 2CV by Andrea & David Sparrow
Citroen DS by Andrea & David Sparrow
Custom VWs by Andrea & David Sparrow
Fiat & Abarth 500 & 600 by Andrea & David Sparrow
Lambretta by Andrea & David Sparrow
Mini & Mini Cooper by Andrea & David Sparrow
Motor Scooters by Andrea & David Sparrow
Porsche by Andrea & David Sparrow
Triumph Sportscars by Andrea & David Sparrow
Vespa by Andrea & David Sparrow
VW Beetle by Andrea & David Sparrow
VW Bus, Camper, Van & Pick-up by Andrea & David Sparrow
VW Custom Beetle by Andrea & David Sparrow

SpeedPro Series
How to Blueprint & Build a 4-Cylinder Engine Short Block for High
  Performance by Des Hammill
How to Build a V8 Engine Short Block for High Performance
  by Des Hammill
How to Plan and Build a Fast Road Car by Daniel Stapleton
How to Build & Modify Sportscar/Kitcar Suspension & Brakes
  by Des Hammill
How to Build & Modify SU Carburettors for High Performance
  by Des Hammill
How to Build & Power Tune Weber DCOE & Dellorto DHLA Carburetors
  Second Edition by Des Hammill
How to Build & Power Tune Harley-Davidson Evolution Engines
  by Des Hammill
How to Build & Power Tune Distributor-type Ignition Systems
  by Des Hammill
How to Build, Modify & Power Tune Cylinder Heads Second Edition
  by Peter Burgess
How to Build Your Own Tiger Avon Sportscar by Jim Dudley
How to Choose Camshafts & Time them for Maximum Power
  by Des Hammill
How to Give your MGB V8 Power Updated & Revised Edition
  by Roger Williams
How to Improve the MGB, MGC & MGB V8 by Roger Williams
How to Modify Volkswagen Beetle Chassis, Suspension & Brakes for High
Performance by James Hale
How to Power Tune Mini Engines on a Small Budget by Des Hammill
How to Power Tune the BMC 998cc A-Series Engine by Des Hammill
How to Power Tune BMC/Rover 1275cc A-Series Engines
  by Des Hammill
How to Power Tune the MGB 4-Cylinder Engine by Peter Burgess
How to Power Tune the MG Midget & Austin-Healey Sprite Updated Edition
  by Daniel Stapleton
How to Power Tune Alfa Romeo Twin Cam Engines by Jim Kartalamakis
How to Power Tune Ford SOHC 'Pinto' & Sierra Cosworth DOHC Engines
  Updated & Revised Edition by Des Hammill
How to Power Tune Jaguar XK Engines by Des Hammill
How to Power Tune Rover V8 Engines by Des Hammill

General
AC Two-litre Saloons & Buckand Sportscars by Leo Archibald
Alfa Romeo Berlinas (Saloons/Sedans) by John Tipler
Alfa Romeo Giulia Coupe GT & GTA by John Tipler
Anatomy of the Works Minis by Brian Moylan
Automotive A-Z, Lane's Dictionary of Automotive Terms by Keith Lane
Automotive Mascots by David Kay & Lynda Springate
Bentley Continental, Corniche and Azure, by Martin Bennett
BMW 5-Series by Marc Cranswick
BMW Z-Cars by James Taylor
British Cars, The Complete Catalogue of, 1895-1975
  by Culshaw & Horrobin
British Police Cars by Nick Walker
British Trailer Caravans 1919-1959 by Andrew Jenkinson

British Trailer Caravans from 1960 by Andrew Jenkinson
Bugatti Type 40 by Barrie Price
Bugatti 46/50 Updated Edition by Barrie Price
Bugatti 57 2nd Edition - by Barrie Price
Caravanning & Trailer Tenting, the Essential Handbook by Len Archer
Chrysler 300 - America's Most Powerful Car by Robert Ackerson
Cobra - The Real Thing! by Trevor Legate
Cortina - Ford's Bestseller by Graham Robson
Daimler SP250 'Dart' by Brian Long
Datsun/Nissan 280ZX & 300ZX by Brian Long
Datsun Z - From Fairlady to 280Z by Brian Long
Dune Buggy Handbook by James Hale
Fiat & Abarth 124 Spider & Coupe by John Tipler
Fiat & Abarth 500 & 600 by Malcolm Bobbitt
Ford F100/F150 Pick-up by Robert Ackerson
Ford GT40 by Trevor Legate
Ford Model Y by Sam Roberts
Harley-Davidson, Growing up by Jean Davidson
Jaguar XJ-S, by Brian Long
Karmann-Ghia Coupe & Convertible by Malcolm Bobbitt
Land Rover, The Half-Ton Military by Mark Cook
Lea-Francis Story, The by Barrie Price
Lexus Story, The by Brian Long
Lola - The Illustrated History (1957-1977) by John Starkey
Lola - All The Sports Racing & Single-Seater Racing Cars 1978-1997
  by John Starkey
Lola T70 - The Racing History & Individual Chassis Record 3rd Edition
  by John Starkey
Lotus 49 by Michael Oliver
Mazda MX-5/Miata 1.6 Enthusiast's Workshop Manual
  by Rod Grainger & Pete Shoemark
Mazda MX-5/Miata 1.8 Enthusiast's Workshop Manual
  by Rod Grainger & Pete Shoemark
Mazda MX-5 (& Eunos Roadster) - The World's Favourite Sportscar
  by Brian Long
MGA by John Price Williams
MGB & MGB GT - Expert Guide (Auto-Doc Series) by Roger Williams
Mini Cooper - The Real Thing! by John Tipler
Mitsubishi Lancer Evo by Brian Long
Motor Racing at Goodwood in the Sixties by Tony Gardiner
MR2 - Toyota's Mid-engined Sports Car by Brian Long
Porsche 356 by Brian Long
Porsche 911R, RS & RSR, 4th Ed. by John Starkey
Porsche 914 & 914-6 by Brian Long
Porsche 924 by Brian Long
Porsche 944 by Brian Long
Rolls-Royce Silver Shadow/Bentley T Series Corniche & Camargue Updated
  Edition by Malcolm Bobbitt
Rolls-Royce Silver Spirit, Silver Spur & Bentley Mulsanne
  by Malcolm Bobbitt
Rolls-Royce Silver Wraith, Dawn & Cloud/Bentley MkVI, R & S Series
  by Martyn Nutland
RX-7 - Mazda's Rotary Engine Sportscar by Brian Long
Singer Story: Cars, Commercial Vehicles, Bicycles & Motorcycles
  by Kevin Atkinson
Taxi! The Story of the 'London' Taxicab by Malcolm Bobbitt
Triumph Motorcycles & the Meriden Factory by Hughie Hancox
Triumph Tiger Cub Bible by Mike Estall
Triumph Trophy Bible by Harry Woolridge
Triumph TR2/3/3A, How to Restore, by Roger Williams
Triumph TR4/4A, How to Restore, by Roger Williams
Triumph TR5/250 & 6, How to Restore, by Roger Williams
Triumph TR6 by William Kimberley
Turner's Triumphs, Edward Turner & his Triumph Motorcycles
  by Jeff Clew
Velocette Motorcycles - MSS to Thruxton by Rod Burris
Volkswagens of the World by Simon Glen
VW Beetle Cabriolet by Malcolm Bobbitt
VW Beetle - The Car of the 20th Century by Richard Copping
VW Bus, Camper, Van, Pickup by Malcolm Bobbitt
Works Rally Mechanic by Brian Moylan

First published in 2002 by Veloce Publishing Ltd., 33 Trinity Street, Dorchester, DT1 1TT, England. Fax: 01305 268864/e-mail: info@veloce.co.uk/
website: www.veloce.co.uk.
ISBN 1-903706-21-1/UPC: 36847-00221-3 (MX-5 edition), 1-903706-51-3/36847-00251-0 (Miata edition)
© 2002 Brian Long and Veloce Publishing Ltd.
Readers with ideas for automotive books, or books on other transport or related hobby subjects, are invited to write to Veloce Publishing at the above
address.
British Library Cataloguing in Publication Data - A catalogue record for this book is available from the British Library.
Typesetting (Bookman), design and page make-up all by Veloce on AppleMac. Printed and bound in the EC.

www.veloce.co.uk

CONTENTS

www.velocebooks.com

FOREWORD

Mazda has its own theory for developing a fun-to-drive sports car. It is a basic concept that focuses on vehicle features such as 50:50 weight distribution, keeping yaw inertia moment and weight to a minimum, and the centre of gravity as low as possible.

The many engineers who have worked on the MX-5 over the years have always kept these principles in mind. It sounds like a simple theory to follow. However, realizing it is a challenge which requires great energy.

It was in 1986 that I first became involved with the MX-5 project; at that time, I worked as a chassis engineer. I remember discussing this theory with Toshihiko Hirai, who was the Program Manager at the time. With Mr Hirai as a leader, our engineers worked together to implement it in the initial development stages.

The devotion of these men and women produced an automobile with global customer appeal. The first generation MX-5 achieved approximately 450,000 sales, and was loved by sports car enthusiasts all over the world. The fun and excitement associated with the MX-5 drive experience come as a direct result of us practicing those three basic concepts.

Throughout the Roadster's history, we have focused on maintaining this theory. When I was appointed the MX-5 Program Manager, I was determined to make a superior car without harming the model's excellent reputation in the LWS sector of the market. I wanted to keep Mazda's basic sports car principles, making sure they would be inherited by future engineers in order to truly serve our customers.

During the development of the second generation car, there was one thing that was engraved on my mind - to first define what should not be changed. The term 'Full Model Change' sometimes lures us to change what does not necessarily have to be. We have learned from previous updates that the basic virtues of a vehicle are all too often spoilt for the sake of change. It sometimes ruins the product.

I strongly believe that we had to maintain the true essence of the MX-5, and felt that the key lay in the very soul of the Mazda Roadster. Eventually, we came to the conclusion that a lot of the fun one experiences from driving the MX-5 was down to the car's nimbleness. Thus, it should remain light - a true LWS.

We do not have to change what does not need to be changed. However, weight increases are now an unavoidable issue in order to comply with the latest collision and emission regulations. I recognized that the most important thing was to offset this additional weight.

Over the years, we have received many requests to make the interior more spacious; calls for additional comfort equipment (such as the installation of tilt-steering, adding more adjustment

Kijima-san with the author,
September 2001.

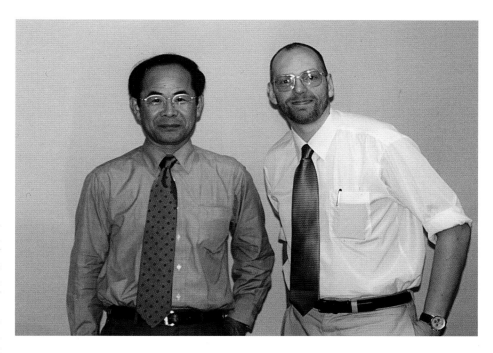

on the seats, upgrading to an electrically-operated soft-top, and so on) and, of course, power increases. We considered all of these wishes, but ultimately concluded that we should not make a bigger or heavier car.

Ironically, the decision not to change the size of the vehicle has become the hardest part of my work to execute. It is a challenge for me to repress the desire to address every request. However, I must focus on keeping faith in the LWS' true value. On the other hand, it is also a challenge not to fall into the same rut as the original lightweight sports models, which were left behind because their makers failed to understand what the customers wanted.

More than 150,000 units of the second generation MX-5 have now been sold to enthusiastic customers all over the world. There have been

so many reasons for change. However, I believe our decision not to change the vehicle size was the right one.

I would like to take this opportunity to offer my sincere thanks to the global customer base that has supported the MX-5. Without your generous support, the MX-5 could not have achieved the success that it has today.

Your enthusiasm has been a tremendous source of energy for us - the engineers - making it easy for us to develop the MX-5 with

confidence and pride. Your continuous support for the Mazda marque and its products is highly appreciated.

Finally, I would like to give a special thank you to Brian Long for his great efforts in writing this book for followers of MX-5 lore. I hope you will enjoy it.

Takao Kijima
MX-5 Program Manager
Mazda Co. Ltd.
Hiroshima, Japan

PREFACE

I have to admit, I wasn't always a great fan of Mazda. Then, in 1991, my great friend, Simon Pickford, and I, travelled down to Le Mans in his ageing Daimler SP250 to see our beloved Jaguars thrash the opposition as they had in the previous year.

During the race, we had commented on the glorious exhaust note of a striking green and orange machine that kept bombing around, lap after lap, but never gave it much attention. However, the Big Cats were beaten and, at the end of the 24 hours, it was this car - a Mazda - that was declared the winner. From that moment on, I had to respect the Mazda marque, as it had proved itself in the world's toughest form of competition.

Shortly afterwards, I met Miho, the Japanese girl who would later become my wife, and began to spend a lot of time in Japan. This sparked off a real interest in the Japanese motor industry, with Toyota and Nissan sports cars becoming a pet subject. We also visited a number of Mazda tuners, and I fell for the rotary-engined RX-7 in a big way - a fast and complex Grand Tourer, it was my kind of car.

When Rod Grainger of Veloce asked me if I would write the history of the MX-5, I must say I had my doubts. With a 1968 Alfa Romeo 1750 Spider Veloce in the garage, the little Mazda had never really appealed to me. But, because of my admiration for the RX-7, I took on the project, hoping in the back of my mind that if I did the MX-5 book first, maybe Rod would ask me to do a volume on the RX-7 later.

My neutral attitude towards the project has doubtless helped, for as I started my research in the autumn of 1997, I was able to see how thorough Mazda had been and the real enthusiasm behind the concept, without falling into the trap of getting carried away by the myth and hysteria that seems to surround all cult cars.

Personally, I hate to read a book written by someone who obviously loves the car he or she is writing about, for they are rarely able to find or see faults, or even want to go looking for them in the first place. However, I have to admit, even from my standpoint, that I didn't find many shortcomings. Originally dismissing the MX-5 as too contrived, too clinical, I now have a great deal of respect for the vehicle and the people behind it, and can see why the MX-5 has gained hoards of fans all over the world.

Brian Long
Chiba, Japan

6

INTRODUCTION, ACKNOWLEDGEMENTS & NOTES ON THIS SECOND EDITION

Introduction

When the Mazda MX-5 was launched in 1989, it took the world by storm. Journalists from all corners of the world ran out of superlatives - nothing had created such a strong impression since the first appearance of the Datsun 240Z. Mazda introduced its inexpensive convertible - which had all the fun of older machines without the hassle - at just the right time. As many contemporary commentators stated, Mazda had reinvented the sports car.

Before long, the MX-5 (also known as the Miata and Eunos Roadster, depending on the market) had gained a reputation that was the envy of the motor industry. The team in Hiroshima was not prepared to rest on its laurels, though, and brought out special versions and a whole series of stunning prototypes. By the end of 1997, the best part of 450,000 examples had been built, and a mini-industry for aftermarket parts had grown up around the vehicle in virtually every country in which it was sold.

At the 1997 Tokyo Show, Mazda unveiled the Second Generation MX-5. Although it looked similar to its predecessor, it incorporated a whole host of improvements and, despite some new competition from MG and a string of other manufacturers, seemed set to keep the MX-5 as the most popular sports car on the market.

In a bid to counter the threat posed by a never-ending stream of new open cars, in the summer of 2000, Mazda gave the model a facelift, with more power and some subtle styling refinements for the body and the interior. Thankfully, enthusiasm for the little Roadster still runs as high as ever.

Acknowledgements

A book is never just the work of one person. Firstly, I must thank my wife for her hour-upon-hour of translation work, and subsequent marathon sessions at the typewriter. Without Miho, the book would be missing the Japanese angle almost completely, and the importance of the home market should never be overlooked.

At Mazda in Japan, I would like to acknowledge the help of Tamotsu Maeda and Kensaku Terasaki, and reserve a special thank you for Mayumi Handa - by now, she must dread every fax that comes in from abroad! Having pestered so many of the staff, including Shunji Tanaka and Koichi Hayashi, I sincerely hope that the team in Japan is pleased with the results.

I would also like to thank Mazda in America, particularly Brian Betz and Ellen Clark, Takahiro Tokura of Mazdaspeed, Mazda UK, and Bill Livingstone and Alan Beasley of IAD. In addition, many thanks to the various companies which supplied material, such as VeilSide, KG Works, Moss, and so on, plus the many shops that provided me with old brochures.

Behind the scenes, Michitake Isobe (a fellow author and translator), was a great help, as was another friend of ours, Sachiko 'Miko' Miyoshi. There was also Kenji Kikuchi of Nigensha (Car Graphic); Ian Robertson - a Sales Executive at Coventry Mazda, and a true MX-5 enthusiast, who put up with my many requests; Paul Grogan of the MX-5 Owners Club, who was kind enough to help with historical material and read the proof for me, and Peter Hunter - as usual, a mine of information on all things Japanese.

Notes on the second edition
It is perhaps ironic that, after reading my book, one reviewer stated it was a shame that it was written by someone who obviously loved the MX-5. The person in question obviously didn't read my Preface, but I can see why he jumped to that conclusion. The reality, of course, is that contemporary reports were so complimentary, when I have quoted them it looks as if I am giving a one-sided account. Not so: there was simply so little negative prose.

Since the original book was published, I have to admit that I've caught the MX-5 bug. When the new 160bhp model came out in Japan, I ordered one on the first day of sales, joined the RCOJ, and became friends with many more Mazda people, largely following my research for the RX-7 volume that I did eventually get to do for Rod.

However, as a historian, I will do my upmost to keep a neutral attitude whilst revising and updating this latest edition.

In addition to those who were kind enough to help last time, I would like to give the following people a special mention. Takaharu Kobayakawa is an extraordinary man, and it is with great pride that I am able to call him a friend. Over the years, he has done so much for the Mazda marque, among other things, orchestrating that historic Le Mans victory in 1991. If we talk about it, he will often say: "Did you see it? Oh, yes. Of course you were there. You were waving a Jaguar flag ...!"

Tom Matano wrote me a very special letter after the first book was published. It is something I shall treasure, and I want to thank him for his help on this project. Takao Kijima was also quick to react to my efforts, and it is a great pleasure to have a Foreword from this engineering genius. Masanori Mizuochi has also been very kind. Along with Hirotaka Tachibana, he filled me in with more detail on the M2 side: he also put me in touch with Shigenori Fukuda, who spent a lot of his spare time to confirm statements made in the text - I'm extremely grateful for the help and enthusiasm shown by all these legendary Mazda figures.

Meanwhile, the delightful Mayumi Handa has escaped to another department, so it is now Ryota Ogawa who has to put up with my many requests. Ogawa-san, your help on this book - and the RX-7 project - is very much appreciated. I would also like to thank Jim Bright, now stationed out here in Japan, and Jennifer Newton at the Mazda Information Bureau in the States.

Finally, the back cover features the work of another good friend of mine, Yoshihiro Inomoto. His superb drawing of the first generation model shows why he is known throughout the world as 'The Cutaway King'.

**Brian Long
Chiba, Japan**

1

A BRIEF HISTORY OF MAZDA

The history of the Japanese motor industry is a complex one, moulded and shaped by government decisions taken in the early 1930s and the reconstruction of Japan following the Second World War.

Mazda's origins date back to January 1920, with the founding of the Toyo Cork Kogyo Company Ltd by Jujiro Matsuda. As the name suggests, the Hiroshima-based firm initially concerned itself with cork products, but in the following year, Matsuda decided to move into the manufacture of machinery.

Matsuda was born in August 1875, and, despite being brought up in the fishing trade, developed an early interest in metalworking. By the age of 19 he had his own business; sadly, destined to fail. After various other enterprises, Matsuda eventually decided to move into the supply of cork, as the First World War stopped exports from Europe and left Japan in short supply. When Europe started exporting again, Matsuda guided the company back into light industry.

The car was still not a popular means of transport for the Japanese at that time. In the early 1920s, there were still fewer than 15,000 vehicles in the country, so automobile production was not considered commercially viable. However, a few two-wheeled machines were built following the devastating Kanto earthquake of 1923.

That year brought a flurry of

Jujiro Matsuda - entrepreneur and founder of the Mazda marque.

imported trucks and buses from the United States to get the country mobile again. Most of Japan's population was centred around the Tokyo Bay (Kanto) area, and the earthquake had totally destroyed thousands of buildings, and most of the communications in Tokyo and Yokohama. Matsuda's Hiroshima-based concern, on the

The first vehicle to bear the Mazda name was a three-wheeled truck. Commercials of this type were built throughout the 1930s.

other side of the country, was not affected, and did its best to ease transport problems by building small two-stroke motorcycles.

Although the firm still dealt in cork (this section of the business wasn't sold off until 1944), light industry became increasingly important. In line with this gradual shift in emphasis, in July 1927, the business was renamed the Toyo Kogyo Co. Ltd, which roughly translates as the Orient Industry Company.

The Mazda marque

Production of Toyo machine tools began in 1929, but, by 1930, thoughts were already turning toward motor vehicles. Design work was initiated on a three-wheeled truck (the 482cc Mazda DA), which entered production in October 1931.

As an aside, there is an interesting story behind the choice of the Mazda name. In Persian mythology, the "lord of light and wisdom" was called Ahura Mazdah. The Mazdah title sounded good in almost any language and had an ideal meaning, with the added bonus that the founder's family name was Matsuda (in Japanese, it sounds very similar to Mazdah). Subsequently, the letter 'h' was dropped and the Mazda marque was born.

The DA was a great success,

and, within a few months of starting production, Toyo Kogyo began exporting the three-wheeled Mazda to Manchuria, an area of China occupied by Japan. Toyo Kogyo continued to develop the three-wheeler, giving it a larger engine, and also started to manufacture gauge blocks and machine drills.

The company's capital increased no fewer than four times during 1934, and the factory - based in the Fuchu area of Hiroshima - was duly enlarged. However, military considerations soon led the government to pass the 1936 Motorcar Manufacturing Enterprise Law. Although only Nissan, Toyota and Isuzu complied with the new law at the time, it effectively ended the activities of foreign car companies, with both Ford and General Motors initially cutting back production and then closing their factories in Japan during 1937.

Toyo Kogyo was forced to make munitions for the Army, although a few three-wheelers continued to leave the factory, despite the Enterprise Law. By 1940, Mazda had built a small prototype coupé, but before it could be developed further, production switched completely to armaments in the build-up to the Pacific War.

After the attack on Pearl Harbour, America declared war on Japan, but no-one could have

foreseen the dreadful events that would follow. On 6 August 1945, Hiroshima became a scene of complete devastation. A broadcast from Tokyo Radio stated: "Most of Hiroshima no longer exists. The impact of the bomb was so terrific that practically all living things, human and animal, were literally seared to death by the tremendous heat and pressure engendered by the blast." The Toyo Kogyo factory, partially sheltered by a hill, was just far enough away from the centre of the blast to escape heavy damage. Sadly, though, the bomb dropped by *Enola Gay* claimed 78,000 lives and injured countless others. The end of the Second World War came later that month, but it was many years before some kind of normality was restored to the lives of those - on both sides - who suffered as a result of the conflict.

Post-war growth

Although the factory was being used as a makeshift hospital and 'town hall', Toyo Kogyo managed to resume production of the Mazda three-wheelers at the end of 1945. Three years later, the company's capital had doubled, and up to 200 vehicles were being built each week. Larger commercials were announced in 1950, but it was another decade before the company moved into the passenger car business.

Various laws were passed to help the Japanese motor industry, and gradually it found its feet.

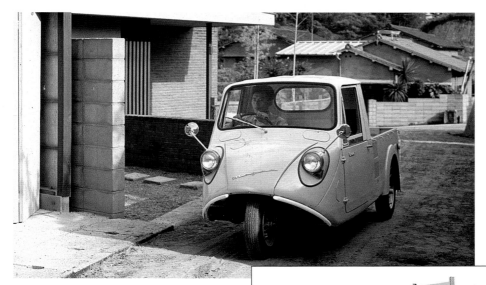

A rare contemporary colour photograph of the K360 three-wheeler, built shortly after the Second World War.

Mazda's three-wheeler acquired a more substantial appearance with the arrival of the CT series in 1950 (this is the 1953 CTA). Three-wheelers continued well into the 1960s, the T2000 of 1962 vintage having a two-ton load carrying capacity.

Production rose steadily, new roads were built, and Tokyo streets began to fill with Japanese cars rather than ageing imported models. Steel and components were being produced in Japan, as by now most of the factories had been returned to their previous owners by the Occupational Forces, thus lessening the need to buy from foreign countries.

Commercial vehicles continued to sustain the Hiroshima concern, but, in April 1960, the company introduced its first car - the R360 Coupé. It went on sale in May with an air-cooled, V-twin engine mounted at the rear; although the 356cc unit developed only 16bhp, the R360 could be bought with either a manual or automatic transmission and was capable of 56mph (90kph). It sold exceptionally well, with over 20,000 being built in the first year.

After the war, a number of Japanese manufacturers had taken the opportunity to enter into technical co-operation agreements with companies in the west. The Toyo Kogyo concern was quite late in taking up this offer, but eventually, in mid-1961, signed a deal with NSU of Germany.

NSU held the rights to the Wankel rotary engine, a rather

The first Mazda car was the R360 Coupé of mid-1960, powered by a tiny air-cooled V-twin. Over 20,000 examples were sold in the first year of production.

advanced piece of engineering. It was felt that being the first vehicle builder in Japan to acquire this technology would enable Mazda to catch up with the likes of Nissan and Toyota, thus ensuring its survival.

Over the next five years, while the rotary engine was being developed, Toyo Kogyo introduced a number of new Mazda cars - the Carol P360 and P600, the first generation of Familia models, and the Luce 1500. (The coachwork on the latter was designed by a famous Italian styling house; in fact, Giugiaro has been credited with the design during his time with Bertone.)

Meanwhile, cumulative production of cars and commercials reached one million units in March 1963; two years later, the Miyoshi Proving Ground was completed. By this time, Toyo Kogyo was the third largest car producer in Japan, continually expanding operations

at a staggering rate. In 1966, a new passenger car plant opened in Hiroshima, and, in the following year, full-scale exports for the European market began.

The rotary revolution

Toyo Kogyo - under the leadership of Jujiro Matsuda's son, Tsuneji, since 1951 - was certainly a forward-thinking organisation, installing its first computer system at Hiroshima as early as 1958. Six years later, at the 1964 Tokyo Show (held at Harumi that year), the Mazda Cosmo Sport 110S made its debut.

Powered by the company's first Wankel engine, it was extremely advanced, and gave the Rotary Engine Development Division more

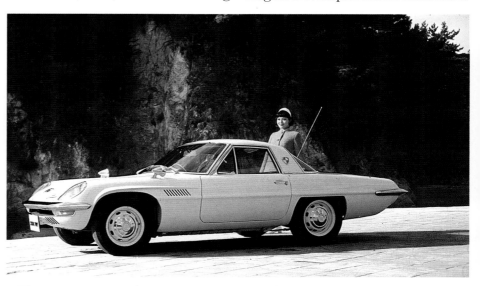

The rotary-engined Cosmo Sport 110S of 1967. Around 350 of these early models were built before the Cosmo underwent a minor facelift in mid-1968. Its high price tag limited total sales to just over 1500 units over a six year production run.

A British advertisement dating from March 1970 for the Mazda R100 Coupé. Known in Japan as the Familia Rotary Coupé, it was also sold in the United States, but acquired round headlights for that market.

1967, by which time the company's engineers had perfected the power unit. Selling at 1,580,000 yen, it was very costly (only the Toyota 2000GT was more expensive in the sports car sector of the Japanese market), and this was reflected in a total run, from 1967 to 1972, of just 1519 units.

In October 1969, the Japan Automatic Transmission Company (JATCO) was formed; a joint venture between Toyo Kogyo, Ford and Nissan for the manufacture of automatic gearboxes. The rotary engine passed Federal tests that year, and exports to the United States began shortly afterwards. The first cars - with both rotary and more conventional powerplants appearing in the line-up - arrived there in the spring of 1970. Within a year, Mazda dealerships were selling vehicles before they even

than a few teething problems in the early days. It underwent an extraordinary period of development before going on sale to the public, with a total of 60 pre-production models road tested. Consequently, the Mazda Cosmo did not go on sale until 30 May

The elegant lines of the Luce Rotary Coupé - a pillarless two-door model based on the Luce 1500 saloon.

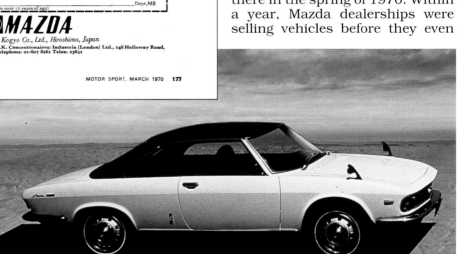

13

The home market Savanna GT of 1972, better known abroad as the RX-3. Like the RX-2 (which was also rotary-engined), it came as an attractive coupé (as seen here) or with four-door saloon bodywork. An estate version augmented the RX-3 range.

had time to unload them from the transporters.

Following the death of Tsuneji Matsuda in November 1970 (he was 74), the reins were passed to his son, Kohei, the third generation of the Matsuda family to head the company. There was a whole string of important introductions during the early 1970s: the Mazda Capella (RX-2) was followed by the Savanna (RX-3) and, in 1972, the Luce (RX-4) made its debut. Mazda cars were now beginning to outsell trucks year after year. By the end of 1972, cumulative production had reached a staggering five million units, and the Mazda Technical Centre had been established in Irvine, California.

The oil crisis held up a number of interesting projects, such as the X020G 2+2 coupé. Rotary units, some rated up to 200bhp, were being prepared, but the timing, sadly, was all wrong, and sales of rotary-engined models as a whole began to suffer as fuel economy became an overriding consideration with new car buyers. As a result, Toyo Kogyo soon ran into financial troubles and had to turn to the Sumitomo Bank for help to keep the business afloat. The company eventually received the bank's backing, but the Matsuda family lost some of its power in the process.

The RX-7 Savanna

1977 saw the introduction of the Familia (the original GLC/323,

Opposite: The RX-7 was an instant hit in Britain. Tom Walkinshaw won his class in one in the BTCC in 1979, whilst Win Percy took the Championship outright with the RX-7 in 1980 and 1981. Walkinshaw had prepared Percy's car, and these are TWR-modified road cars from 1981. From left to right: the front-wheel drive 323, the 626 Coupé, and the RX-7 Turbo.

An official photograph of the 1973 RX-4 Coupé from the UK concessionaires. The era known as the 'Sporting Forties' (1965-1974 in Japanese Emperor years) spawned a number of exciting vehicles from the Land of the Rising Sun.

Although not the most interesting Mazda ever built, the Familia (known as the GLC in America and the 323 elsewhere), with its conventional fuel efficient engine, helped Toyo Kogyo to survive an uncertain period in the company's history. This American advert dates from early 1978.

The Mazda RX-7, seen here in home market Limited form, was immensely popular in America, despite the fuel crisis and unfavourable exchange rates. An excellent competition record in the United States probably helped convince enthusiasts, and the car also received a number of awards in Japan.

powered by a conventional four-stroke engine), which doubtless helped combat the downturn in Mazda sales. However, it was the car launched the following year that was significant to enthusiasts of sporting machinery.

Things were starting to happen in Japan as far as the sports car world was concerned. Nissan had been building the highly-successful Fairlady Z since late 1969, but, during 1978, it took a distinct move upmarket. Mazda had launched the RX-7 (known in Japan as the Savanna) in March 1978, and, in effect, this took the market position of the old Fairlady Z as a cheap but competent sports car, selling for 1,230,000 yen.

As Kohei Matsuda said in late-1977: "A two-seater sports car may well represent the ultimate design compliment for the rotary engine." He was absolutely right. The Mazda marque had already acquired a reputation among motorsport enthusiasts for its sporting machines, but the rotary-engined RX-7 established the Japanese car maker all over the world, and signalled a turnaround in the fortunes of the Wankel power unit.

Of course, the RX-7 was admired on the home market as well, and duly received the 'Japanese Car of the Year' award. However, by the time it was officially

put on sale, Yoshiki Yamasaki had become the head of the company - the first non-Matsuda family member to do so since 1922.

Revival, and links with Ford
Sales started to pick up again after the introduction of the conventionally powered Familia family car and the immensely popular RX-7. Cumulative production reached ten million vehicles in 1979, but, in November that year, Ford acquired a 24.5 per cent equity stake in Mazda. Within three years, Mazda was marketing Ford brand vehicles through its Autorama sales channel in Japan. This arrangement actually worked both ways, as a number of Mazdas (such as the B-series pick-up) had been badged as Fords in the States, and vehicles were later developed jointly on both sides of the Pacific.

In the meantime, 1980 brought with it the introduction of the front-wheel drive Mazda Familia (also known as the GLC or 323 depending on the market). The Familia was presented with the coveted 1980-1981 'Japanese Car of the Year' award, and over one million had been produced by 1982.

As a matter of interest, Japanese manufacturers built seven million vehicles between them during 1980, helping Japan to become the world's number one

car-producing country. Mazda (North America) Inc. - better-known as MANA - was established during 1981, and became a key organisation in the initial stages of the MX-5's development. Despite unfavourable exchange rates, almost 170,000 Mazdas were sold in the States that year, with the GLC being a bestseller in the economy sector, and the facelifted RX-7 appealing to the enthusiasts.

1982 saw the introduction of the fwd Mazda Capella (or 626). It was immediately given the 1982-1983 'Japanese Car of the Year' award in its native country, but it also received a large number of prestigious accolades overseas, including being named *Motor Trend* magazine's 1983 'Import Car of the Year'. Sales in America continued to climb as the Mazda range attracted an ever wider audience.

Toyo Kogyo entered into an 8 per cent capital tie-up with Kia Motors in 1983, and cumulative production reached 15 million units. From a very small beginning, the Mazda marque had grown at great speed, and now had a range of vehicles which could compete in all markets, challenging established manufacturers throughout the world. However, Toyo Kogyo was not yet satisfied with its achievements ...

2

BIRTH OF THE MAZDA ROADSTER

The Toyo Kogyo business was renamed the Mazda Motor Corporation on 1 May 1984, with Kenichi Yamamoto elected President shortly after his 62nd birthday. Born in September 1922, the former MD had served Toyo Kogyo for many years, and had been the company's Chief Engineer since January 1978.

Yamamoto had seen a vast number of changes along the way in both technology (he had been responsible for designing a V-twin engine for the three-wheeled Mazda trucks shortly after the war, and was heavily involved with the R360 and its descendants; he was also one of the key people behind the development of the Mazda rotary engine), and in the growth of the company as a leading car manufacturer. However, behind all of Yamamoto's achievements in the field of engineering was an underlying enthusiasm for his work - an important factor which would have a bearing on the future.

MANA

Mazda (North America) Inc. (or MANA) had a Product Planning & Research (PP&R) arm, which was managed by Shigenori Fukuda. The idea behind this department was that its findings would give Mazda a much better feel for its market, so that future vehicles could be tailored specifically to suit the tastes of different countries.

One of the first Americans to join the PP&R office was Bob Hall,

Kenichi Yamamoto, RJC 'Person of the Year' 1991-92, and a key figure in Mazda's automotive history.

a true car enthusiast with a background in automotive journalism. Hall, having been brought up around British sports cars, was keen on the idea of a modern equivalent. In fact, when casually asked at the end of a meeting with Kenichi Yamamoto in the spring of 1979 (when Hall was still working as a journalist), what he would like to see Toyo Kogyo building, he suggested that Mazda should make a lightweight sports car that would sell at a price even cheaper than the RX-7's.

The MANA team actually drew a diverse range of sports car proposals, but, in reality, it was the lightweight open two-seater that appealed the most.

An original design sketch from Tom Matano, dated March 1984.

A roadster with a detachable hard-top in place. A closed coupé was also investigated, at least on paper.

Another of the design drawings submitted by MANA for its ideal lightweight sports car. According to Fukuda-san, hundreds of sketches were produced, a number of the proposals resembling vehicles like the Morgan three-wheeler, Lotus Seven, and the Porsche 550 Spyder.

On a trip to the 1983 Pebble Beach concours event, Hall soon found he was not alone in this idea. Fukuda, one of the group evaluating the RX-7 in the all-important American market, was asked by Hall what type of car he would like to design next. His reply was "a lightweight sports car." Naturally, this drew quite an eager response, and Hall's Japanese soon turned into excited English. Needless to say, by the end of the journey (after Hall had been stopped for speeding as his enthusiasm grew by the mile), Fukuda-san's English had improved no end!

Not long after this, an appraisal entitled *What is a Sports Car to an American?* was sent through to Head Office. This was quite a lengthy piece, but the most important paragraphs read as follows: "Sports cars must have a degree of performance, but more importantly, they must be fun to drive. A low-cost sports car doesn't need 0.81g lateral acceleration or 0-60 in 8.5 seconds. It has to, as one journalist succintly put it, 'feel faster than it is, but it doesn't have to be fast in absolute terms.' Of course, a sports car musn't be a sluggard either, so it is a classic example of searching for the happy medium.

"Appearance (particularly one's first impression) and performance are obvious things which make a sports car, but there are a couple of intangibles, too. Not the least of these is image. If you look back in

history, all (not some or most, but all) of the successful sports cars have developed a cult-like following of enthusiasts, a core of people who have an almost maniacal enthusiasm for the particular make and model of car they own - MG or Lotus Elan enthusiasts, for example. Most of these people would never race or rally their car, but they won't buy anything else. This image is essential to a successful sports car. The MGs all had it - Saab's Sonnet never did. Any TR-series Triumph possessed this element, but try as hard as it could, Sunbeam wasn't ever able to develop such an image for the Alpine.

"There have also been a lot more successful convertible sports cars than coupés, at least in the United States and Canada. The Opel GT, Marcos 1800, Glas 1700 GT, Lancia Montecarlo (Scorpion in America), Simca 1000 and (in later forms) Saab Sonnet were all pretty, but there wasn't a convertible (or a success) among them. Even Targas are not open cars to most sports car owners. This is not to say that a light sports car cannot succeed without a convertible [top], but an $8000 convertible among a flock of $9000 - $12,000 coupés and Targas should be as popular as beer at a baseball stadium."

It was obvious that the people at MANA thought America was in need of an affordable sports car. At this stage in the proceedings,

however, nothing was heard from Hiroshima.

An LWS
A friend of the author's, Yoshihiko Matsuo, Chief Designer of the original Fairlady Z (240Z) and now a design consultant, gave his definition of a modern sports car in a recent interview: "It must be a two-passenger automobile with attractive body styling designed for high speed, highly-responsive driving. The engine must have reserves of power even at high rpm. It should have a manual transmission with a good feel and a fully functional cockpit, and support pleasant high speed handling. To state it as a category, I would say that sports cars belong to a category somewhere between specialty cars and racing prototypes. Also, I believe, there are two main types of sports cars; one the Lightweight Sports Car and the other the Super Sports Car."

The Mazda RX-7 wasn't exactly lightweight, but it was nearer the lightweight concept than most. Weighing in at around 1100kg (2420lb), it was substantially lighter than Nissan's S130 series Fairlady (280ZX), and the recently introduced Z31 models. But the RX-7 was destined to follow the Fairlady in its move upmarket: the P747 would be bigger, faster, heavier, and better-equipped. In other words, the second generation RX-7 was going to be a Super Sports Car.

The first generation RX-7 sold in massive numbers in the States, just like the original affordable Japanese sports car of the Seventies, the 240Z. The Toyota Celica was another success story. Of course, exchange rates at the time helped, but these cars were not the pure flukes some would have you believe - nothing in Japanese business happens by chance. By careful research, the Japanese had found the formula: offer excellent value-for-money in an attractive, reliable package, and it's a licence to print money.

However, with the new RX-7 scheduled for the 1986 model year (work had started on it in 1981), this was going to leave a void in the market as far as Japanese manufacturers were concerned. Toyota immediately spotted this niche and tried to fill it with the mid-engined MR2, but in America - the world's biggest sports car market - it was not as successful as was hoped, probably because Pontiac brought out the Fiero just beforehand. Honda also saw the gap and launched the sporty front-engined, front-wheel drive CRX, but this could never be considered a true sports car in the great tradition of the S500, S600 and S800 roadsters.

The Mazda marque was flying high in the States at that time, with the RX-7 dominating the IMSA racing scene and the SCCA Pro-Rally series. Kenichi Yamamoto knew that a true LWS - an abbreviation of lightweight sports car, a term used within the trade in much the same way as MPV (multi-purpose vehicle), and so on - would potentially have the market to itself and further strengthen Mazda's sporting image.

Yamamoto had got the sports car bug after Hirotaka Tachibana of the Experimental Department and Takaharu Kobayakawa (one of Yamamoto's most respected engineers who had been Chief Engineer on the RX-7 since 1986) - both LWS enthusiasts of the highest order - had encouraged him to take a business trip to Tokyo via the mountain roads around Hakone in a Triumph Spitfire. After this, he knew that Mazda should try and develop a similar vehicle. Judging by MANA's essay sent to Hiroshima in 1982, the staff there also thought the market needed an entry level sports car as well.

The Mazda Technical Research Centre in Hiroshima was still in the planning stage (it opened in 1985), so as something of a stop-gap, in November 1983, the company established a programme to allow its designers to think up and develop ideas for vehicles outside their recognised range. This programme was given the bizarre name, 'Off-Line, Go, Go'.

Michinori Yamanouchi, Mazda's Managing Director, hoped that this programme would encourage the engineering and design staff to take a fresh approach and, indeed Off-Line, Go, Go (or OGG) elicited some novel proposals. The subject of this book was one of the projects to be tackled off-line - a lightweight sports car.

A competition

Once the LWS project had been chosen, there was the matter of which layout to go for. It was decided that the three main possibilities - FR (front engine, rear-wheel drive), FF (front engine, front-wheel drive), and MR (mid-engine, rear-wheel drive) - would be split so that each idea could be developed properly. After some far from subtle hints, the FR layout went to MANA in the States, while the FF and MR cars were assigned to the Tokyo Design Studio in Japan. The resulting designs would then go through two rounds of judging in Hiroshima and, ultimately, a winner declared. Masakatsu Kato, who was behind many of Mazda's concept cars, was given the task of overseeing the project, code number P729.

Although there were no firm plans for the LWS as yet, Mazda was seriously considering producing a Familia Cabriolet. Mark Jordan, who had joined MANA in January 1983, was put in charge of the project. The son of Chuck Jordan (the head of design at General Motors), he came from talented stock. A car was duly built, and the model eventually joined the Mazda line-up.

However, the team at MANA was far more interested in the LWS project. By this time, Fukuda,

August 1984. The first model from MANA which set the LWS project in motion. Tom Matano said his team had set out "to recapture the spirit of the British sports car," but no-one could have anticipated at the time the huge success of the subsequent production model.

The Tokyo Design Studio's FF coupé in profile. The drawings based around this layout were perhaps better than the full-sized clay, although the nose was very attractive. A convertible had also been suggested in the early stages of the design process.

first place, Matano's view concerning the background to the project was quite significant: "I think what we're looking for is the simplicity of the era, say, the Sixties. We want to get back to a relationship between car and driver that simply brings fun [to the owner]. At a time when the British sports cars had all gone ... due to either safety rules or emission rules and so forth, the fun element was really disappearing out of the market. And again, another urge was to provide the type of car that we loved when we were younger ... [We thought] a small sports car with a convertible [top] has to have a place in the future as it had in the past."

Shortly after Matano joined the team, a layout engineer by the name of Norman Garrett III signed up for

Jordan, and stylist Masao Yagi (Fukuda's assistant who had been sent to the States from Hiroshima), had already began working on their ideal open sports car. Tsutomu (Tom) Matano joined MANA at the end of 1983 as head of the design section, having previously worked for GM and BMW, earning an excellent reputation along the way.

Tom Matano wasn't particularly happy with the facilities at MANA when he first moved there (most of MANA's money at that time came from fitting air conditioning units bought in the States), although the LWS project that he took over had great appeal. "When I joined Mazda," he said, "the first project I worked on was the Miata, and I thought this was a good chance for me to really put my emotions and passions together to make a car."

Having said that it was the Bertone-styled Alfa Romeo Giulia Canguro of 1964 which inspired him to become a car designer in the

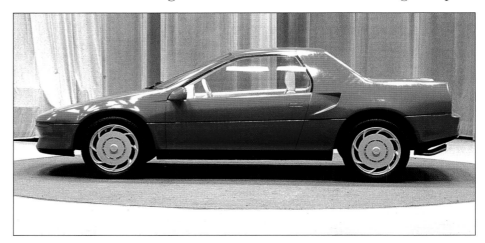

The MR design submitted by Sato and Suzuki. An interesting proposal, the overall dimensions were very close to those of the recently introduced Toyota MR2.

MANA as well. Given that the American LWS would use an FR layout (the one preferred by most traditional sports car enthusiasts and the MANA team itself), Garrett decided to use components from the existing range - an old rwd GLC (323) engine and transmission, and MacPherson struts all-round for the suspension.

Although a fresh approach could have been used (that was the reason behind the formation of OGG, after all), it was hoped that by using parts which could be easily sourced from within the organisation, the project stood more chance of being accepted.

Meanwhile, two lightweight coupés were being designed in the Tokyo Design Studio; one, a front-wheel drive model (FF), and the other, a mid-engined (MR) vehicle. The FF design had a distinct advantage, as the 323 was moving in this direction and would make an obvious donor car if the design was allowed to progress. The success of the Honda CRX also helped promote this configuration.

Having been involved with the RX-7, Yoichi Sato was quite keen to produce a car to compete with the CRX, and set about his task with the help of Hideki Suzuki in their small office in the Gotanda district of Tokyo, not far from Haneda Airport. Early drawings included a convertible but, eventually, an attractive coupé was settled on. However, the mid-engined vehicle, with its wedge shape and sharp

A rear view of the MR model. In fact, the MR layout was always going to struggle, as Masaaki Watanabe had built an experimental mid-engined 323 and dismissed it on NVH (Noise, Vibration and Harshness) grounds.

roofline, was more distinctive. Indeed, when the competitors met for the first round of the contest in April 1984, it was the MR machine that looked the most impressive on paper.

The MANA proposal was not totally without support, though, as Toriyama-san (Mazda's export man and MANA President) was quite enthusiastic about the open car.

Seconds out, Round Two ...

When the second round of competition was held in August, the FF design was looking odds-on favourite. The MR design, meanwhile, had an uphill struggle on its hands. In reality, it was almost doomed from the start, as Masaaki Watanabe had already built a Familia with the MR layout and declared it unsuitable for

A front view of the FR model. Note the stylish air intake and small door mirrors.

The attractive Kamm tail of the Duo 101. Neat touches abound, such as the hidden door releases and the fairing on the rear deck.

MANA's Duo 101 in profile.

dimensions very close to those of the recently announced Toyota MR2, and with the Pontiac Fiero also available, the mid-engined sports car market was probably better catered for than it had been since the 1970s.

The second phase of the competition was to present full-scale clays, and, through this process, the MANA proposal suddenly came alive. Even Sato was impressed, saying: "Their full-size model was a quantum leap from those flat sketches."

The design (which was actually the first clay to be built at the Irvine studio) was christened the 'Duo 101' by the staff at MANA - Duo apparently signifying that either a hard- or soft-top could be used.

Fukuda and Hall put forward a whole host of reasons outlining why the FR layout was more suitable in a car of this type, and even put together a video presentation to try and sway the judges' decision. It was a very professional approach which ultimately paid off. The MANA team won and was therefore destined to play an important part in the early stages of Mazda's LWS project.

A brave decision?

The decision to go for the convertible may have seemed a brave move, but, in retrospect, there was an obvious hole in the market. The Alfa Romeo Spider was suffering from a lack of investment and ongoing development, and the Fiat

production. Extra bulkheads would have insulated the noise and heat build-up, but, naturally, weight then increases as a result. It had

Spider, latterly badged as a Pininfarina model, was about to fade away.

There wasn't really much else available, unless one was willing to look at low-volume models, special conversions on existing coupés, or very expensive convertibles. But it wasn't always this way: look in any American monthly magazine from the 1960s and there will almost certainly be more adverts for open British sports cars than for any homegrown products. However, by 1970, British manufacturers had completely lost their stronghold on the American market.

Forthcoming Federal regulations seemed to signal the end of the convertible, but it's much too easy to cite this as the sole reason for the extinction of the cheap sporty models eminating from UK shores. In fact, a number of factors contributed, with the car builders having to take at least some of the blame for poor build quality, archaic specifications, and a distinct lack of customer care.

Reliability problems were another factor. The author has owned a string of cars which would appeal to the enthusiast, so can confirm as well as anyone that the occasional problem is accepted and passed off as thoroughbred temperament. However, after a while it soon becomes wearing, and,

with the introduction of the Datsun Fairlady roadsters (and then the legendary 240Z), many sports car enthusiasts were converted to Japanese products which not only spent more time on the road instead of in the garage, but also offered exceptional value for money.

This spoilt the Americans, who witnessed the qualities of Japanese cars in SCCA racing as well. When the Triumph TR7 eventually became available as a convertible (it was designed as a pure coupé from the start as it was thought soft-top cars would be banned in the US), an American magazine carried out a loyalty survey to see if existing owners would buy another. In stark contrast to cars like the 240Z and RX-7, the results were some of the worst recorded. In Europe, too, although sports car buyers were a little less receptive to these Oriental impersonators, the Japanese were certainly making inroads.

Japan had not built many convertibles since the war, and most of them from the early 1980s were coupés converted to cabriolets by third parties. Avatar did this with the first generation RX-7 before Mazda produced its own convertible on the second generation RX-7. Other notable examples included ASC's work on the Celica, and Richard Straman's 300ZX and

cheap little roadster based on the Honda Civic. Interestingly, all of these conversions were carried out in North America.

Looking further back in history, the Datsun DC-3 was probably the first purpose-built Japanese convertible, sold during 1952. Nissan built a few soft-top prototypes before launching the Datsun Fairlady Roadsters. There was also a prototype 240Z drophead, which, sadly, failed to make it into production due to proposed Federal regulations threatening to stamp out open cars. There was also the Mikasa, but very few were sold. Other rarities included the Prince Skyline Sport Convertible and Daihatsu Compagno. Honda built a run of successful roadsters, and Toyota took the roof off a 2000GT for a James Bond movie, but it wasn't until the third generation Celica that Toyota listed a convertible in its line-up. The examples mentioned here show that the Japanese had hardly flooded the market with convertibles, the best-selling models having gone out of production in the late 1960s.

Ultimately, the American authorities didn't pass the regulations outlawing the soft-top, but even though the convertible's future seemed assured, surprisingly few manufacturers took the opportunity to build one. The consensus of opinion seemed to be that the convertible market had simply ceased to exist after

1970. Maybe Mazda was right to explore the possibilities, and, by using the OGG route, the company didn't have to commit itself fully until totally satisfied there was still sufficient interest. Although the LWS project was not guaranteed production status at this stage, the team at MANA was convinced it would eventually find its way into the showrooms.

IAD

In September 1984, International Automotive Design, better-known as IAD, was asked by Mazda to become involved with the LWS project. Based in Worthing in the south of England, IAD was founded by the late John Shute (an ex-GM body engineer and avid collector of MGs) in the early 1970s. Shute was well-known in the trade, and IAD soon gained an excellent reputation for developing prototypes.

Mazda wanted its new car to have a British flavour and actually commissioned IAD not only to build

A rear view of the V705. Note the exceptionally large rear screen area and the Toyota reference on the number plate - typical British humour.

a running prototype based on the Duo 101, but also to carry out evaluations on a number of British classics. Cars - including the first Lotus Elan - were tested at the MIRA facility in the centre of England and reports compiled.

A fibreglass lookalike open body and makeshift interior were constructed around mechanical components from a selection of Mazda models: the 1.4 litre engine and transmission came from a rwd Familia, the front suspension and wheels were taken from an early RX-7, and the rear suspension was from a Luce (929). The interesting part of the prototype was the use of

a backbone chassis, designed and built in-house by IAD.

Given the code number V705 by Mazda, the car - with its fibreglass body (a feature Kato had insisted on at this early stage), backbone chassis and FR layout - was, in effect, the Japanese equivalent of the original Lotus Elan. The V705 was fully-functional and, under the direction of Project Manager, Bill Livingstone, it was eventually completed in August 1985.

California dreamin'

The enthusiastic team at MANA had done little on the LWS project

When the IAD-built V705 prototype arrived in America for its Santa Barbara excursion, the RX-7 wheels were changed for some multi-spoke items that would not give a clue to the car's true identity. Arriving on the back of a car transporter wrapped in a grey cover, the vehicle was made ready for its drive around the local area, but its number plates from a Mazda distributor soon gave the game away.

since it was handed over to IAD, but work had recently started again to enable some subtle design changes to the body, the eventual result being the S-2 clay. In the meantime, on 17 September 1985, Mazda staff from Japan and America met up in Worthing to view and drive the IAD prototype in England.

On the first day, the car was viewed in the IAD works, but on the second day the group, led by Masakatsu Kato, was taken to the Ministry of Defence test track not too far from IAD, where the V705 was compared on a high speed loop, a road course and a skidpan with a Fiat X1/9, a Toyota MR2, and the new Reliant Scimitar. Everyone was exceptionally happy with the vehicle. Mark Jordan wrote in his report that IAD "did an excellent job. After testing the car, it felt very pleasing ..."

The car was then scheduled to be shipped back to Japan, but, on the orders of Managing Director, Masataka Matsui, newly-appointed head of the Technical Research Centre, it was sent to the States instead. Matsui wanted to see the new machine in its natural environment, which made sense, but it was also very risky as the car could have been spotted by someone from the motoring journals. For this reason,

somewhere that wasn't too busy had to be chosen. After much deliberation, Santa Barbara seemed the ideal place.

In mid-October, Matsui arrived in California to see the new car in the setting it was designed for. MANA had assembled a small group of cars for comparison (an RX-7, a Triumph Spitfire, and a Honda convertible by the Straman concern), and took the V705 to Santa Barbara on a car transporter. Anyone remotely interested in cars immediately came to look at the new vehicle, which wasn't exactly anonymous as it carried Californian plates borrowed from a local distributor.

Unfortunately, whilst out driving, the Mazda crew came across a number of journalists testing cars, and the registration plates quickly gave the game away. Bob Hall, being an ex-writer, explained the situation and somehow managed to get the motoring scribes to agree not to publish any photographs.

In retrospect, Fukuda thought it was a mistake to expose the car so early. Overall, though, it was a highly successful day. Matsui was more than happy with the public response at this impromptu clinic. At dinner with the MANA team that evening, Matsui was convinced that the LWS had potential and declared

"I think we should build this car." More importantly, when he returned to Hiroshima, he gave the LWS project his full recommendation.

Virtual reality

1985 saw the introduction of the all-new fwd Mazda Familia (323) series in Japan, and the second generation Savanna RX-7. The RX-7 was duly named 1986 'Import Car of the Year' by Motor Trend magazine.

A number of interesting concept cars appeared as well. Suzuki displayed its R/S1 LWS at the 1985 Tokyo Show. However, somewhat surprisingly, despite favourable reactions, the vehicle never made it into production, so the way was still clear for Mazda. The Hiroshima marque displayed the MX-03, a four-wheel drive, four-wheel steer coupé designed by Kato, at the same event. With 2+2 seating, it was sportier than the MX-02 from two years earlier (which was quite staid by comparison), but was destined to remain a prototype.

Shigenori Fukuda returned to Japan to take up the post of General Manager of the Design Division. Having been closely involved with the LWS project from its birth, Fukuda was obviously keen to see it through to the end, as it was the epitome of his 'Romantic Engineering' concept. However, the LWS was still not guaranteed a place in the Mazda line-up. At the end of the 1980s, Fukuda stated

Toshihiko Hirai, the MX-5's Chief Engineer, pictured by the author during a recent trip to Hiroshima. He is now a highly successful university lecturer.

The third and final clay produced by MANA. The front indicators were a little too large, and the shape of the air intake and tail graphics were further refined in Japan.

that "the project was interrupted several times." In fact, Shunji Tanaka feels that had Fukuda not returned to Japan, the LWS might never have seen the light of day.

There were a number of reasons for having doubts about the LWS's future. Mazda had already approved its new MPV which, with the benefit of hindsight, was an excellent move (Japan's roads are full of these utility vehicles nowadays), but was also pushing for a new model in the Light (or *Kei*) class. The tiny K-car was a proven winner, and, with limited resources available, many in the company recommended that this route should be taken and the LWS project suspended.

Fortunately, this immediate problem was overcome via a joint engineering agreement with Suzuki in relation to the Light Car; Mazda now had the resources to enable it to do the MPV, the K-car (the Carol) *and* the LWS, but the men in the finance department were still not too happy. America was always

going to be the main market for an open sports car, and the value of the yen was making life hard for Japanese exports.

The first major Japanese sports car success in the US market, the Datsun 240Z, hit the shores of America in 1970. The floating exchange rate system was introduced in 1971, and almost immediately the yen began to strengthen against the dollar. By 1972, 300 yen would buy a dollar instead of the 357 needed at the start of the previous year.

With the oil crisis of 1973, the yen was quoted at 253 per dollar before the greenback recovered dramatically. By the end of the 1970s, when Mazda's RX-7 arrived on the scene, the rate had dropped to below 200 yen to the dollar, and was still moving in the same direction. 1985 had seen the yen moving strongly against the dollar, pushing prices in export markets up to unprecedented levels, which had an obvious effect on sales.

This was not such an easy problem to resolve, as the thinking behind the LWS was that it should be cheap enough to tempt people into buying what was, at the end of the day, something of an indulgence.

In January 1985, AutoAlliance International Inc., a 50/50 venture with Ford, was established in Flat

Rock, Michigan. Having a manufacturing plant in the States would overcome currency fluctuations (MX-6 production began in September 1987, followed shortly by the Ford Probe, and later the 626), but there were no plans to build the LWS there.

With initial sales projections pointing towards 1800 units a year for Japan, 30,000 for North America and around 3600 for Europe, the volume was hardly massive. Careful design, to keep production costs down, would ultimately be the car's saviour (although, luckily, these figures proved grossly underestimated).

In the meantime, progress was slow. MANA eventually completed the S-2 clay in December 1985. When it was officially presented to the Board the following month, Yamamoto was fully behind the LWS idea, saying it had "a smell of culture." Mazda's Managing Director, Takashi Kuroda, also expressed his support, and, for this reason, on 18 January 1986, the P729 was grudgingly given approval. But then there was another, unexpected delay ...

Kato, who had overseen the project since inception, decided to step down from his position as head of P729 and concentrate his efforts on new ideas within the recently opened Technical Research

Centre. Naturally, this meant a replacement had to be found. Fortunately, Toshihiko Hirai, previously in charge of the Familia (323), made it known that he would like to be considered for the LWS project. Born in 1935, Hirai was well-respected and had a proven record with the successful 323 range. With his vast engineering experience and a spell in the Service Department, he was declared the ideal man for the job and, in February, duly took up his new post as the P729's Chief Engineer.

In the same month, MANA was told it could start on the third and final clay model (the S-3). Work began in earnest in the middle of March, with Tom Matano and Koichi Hayashi responsible for the majority of input, ably supported by Mark Jordan and Wu-Huang Chin.

Matano wanted to develop a family resemblance between the "faces" of the various cars in the Mazda range - a frontal view that would immediately single out the vehicle as a Mazda. Using BMW and Mercedes-Benz grilles as examples, he went on: "To us, this is a graphical way of identifying the car. It's great if you have a [long] heritage, and so forth, that establishes you in such a way, but at this point in Mazda's development we wanted to upgrade our image ... To achieve that, we wanted to have something like a body language to [distinguish] the Mazda for that time.

"I always look for the movement of the highlights on a car. It's almost like a drama, or a symphony in some cases; like a Jaguar is a symphony. Every moment that lights move on a surface by driving [along], really [tells] the whole story of a car."

Matano dislikes the use of fussy lines and heavy creases in styling. He said: "I often think of water, dropping onto the roof, following the curvature, going down the roof to the pillar, to the bottom of the pillar, to whatever. And every time this water has to think which way shall I go down - if the water has to think that way - the design is not right yet. You know, it's not natural yet.

"Because it's a convertible, the rear end is very important to identify the car. And yet we don't really want to have a spoiler just for the sake of it, so it's there but it's not really obvious."

During May, the project was considered advanced enough to call a joint meeting between the MANA staff and a large delegation from Japan. As far as the American team was concerned, the project was finished.

A return to Worthing

Once the decision was finally taken to embrace the lightweight sports car, Mazda again turned to IAD in England - this time to produce five complete running vehicles (engineering mules), and nine bodyshells for test and evaluation.

The mules didn't have the PPF

brace (all will be explained in due course), but otherwise were similar to the future production models. Significant detail changes were made along the way, including the use of a larger fuel tank (the original was far too small to be practical), and redesigning of the hood.

IAD actually carried out the front and rear crash tests, which the LWS passed with flying colours. After the Worthing phase in the proceedings was completed, a number of IAD staff were sent to Japan to personally explain problems encountered and make the transition as smooth as possible. The Mazda roadster was now a reality.

The synthesis of man and horse

The author's point of view regarding sports cars has always been that they have only one main purpose - to be driven. Of course, some of the more exotic designs can be looked upon as works of art - like automotive sculpture - but basically speaking, a sports car is intended simply to provide driving pleasure.

The LWS project's Chief Engineer, Toshihiko Hirai, felt exactly the same way. The Japanese love their cars; they represent personal space in a crowded city, something they can own. Few young people are in a position to buy anything in the housing market other than a tiny flat, as prices are extremely high. Even if somebody does take on a mortgage, repayments often continue well into the third generation of the family! The car is also a way to escape into the countryside, or a means of getting to the fishing port. In other words, even given the prospect of enormous traffic jams at certain times of the day, the automobile is considered a necessity to the enjoyment of life. However, a sports car is not just a means of transport: it has to look and feel special, and make its owner enjoy each and every mile, every corner, every gearchange.

Hirai gathered around him a team of about ten people, including Shinzo Kubo (who had been at MANA for a while, and would later become Hirai's assistant), Kazuyuki Mitate and Hideaki Tanaka (both of whom had been with the project for some time), Takao Kijima and Masaaki Watanabe. Hirai, described by Bill Livingstone as "a very professional engineer," began by listing every minute detail that he expected from a sports car, declaring he would not be happy until this criteria had been met. The list took on an almost legendary status once the journalists got to hear about it!

The concept was originally described as the synthesis of man and vehicle, but this was later changed to the synthesis of man and horse; Hirai wanted the new Mazda to give the driver the feeling of oneness that exists between a good rider and a thoroughbred stallion.

An interview with Shunji Tanaka (Chief Designer on the M1 body)

Mr Tanaka: "Today, there are many open two-seater cars on the market. However, in 1986, there was nothing resembling the open two-seater concept available, and it was hard even to carry out market research effectively. I remember that at the time we really struggled to get this car into production."

Miho Long: "Could you tell us your favourite parts of the design, and why?"

Mr Tanaka: "I like the rear view when the car is open - I believe the rear view of a sports car has to be cute! I would also suggest the tail lamps, which are as one with the body. I wanted them to resemble a *fundo* [a balance weight from old-style weighing scales], so I shaved a tail lamp housing myself to get exactly the shape I desired."

Miho Long: "Which would you say was the hardest part of the body design to execute?"

Mr Tanaka: "To create the authentic originality of Mazda and Japan on the body surface. You will notice that the lines enclose an aesthetic consciousness, giving different feelings depending on the angle from which the car is viewed, just like a *Noh* mask.

"Every time I take up a chisel to create a *Noh* mask, I always respect the traditional simplicity and perfect curves which have been handed down over the centuries. Many different feelings and wishes are held within the mask, their appearance depending on the light and changing shadows. It is very characteristic of the Japanese, and completely different from the Western notion of expressing perfection concretely.

"I also wanted to enclose the rhythms - peace, motion, and silence - which exist in the Japanese heart, into the form of the sports car. For peace, I looked towards a statue of the Goddess of Mercy for inspiration, a truly graceful symbol. For motion, I thought of a wild animal when it's hunting, running fast and accurate, and for silence, the tranquility of nature. I wanted the car to melt into the scenery, reflecting the light over its curved surfaces.

"I wanted to establish a new mould which was dynamic and original, yet distinctly Japanese in its origin - a mixture of sensitivity and modern technology."

The final design

The third MANA clay (S-3), arrived in Hiroshima in July 1986, at a time when the studio was packed with other projects. A now familiar figure entered the story when Shunji Tanaka of Design Department No. 1 (Hiroshima), took over as Chief Designer. Initially, Tanaka struggled to find a surface plate for the clay; considering the project had still not secured the full support of everyone at Mazda, in a country that is usually so organised, one wonders if this had not been planned to delay it still further. However, one was eventually obtained and, in November that year, Tanaka started work on the model.

Tanaka decided that the car was too heavy-looking for his liking. As he said, he proceeded to "take one layer of skin off the MANA

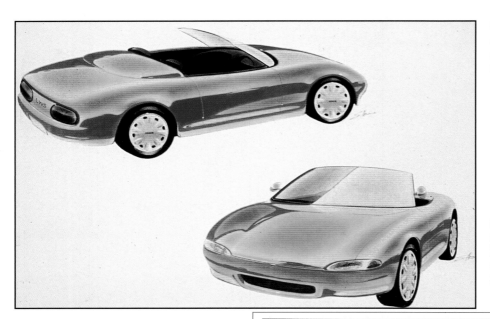

mentioned a hint of Muromachi culture - a great era in Japanese history that brought about the tea ceremony, *Noh* plays, floral art, the Zen sect, and so on. There was very

model from front to rear" to reveal a lither profile. He insisted that the wheelbase be shortened slightly, causing more than a few problems for the layout engineers (MANA had already lengthened it during development of the third clay), the most obvious of which being the need to move the battery from behind the seats to a new location in the boot. The battery then encroached on luggage space, but the stylist stood by his decision. In the end, it helped with weight distribution anyway, so could be regarded as something of a mixed blessing, even though a special lightweight battery was eventually deemed necessary by Hirai.

Tanaka and Hirai had several more arguments during the development of the final model. Tanaka lowered the cowl height but was prevented by the Chief Engineer from going the extra 20mm (0.79in.) he really wanted, although he did manage to change the width of the air intake. When Hirai found out after taking a ruler to the model, it was too late to change it!

Mazda thought that the car had to have spirit, incorporating the "beauty of Japan," so the brief

The MX-5 is definitely starting to show through in this proposal.

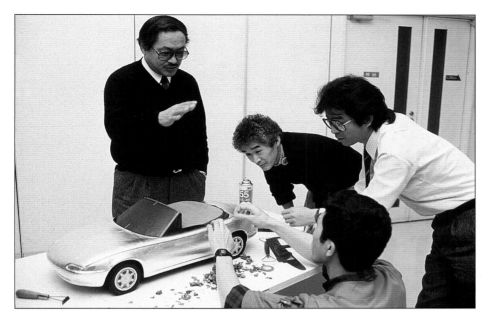

Work on a scale model of the Mazda sports car. Shunji Tanaka (left) makes a point, while Satoru Akana (one of the Hiroshima-based designers, seen here on the right) looks on.

little further intervention from the management and marketing people. Tanaka (who was born in 1947 and joined Mazda in 1971) sculpted *Noh* masks as a hobby, and used them for his inspiration. The simple mask's facial expression doesn't actually change, but as soon as a *Noh* actor wears it, by careful movements the mask can change expression through the use of light, shadow and different angles.

The modeller, Shigeru Kajiyama, had the unenviable job of interpreting Tanaka's vision to make light dance on the car's profile, regardless of whether it was in motion or stationary. When the clay model was completed, the data was loaded into a computer and it was found that the LWS had 260 different faces. By comparison, other Mazda cars have around 80 different faces.

The LWS taking shape in Japan, based on MANA's S-3 clay. The Americans had been worried that Tanaka would drop the pop-up headlights; in actual fact, Fukuda (seen pointing in the background) wanted the headlamps placed under clear covers, but regulations dictated that the pop-up arrangement remained. Note the Minilite-type wheels.

Shunji Tanaka (in the foreground, on the left) checking on progress. The scale model in the background, complete with removable hardtop, was a masterpiece.

Tanaka's finished design. His modifications actually brought the final shape nearer to the original Duo 101 clay submitted by MANA when the project first started. From quite an early stage, Tanaka had removed the black rubbing strip and replaced it with a crease line instead. From this clay, a glassfibre model was built, which was subsequently sent to America to take part in a clinic.

Three views of the glassfibre model that went to the States to take part in a clinic held at the Pasadena Convention Centre in 1987.

After working on the clay model for about three months, in between his other work on the Luce, RX-7 and MPV (which were considered by Yamanouchi to be more important at the time), a resin mock-up of the body was produced. This was duly sent to California for appraisal at the end of March 1987, by which time Watanabe and his team had sorted out the vast majority of engineering details. Although the staff at MANA were dreading the results (they had been told that Tanaka had been quite brutal with his modifications), they were all suitably impressed and immediately sent a fax through to Hiroshima to convey their congratulations.

It was one thing to impress your colleagues, but the true test came at a clinic held at the Pasadena Convention Centre, when 240 people were invited to give their views on the anonymous vehicle. It received an overwhelming yes vote, which was almost certainly a key factor in the decision to finally go ahead with the project. The importers in America were fully behind the car, so everything was now in place, signed and sealed. There was no turning back.

Engine

A rotary engine was dismissed at the start of the project. Managing Director, Takashi Kuroda, said that from a marketing point of view, the rotary was better suited to higher powered prestige models. Cost was

also an important factor. Masakatsu Kato was also opposed to the rotary but for different reasons: if an existing unit was to be used, the chassis would require costly modifications to enable it to handle the extra power (which would also add a substantial amount of weight), or a new smaller engine would have to be built.

Sensibly, it was decided to adapt an existing unit to cut down on development time and costs. The fuel-injected, 1.6 litre, twin-cam engine from the Familia GT was selected, and suitably modified to enable the four-cylinder block to be installed longitudinally, instead of in its usual transverse position. Having only recently ushered in the FF layout on the 323 range

A sectional view of the B6-ZE (RS) engine.

Tominaga and his team as the starting point for what would eventually amount to a new engine. The bore and stroke were retained (78 x 83.6mm, or 3.1 x 3.3in.), which gave a cubic capacity of 1597cc. The block, with five main bearings, was of cast iron, while the head was cast in aluminium alloy. Double overhead camshafts remained a feature, operating four valves per cylinder, although the timing was changed to allow higher rpm. The cast iron crankshaft and flywheel were subtly altered, and this attention to detail resulted in an engine with a 7200rpm red-line.

But, in typically Japanese fashion, the detailing went much further - even the induction system, cam covers and timing belt cover were stylized to make the engine attractive to look at, and to bear a passable resemblance to Lotus, Alfa Romeo and Fiat twin-cam units! Another novel feature was the cast aluminium sump, complete with cooling fins, in the best Italian tradition.

Fuel-injection was retained, for although twin carburettors would have been nice from an aesthetic point of view (as well as following a traditional sports car line), emission regulations soon scuppered that idea. An L-Jetronic EFI system with a pendant-type airflow meter was employed, and Tsunetoshi Yokokura (who had previously worked on the B6-DOHC engine), designed both the intake and exhaust porting and manifolds. To

The engine and five-speed gearbox used in the P729 lightweight sports car.

(which was almost universal on small cars by this time), it is somewhat ironic that this conversion was necessary.

However, the B6-DOHC was found to be less than ideal. Hirai wanted a high- and free-revving engine and, in its standard form,

this unit, having been tuned to give low-end torque instead of top-end power, was hardly suitable for its proposed new application. The turbocharged version, available in Japan, was also quickly dismissed.

The water-cooled B6 was therefore adopted by Kazuo

33

The drivetrain for the LWS was quite short, with the engine mounted a long way back. It was the first car to employ the Power Plant Frame, or PPF. Weighing less than 5kg (11lb), it effectively turned the engine/gearbox and back axle into an integral unit and made a notable difference in refining power delivery.

save weight, the free-flow exhaust manifold was produced in stainless steel rather than the more commonly used cast iron.

Interestingly, instead of using a distributor, it was decided to employ a crank angle sensor, as the old Familia-type distributor would have been in the way of the wiper motor. Although this computer-linked device cost a fortune compared to the more traditional ignition set-up, it ultimately gave a much smaller and lighter package. Other weight saving measures included the use of an aluminium and plastic radiator which was cooled by a particularly small electric fan.

The new engine was designated the B6-ZE (RS), and with a compression ratio of 9.4:1 produced 120PS (the Japanese measurement of power, which is roughly the same as European bhp) at 6500rpm. Maximum torque (of 100lbft) came in very high up the rev range, at 5500rpm, confirming the sporting nature of the unit. The engine was mounted as far back as possible to bring the weight nearer the centre of the car.

Drivetrain

The gearbox was developed from the proven M-type, five-speed transmission that had seen service in the two-litre Luce and normally-aspirated RX-7. The main changes concerned the shift linkage, which was modified to give a very short stroke between the gears; indeed, when the Mazda engineers had finished, the stubby gearlever travelled just 50mm (2in.) from any gear into the neutral position, prompting one tester to compare it to operating a rifle bolt. However, that was not all, as the synchromesh was improved, and a subtle 'click' as the lever reached its stop was built in to enhance the positive feel of the 'box.

After reviewing the specifications on a number of sports cars, close and evenly spaced gear ratios were chosen. With a 4.3:1 final-drive, a 3.14:1 first gear gave a maximum speed of 33mph (53kph); the 1.89:1 second gear allowed 54mph (86kph); third, at 1.33:1, gave 77mph (123kph); the direct fourth gave 102mph (163kph), and a 0.81:1 overdrive top, an estimated 117mph (187kph).

The clutch was a single dry plate unit. Power was taken from the gearbox to the back axle via a single-piece propshaft (with the engine located so far back, a two-piece propshaft was deemed unnecessary). A viscous-coupled, limited-slip differential was made available as an option.

Having designed a novel way of bracing the driveline for the forthcoming third generation RX-7, at the end of 1986, Mazda decided to use what it called a Power Plant Frame (or PPF) on the LWS as well. Having tested the idea on an early engineering mule, the system was later adopted for production. The PPF was basically an aluminium bracing piece linking the engine and differential which had been refined and lightened through the use of computer technology; its purpose was to improve throttle response (by stopping the differential unit twisting on its mounts) and reduce drivetrain shudder.

On the subject of throttle response, throttle travel was some 65mm (2.5in.) on the LWS, as opposed to the usual 45mm (1.8in.) on most Mazdas, thus giving the driver more precise control. The throttle pedal was drilled to evoke memories of earlier sporting machines. Incidentally, an automatic gearbox was not offered immediately but was promised

The front suspension.

The rear suspension.

for the future.

Chassis

Having originally been under the auspices of the Technical Research Centre, the job of developing the suspension eventually fell to Takao Kijima and Fumitaka Ando. Kijima was perhaps the ideal person for the job, having thought up the idea of the DTSS system for the second generation RX-7.

It was declared early on that the independent suspension would be via double wishbones all-round. Although it would have saved both time and money to use components Mazda already had in service, unequal length A-arms were unrivalled for sports car suspensions, so a new set-up was designed from scratch. Originally, aluminium alloy suspension components were envisaged, but the associated production costs curtailed this line of thought as the LWS was, after all's said and done, supposed to be an affordable sports car. Instead, the A-arms were fabricated from high tensile steel sheet, a material which was strong, reasonably light, and cheap to manufacture.

Up front, a combined coil

Cutaway drawings showing the layout of Mazda's new sports car.

spring/gas-filled shock absorber sat in between the wishbones on each side; an 18mm (0.71in.) anti-roll bar was used. At the rear, Kijima - famous for his perfectionism - allowed the forward lower suspension bush to deform slightly under cornering to give the rear wheel a minute amount of toe-in: an ingenious idea. Again, combined

35

coil spring/damper units were used, along with a 12mm (0.47in.) diameter anti-roll bar.

Spring rates were completely different to those of the Familia: 1.6kg/mm at the front and 1.4kg/mm at the rear. The rates for the 323 were quoted as 2.7kg/mm and 2.1kg/mm respectively. Staff from Bilstein spent a great deal of time, alongside the Mazda team in Japan, on the shock absorber settings, thus ensuring the correct amount of damping for the various types of roads around the world.

The pressed steel front subframe not only carried the suspension pick-up points, but the steering gear as well. As the engine was placed so far back, the rack was mounted ahead of it on the front of the subframe. Rack-and-pinion steering was employed, with a ratio of 18.0:1, as opposed to 23.5 on the Familia. This gave 3.3 turns lock-to-lock, but, being such a light car, steering effort remained acceptable at slower speeds. The optional power steering had a 15.3:1 ratio (it was 16.4:1 on the Familia), which translated into just 2.8 turns lock-to-lock.

Drum brakes would probably have been more than adequate for the car's weight and performance (the Porsche 924 had drums at the rear, and drums do provide a better handbrake), but for marketing reasons it was decided that discs all-round would be better.

The Familia was available with this system and its components provided an ideal basis on which to work. Ventilated discs of 235mm (9.3in.) diameter were employed at the front, while solid items of 231mm (9.1in.) diameter were used at the rear. The pads had a slightly larger area than those of the Familia, and the servo was changed to provide the driver with a more progressive feel.

Attention to detail was again much in evidence: The front calipers were at the trailing edge of the discs, with the rear calipers on the leading edge, thus ensuring that the weight of the braking system was kept within the wheelbase. The handbrake mechanism, which worked on the rear discs, featured an automatic adjuster.

Finally, the wheels and tyres also came under the spotlight. Shunji Tanaka had come up with an alloy wheel resembling the original Minilite, but given the weight that Hirai wanted, the wheel's would-be manufacturer suggested removing one of the spokes. The 5.5J x 14 alloy wheels were thus destined to have seven spokes instead of eight, although pressed steel wheels of a similar size were fitted to basic models.

As for the tyres, Mazda approached various companies with a request for a lighter type than those already on the market. Eventually, around 2.5kg (5.5lb) was saved on a set of four 185/60 HR14 radials. A spacesaver spare was specified to keep weight down to a minimum, and this was placed as close to the rear bulkhead as possible in order to maintain the car's ideal weight distribution.

Body

Hirai once again had very strong views on what the body should be like: "Very light and very stiff." Masakatsu Kato knew that a fibreglass body and backbone chassis, as used on the IAD prototype, was not an ideal recipe for mass-production. This conclusion was not a new one, as Daimler established as far back as 1958 (when it was looking at the details on the SP250 project) that once production reached 3000 units a year, it was cheaper, long-term, to tool-up for steel bodies.

Modern techniques had increased this threshold figure substantially, but the conclusion was basically the same. With high volume sales envisaged for Mazda's LWS, fibreglass was out of the question. Aluminium was also rejected because, although it had an obvious weight advantage, it was a very expensive material compared with steel. However, in Hirai's endless quest for weight reduction, some aluminium would eventually be used for panelwork.

Mazda's GNC-2 computer programme was used to enable the engineers to reduce weight whilst at the same time retaining vehicle rigidity. The car's body was an incredibly light structure, but strength was guaranteed by the thoroughness of Hirai's team. On

After the Pasadena clinic, Tanaka set about the subtle detailing to make the car ready for production. The tail was made softer, rear overhang was increased by 30mm (1.2in.), and the famous door handles at last made an appearance. With so many subtle lines, Naoyuki Ikemizu said the tooling for the panels was very difficult to make. This final prototype had raised 'Mazda' script on the front bumper, and the shield-shaped badge on the nose carried a star above an abstract bird with opened wings.

average, stress measurements are taken and analyzed at approximately 5000 points but, in the case of the LWS project, no less than 8900 readings were used to ensure the body would be free of the problems one usually associates with open cars, such as scuttle shake. Designing the car as a convertible from day one was an added advantage, of course, as converting a coupé into a drophead always involves compromises.

The bodyshell was of all-steel welded unitary construction, although in order to reduce weight forward of the centreline, it featured an aluminium bonnet, while the bootlid was actually made out of thinner gauge steel than that found in the rest of the body. In all, the steel parts of the car accounted for just 16 per cent of the P729's total weight.

The front bumpers were faced with urethane, while the rear bumper used polypropylene. Both were backed by impact absorbing, blow-moulded plastic, and mounted on the bodyshell via lightweight polycarbonate brackets. This arrangement, compared with more traditional bumpers, significantly reduced weight at the car's extremities. In addition, side impact bars within the doors were tubular to further reduce weight.

The overall dimensions of the roadster read as follows: length 3970mm (156.3in.); width 1675mm (65.9in.); height 1235mm (48.6in.),

The roadster's body as seen by the GNC-2 computer software.

and wheelbase 2265mm (89.2in.). Ground clearance was 140mm (5.5in.), while the front and rear track measurements were 1405 and 1420mm (55.3 and 55.9in.) respectively.

Although not particularly impressive by today's standards, for an open car the Cd figure of 0.38 was more than respectable, although it did rise to 0.44 with the hood down. Luggage space in the boot, incidentally, amounted to just 125 litres (4.4 cu ft).

Interior
Above all, the cockpit was designed to be functional, and rightfully so - it was said to represent the simplicity of a Japanese tea room. Of course, weight was kept to a bare minimum, although the interior was fully trimmed.

Early designs had been a little too futuristic, so Kenji Matsuo decided to resort to a T-shaped theme like that found on Mazda

sports cars from the past. The cluster of instruments contained five main gauges, with a large 8000rpm tachometer on the left and matching speedo to the right. The small oil pressure gauge sat between and above them, while the similar sized fuel and temperature gauges were low down on either side. The two larger dials had chrome surrounds to make them stand out.

In the tail of the T-shaped arrangement were two of the four eyeballs for ventilation (the others were at each extremity of the fascia) and heater controls, both of which were sourced from the first generation RX-7. However, as *Car Styling* said: "The sense of unity has been pursued by fully using the motif of a circle as seen in the meters and ventilator grille, but the basic touch of quality is somewhat unsatisfactory."

High-backed seats with integral headrests were selected. Many

An early interior concept sketch. Note the 'RX' script on the steering wheel - something that appeared on several of the initial design proposals.

3

Another early sketch. Attractive, sporting, but far too modern for the new LWS. Something more traditional was sought.

presumably to save on production costs). At the other extreme, door trims were very basic, and the cheap-looking handles inside were in stark contrast to the Tanaka-styled items found outside. Indeed, Tanaka commented that a lot of effort had gone into the exterior, but the interior had been produced with cost as a prime consideration.

Finishing touches

By September 1987, drawings had been submitted to enable trial manufacture, with the resulting prototype eventually being passed on to Hirotaka Tachibana of the Experimental Department. Tachibana, who had been with Mazda for many years after leaving the Bridgestone concern, wanted a forgiving vehicle that would reward drivers whatever their level of skill. Above all, he wanted the car to feel responsive, and had the suspension tuned so that it performed at its best at around 60mph (roughly 100kph) - a speed that most can enjoy whilst keeping within the law. Testing was carried out at the Miyoshi Proving Ground, as well as on the roads of America and Europe.

In the Psychoacoustics Lab in Japan, a large number of people were asked their opinion of various exhaust notes. Those involved in the tests came from different age groups and backgrounds, representing a fair cross-section of potential buyers. They recorded their thoughts on set format, pre-printed sheets so that the results

magazines (and even a few people within the company) commented on the somewhat tight, 'cosy' feel within the cockpit, but most testers were happy with the support provided by the seating.

The steering wheel was a four-spoke affair for America (to allow for an airbag), or a three-spoke

design elsewhere. A leather-wrapped wheel was available one way or another - either as standard or as an option - in most markets.

On Hirai's insistence, the sunvisors were made to fold in two to stop them showing over the top rail (although eventually a more traditional design was adopted,

Two of the later designs put forward for the car's fascia.

Tanaka-san reviewing interior proposals with Kenji Matsuo (right), the man ultimately responsible for the final cockpit design.

Tanaka and Matsuo assessing an interior styling buck.

could be analyzed effectively, thus giving the engineers a good idea of what the public expected the ideal sports car to sound like; Makoto Shinhama designed and built an exhaust system out of stainless steel to suit. In line with Hirai's drive to keep everything as light as possible, including the standard three-way catalytic converter, the system weighed less than 18kg (40lb).

As well as having the right exhaust note, Hirai stated that a tight seating arrangement was necessary to give the car the intimate atmosphere he wanted. He said: "In the course of development, we are apt to enlarge

a vehicle by expecting too much. But then, the sense of unity between the rider and the vehicle is lost. That is why we adhered to limits for all aspects of this car." Even so, he was quick to point out that due to the Mazda's wider track, there was more room in the cockpit than that found in the average British sports car of the 1960s.

The roadster was designed to give the full feeling of an open car. That statement may seem a little obvious, but one only has to think of vehicles like the RX-7 Cabriolet and the Jaguar XJ-S Convertible, where the occupants are cosseted from draughts and direct airflow, and compare them to the wind-in-

the-hair experience of a sports car from the 1960s, for instance. Mazda went to extraordinary lengths to get right the movement of air in the cockpit. The large door mirrors were shaped and positioned so that passengers didn't get draughts on their shoulders. It has even been said that a long-haired lady was taken to Miyoshi to see how medium speed runs affected her hairstyle!

Despite having completed its 20-millionth vehicle, as far as the hood was concerned, Mazda didn't have a great deal of experience in this field. The Familia Cabriolet had not been particularly popular, and the introduction of the RX-7 Cabriolet (launched to

Mazda advertising from the mid-1980s. The Mazda team members were certainly perfectionists regarding the LWS project.

A smiling Tachibana talking over the finer points of the LWS with Hirai (seated). The relationship between the two was not always this cordial - a fact that came to the attention of the MD, Michinori Yamanouchi. He delivered them an ultimatum: either work together or leave the project that meant so much to both of them. Masaaki Watanabe can be seen in the background.

commemorate the 20th anniversary of Mazda's rotary-engined automobiles) didn't occur until 1987 (the 1988 model year in the States).

It was declared at a very early stage that the hood had to be designed in such a way that it could be operated quickly with just one hand, rather like the hood on the Alfa Romeo Spider. A lightweight frame was duly built, covered with an unlined material which incorporated a vinyl chloride rear window. The latter could be unfastened via a zip to allow for extra ventilation, or for when the hood was lowered. With the soft-top up (or with a hard-top in place), it was found that noise was amplified within the cockpit, but the same is true of virtually all convertibles.

In addition to the standard soft-top (which was found to be both taut and weatherproof in practice), an optional hard-top was made available. An SMC plastic was employed for its construction to give the best combination of light weight and strength, but first attempts were far from satisfactory. Quality and colour matching were improved, but, even then, Mazda was not entirely happy with all the shades proposed, so only red was sold initially. With a glass rear screen, it fixed at six points and made the body noticeably more rigid.

After everything had been finalized, the basic car weighed just 940kg (2068lb); even then, Hirai thought it was possible to shed more weight. However, Hirai must have been pleased with the weight distribution - most of it being low down and within the wheelbase, just as he wished - with 52 per cent over the front wheels and 48 per cent over the rear. It was an almost perfectly balanced car.

The MX-04

At the 1987 Tokyo Show, Mazda displayed the MX-04. The MX-02 and 03 had been practical cars with seating for four, featuring advanced, but nonetheless conservative, styling. The MX-04 was completely different. Powered by a 150bhp rotary engine, the MX-04 could be fitted with any of three fibreglass body styles: a closed coupé or a choice of two roadsters.

Although the MX-04 was not the prettiest car ever produced by Mazda, some of its features were clues to the future that few picked up on: independent suspension by unequal length upper and lower arms, and a backbone chassis developed by Masakatsu Kato. It is interesting that the headlights on the MX-04 were fixed rather than pop-up, giving the car a similar frontal aspect to the second generation MX-5.

Another debutant at the '87 Tokyo Show (the last to be held at the Harumi site) was the mid-engined Suzuki R/S3. This was the second time in a row that Suzuki had displayed an LWS as its concept car design, and on both occasions they looked suitable for production, giving Fukuda more than a little

cause for concern. Maybe Mazda would have a competitor in the near future?

In fact, Mazda knew it was guaranteed at least one competitor, as Ford (which owned 24.5 per cent of Mazda at the time) was planning to bring out the Mercury Capri, a fwd convertible, using a large number of components sourced from the Familia. Based on Ford's Barchetta, an exhibit at the 1983 Frankfurt Show, it was built in Ford's plant in Australia. Although announced early in 1988, it wasn't introduced until the end of 1989.

The pilot build

The Mazda team must have held its breath when Bitter announced a two-seater convertible at the 1988 Geneva Show. It looked very similar to the P729 and was said to be ready for production, with sales to the US in preparation. Fortunately for Mazda, it was a typical Bitter product - upmarket (and therefore expensive), powered by a large Opel engine, and very low volume.

Shortly after this, the pilot build process began, with 12 cars put together by hand at the plant in Hiroshima. These were labelled S1-1 through to S1-12 and would be the vehicles tested by a select number of journalists well in advance of the launch.

Dennis Simanaitis of *Road & Track* was one of those lucky enough to be chosen to test the three vehicles Mazda had provided for the day. "Last summer," he said,

"I was invited to Mazda's Miyoshi Proving Ground to drive a prototype of the company's all-new lightweight sports car ...

"It helped assess how brilliantly conceived and executed this new car is. Its convertible top is a good example. It had to be easily erected or stowed from the driver seat. It required a latching mechanism that was easy to use. Erected, it had to offer perfect sealing up to 80mph. Down, it had to stow completely below the car's rear deck line. These engineering criteria give a perfect description of the Miata's soft-top, developed in conjunction with the British design specialist, IAD. Its latches, for instance, are large and of a novel over-centre sort that don't need Godzilla for actuation. Though not a heavily padded top of the Germanic idiom, Mazda does get its top materials from the same firm supplying Volkswagen and BMW ...

"Twist the key and you're rewarded with a pleasant burble from the Miata's 1597cc fuel-injected inline-four, essentially the same dohc four-valver powering sporty 323s. One change, a

The new Mazda sports car with (from left to right), Shunji Tanaka, Mark Jordan, Wu-Huang Chin, and Tom Matano. It was to be known as the Eunos Roadster in Japan, the MX-5 Miata in the States, and the MX-5 in all other markets throughout the world.

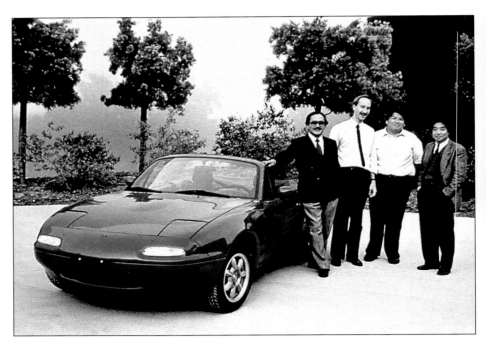

lightened flywheel, emphasizes its sports car intent... Snick the shift lever into first, and you'll experience another element on Mr Hirai's list. The shifter and its actuation are super short and wonderfully positive ...

"Consulting Mr Hirai's list again, engineers worked for a feeling of directness between throttle and rear wheels. I believe a lot of this driveline integrity is achieved by an artfully cast piece of aluminum that connects the engine, transmission and final-drive. Check off another goal successfully met. Handling goals occupy a good portion of the list, and it's in this area that the Miata impresses me the most. Its combination of communication, responsiveness, predictability and forgiveness makes it the best-handling two-seater I've driven in recent memory - and my memory for such things is good ... It was an absolute delight and my post-drive debriefing with Mazda engineers probably sounded like over-hyped ad copy ..."

In Japan, the June 1989 edition of *Car Magazine* noted that "although from the outside it looks like a British lightweight sports of the 1960s, in the way it performs, it is definitely a car from today. After driving it, one is left with a feeling of happiness."

In the meantime, importation and distribution of Mazdas in the States was consolidated with the establishment of Mazda Motor of America Inc. (MMA), and the completion of the Mazda R&D of North America Inc. facility in Irvine, California (MRA, nee MANA). Unfortunately, despite Mazda's best efforts to keep the new car under wraps until its official launch, the cover of *Auto Week* carried a picture of the P729, as well as an article inside; this was at the end of November - a long way ahead of Mazda's planned publicity campaign.

What's in a name?

Throughout the development of Mazda's new sports car, it had been given a number of codenames and designations. Firstly, it was known simply as the LWS, but, as time passed and the LWS was declared an official 'OGG' project, it was given the code P729. Interestingly, despite the second generation RX-7 having already been granted production status, and the fact that work on it was started well in advance of P729 (so one would expect a lower number), it was given the code P747.

Whatever, as P729 took shape, a number of prototypes were built. The first full-size clay produced by MANA was christened the 'Duo 101' by the Americans, but should probably be called the S-1 to comply with future policy.

The handbuilt machine constructed by IAD was designated V705, the V denoting that it was a one-off prototype. Shortly after, the second full-sized styling clay produced at MANA was christened S-2, and the final one, naturally, was S-3, after which, the project was sent to Hiroshima.

The engineering mules, also constructed by IAD in England, were known by the code M-1, the M denoting mechanical. Still using the P729 code, the project was taken through its final stages in Hiroshima until 12 handbuilt prototypes were constructed in 1988. These were named S1-1, S1-2 and so on up to S1-12, but should not be confused with the MANA styling clays.

It would seem reasonable to expect that, once the new sports car reached production status, things would become simpler. However, three different names were chosen for the various markets.

MX-5 production at the Hiroshima Plant Complex, where it was built alongside the RX-7 and a number of other cars in the Mazda range.

The MX series of concept cars (the MX-02 Show Car in 1983, followed by the MX-03 in 1985 and MX-04 in 1987) had the right image, and the LWS was so unlike the rest of the Mazda range that a new designation was needed anyway. The new sports car was therefore christened the MX-5 (presumably MX-05 was dropped as it fails to roll off the tongue quite so easily).

So, the MX-5 was the name used in all markets - I'm afraid not! Both America and Japan decided they needed something different. In the USA, Laguna was a hot favourite, but then marketing boss Rod Bymaster came across the word "meed" in the dictionary. Today, this means "a reward" or "due amount of praise," but Mazda Meed just doesn't appeal. However, apparently its origins lie in an old German word - Miata. It was perfect; the new Mazda would be christened the Miata. However, there was a slight problem - in Japan there was a company with a very similar sounding name.

The Miyata business was founded in Tokyo in 1880, concerning itself mainly with the production of armaments. Although better known nowadays as a manufacturer of bicycles (the company has been in the trade for over a century, after all), Eisuke Miyata had also built a small two-cylinder car as early as 1909. Just before the Second World War, a number of Asahi light cars were constructed, and the company was heavily involved with motorbikes, too. Having produced its first Triumph-based machine in 1913 (also known as the Asahi), it finally stopped building motorcycles in the mid-1960s.

After some negotiations, it was finally agreed that the official designation would be 'MX-5 Miata' in the States, but the home market would use yet another name. On 4 April 1989, Mazda set up the Eunos and Autozam sales channels to augment those already in place. This splitting of the line-up is common practice in Japan where home market ranges are so extensive (Toyota currently lists 45 basic models, for instance, before moving into commercials).

Basically, it gives the dealers the opportunity to compete in different market sectors.

Anyway, after much deliberation, it was decided to call the new sports car the Eunos Roadster and to sell it through Eunos dealerships. The word Eunos, apparently, comes from a combination of the latin word for joy and an abbreviation of numbers. Expressed another way, it could be taken to mean a collection of joy! At last, the LWS had proper names for all markets.

Kenichi Yamamoto had been talking publicly about an 'entry level' sports car from as early as 1985 but, in reality, few were prepared for a car like the MX-5. As will be gathered from this chapter, however, its gestation period was far from smooth and straightforward.

Looking back, Toshihiko Hirai said: "There were times when a small breeze from the wrong direction could have blown the project away," but the future of the car that meant so much to him was now secure, and three months ahead of schedule.

Production took place at the Hiroshima Plant Complex (opened in November 1966), where it was built alongside the RX-7 and a number of other cars in the Mazda range.

3

LAUNCH OF A LEGEND

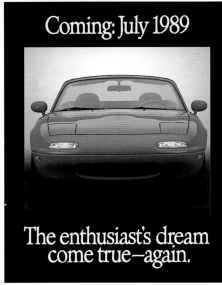

Cover from the American pre-launch brochure, describing the car as "The enthusiast's dream come true - again."

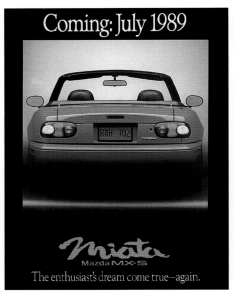

The rear of the pre-launch brochure, aptly showing the tail of the Miata. There were actually two different rear panels to suit the shapes and sizes of registration plates for any given market.

After years of preparation, the Mazda MX-5 was finally unveiled at the 1989 Chicago Auto Show in the United States. The event, which opened on 10 February, saw the debut of two other important Japanese cars - the Nissan 300ZX and Honda's NSX supercar - so some of the initial impact could so easily have been lost. However, at less than $14,000, the Miata was in a completely different price bracket, so a clash was therefore avoided.

To help the Miata get even more press coverage, the so-called 'Club

Racer' was shown alongside the production models. There was a link here with the launch of the original RX-7, when Toyo Kogyo had put a 'competition version' of the new car on display. This was something that nobody seemed to pick up on, presumably because they were too busy filling column inches on the latest Mazda to look into the past. Finished in a bright yellow hue, it seemed that every magazine in the country featured

A page from the first American catalogue, clearly showing the snug cockpit of the Miata.

at least one picture of the Club Racer.

The production models were the most important to Mazda, of course, as it was these that would give the company a return on its investment. The marketing was extremely clever - well co-ordinated and, above all, very thorough. The American public was bombarded with Miata stories; people couldn't even sit down for a quiet evening in front of the TV without seeing one. One American advert showed ghosted images of an Austin-Healey and Triumph TR in the dark. Then day broke with a new, bright red MX-5 sitting in the sunshine outside the garage. The advert implied, with a touch of subtle humour, that the owners of classic British cars more often than not had to contend with the hassle of maintaining or repairing them, sometimes well into the night, whereas the Mazda owner just got into his car and drove it away. As Bob Hall once said, although the

Advertising for the Miata, whether it was on the television or in newspapers and magazines, was quick to point out the concept of the new Mazda - to take the owner back to the simplicity of the fifties and sixties, but to offer it in a modern, more reliable package.

INTRODUCING MAZDA MIATA.
IT NOT ONLY GIVES YOU A GLIMPSE OF THE '90S... IT TAKES YOU BACK, AS WELL.

IT IS A CAR THAT INSTANTLY EVOKES A RUSH OF EMOTION. FOR IT IS, AT ONCE, AN AUTOMOBILE OF BOTH CLASSIC FORM AND VISIONARY TECHNOLOGY.

INTRODUCING THE ALL-NEW MAZDA MX-5 MIATA. A CONVERTIBLE. A TWO-SEATER. A TRUE REAR-WHEEL-DRIVE ROADSTER. IT IS AN AUTOMOBILE BUILT WITH JUST ONE OBJECTIVE IN MIND: SHEER EXHILARATION. AND FOR LESS THAN WHAT YOU MIGHT EXPECT, YOU CAN DRIVE ONE OF YOUR OWN. AT THE HEART OF ITS UNIQUE ABILITY TO STIR THE EMOTIONS IS A 16-VALVE, FUEL INJECTED ENGINE. SHORT THROW FIVE-SPEED TRANSMISSION. PLUS A RACING-INSPIRED 4-WHEEL DOUBLE-WISHBONE SUSPENSION SYSTEM. AND 4-WHEEL DISC BRAKES. A DRIVER'S-SIDE AIRBAG SUPPLEMENTAL RESTRAINT SYSTEM (SRS) IS ALSO STANDARD.

MAZDA MIATA. IT'S DESIGNED TO NOT ONLY PERFORM RIGHT, BUT ALSO FEEL RIGHT. SO DISCOVER THE PURE FUN AND PASSION OF DRIVING A MAZDA MIATA. IT NOT ONLY GIVES YOU A GLIMPSE OF THE '90S... IT TAKES YOU BACK, AS WELL. FOR MORE INFORMATION, CALL THIS NUMBER: 800-424-0202 EXT. 705.

mazda
IT JUST FEELS RIGHT.

"JUST BORN AND ALREADY A STAR..."

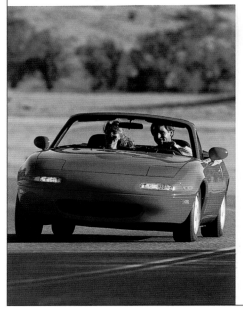

Road & Track editors in their July 1989 issue named the new Mazda Miata one of their five "World's Best Cars"—extraordinary praise in the company of some of the most exotic and expensive cars in the world.

"Just born and already a star. What does this say about the MX-5? That it stole the hearts (and votes) of nine smitten staffers ...what a sports car should be... Pure, simple, undistilled, clear-eyed driving fun..."

Road & Track, July 1989

"Wait till you drive the Miata! You'll love it ...Twist the key and you're rewarded with a pleasant burble...torque is strong across a wide band...a feeling of directness between the throttle and rear wheels...Its combination of communication, responsiveness, predictability and forgiveness makes it the best-handling 2-seater I've driven in recent memory...The lightweight sports car is back!" Road & Track, March 1989

"This car is alive. It breathes and flexes its muscles and generally behaves more like an organism than a machine...a flat-out blast to drive. Nimble, precise, even, smooth-wonderful traits all wrapped up into one neat little package..."

Autoweek, May 22, 1989

"The best sports car buy in America... the appeal of the Miata knows no bounds... clean, elegant design...marvelous road manners...a real sense of excitement as the revs rise...a serious for-real sports car that churns up all sorts of memories of late, great roadsters. The only difference is that this one's a far better, more capable car."

Motor Trend, July 1989

"The Miata MX-5 feels just about perfect, delivering every bit of simple fun its voluptuous, organic shape promises...a car for those of us who were born too late for the English roadster craze...light, agile, and quick, with a seat that supports, a wheel that commands, a shifter that snaps, and an exhaust note of sheer exuberance."

Automobile Magazine, March 1989

"If you were reading this magazine 30 years ago...no one would have dared dream of a two-seater so deft in its execution..."

Car and Driver, March 1989

Shown with optional front air dam, rear spoiler and skirt.

British sports cars of the 1960s had a certain charm, reliability was not a strong point ...

Although the Mazda didn't officially go on sale until July, by mid-1989, *Road & Track* was already naming the Miata as one of the world's best cars, lined up alongside the Ferrari Testarossa, Mercedes-Benz 300E, Chevrolet Corvette ZR1 and Porsche 911 Carrera 4. In one paragraph, the MX-5 project was summed up perfectly: "Just born and already a star. What does that say about the MX-5? That it stole the hearts (and votes) of nine smitten staffers. That in typical Japanese fashion, Mazda has done its homework and come up with a design and a concept that time has all but forgotten: the basic, front-engine, rear-drive, open-top affordable sports car." Shortly after the launch, the same magazine had said: "Mazda hopes to attract 40,000 buyers per year, which sounds a bit optimistic." But the timing was perfect; the Hiroshima concern had beaten the competition in a market many thought had disappeared.

Miata fever seemed to grip the States. As *Road & Track* said: "More than any other car in recent memory - and even fairly distant memory - the Mazda Miata has created a stir of almost embarrassing proportions ..." Deposits were being taken months in advance, and rumours soon spread of people paying ridiculous premiums. It was a re-run of 1970, when the Datsun 240Z first hit the American scene. Demand outstripping supply was the root cause once again, as only 20,000 units were scheduled for the US in the first year.

The American market was given the 1.6 litre twin-cam engine (much the same as that found in other parts of the world), with a five-speed manual gearbox. Introduced at $13,800 (although few people managed to get one for that price), one of the few standard features that made a concession to modernity was a driver's side airbag, but that was the way things were intended to be with the MX-5 - a full set of instruments and comfortable adjustable seats were far more important. One journalist

remarked that the MX-5 was "a refreshing throwback to simpler times."

The basic list price was indeed low. Mazda promoted its new convertible with the phrase "The Return of the Affordable Sports Car." The RX-7 now ranged from $17,000 to a mighty $26,000. On the other hand, if one looks at the other two Japanese sports cars launched in Chicago, the Z-cars had become progressively more and more expensive (the Z32 type 300ZX was launched at $27,300 in its cheapest form), and the NSX made the Z look a snip, even at that price.

A number of options were available for the MX-5. For starters, there were two different packages: Package A, priced at $1145, included alloy wheels, a Panasonic stereo radio/cassette, leather-trimmed steering wheel and power-assisted steering, while Package B (at $1730) included everything in Package A plus cruise control, headrest speakers and electric windows.

Air conditioning, a limited-slip differential, a CD player and fitted overmats were offered separately. The air conditioning was $795, while the LSD was a very reasonable $250. The CD, listed at a hefty $600, reflected the fact that this type of stereo equipment was then quite novel in a car; the floor mats were just $59.

A number of dealer-installed accessories were available, including a tonneau cover, a protective front-end mask (known affectionately in the States as a 'bra'), front and rear spoilers, side skirts, a luggage rack for the bootlid, and various alarm systems.

A removable hard-top was also listed (at $1100) but sold in red only after Mazda had trouble matching the blue and white pigments initially - these shades eventually followed in spring 1990. On the subject of colour schemes, three colours were available in the States: Classic Red, Crystal White and Mariner Blue. Yellow and British Racing Green were expected to join the line-up in the future, but it was a silver hue (Silver Stone Metallic) that made it to the marketplace first.

Press reaction in the States

The July 1989 edition of *Road & Track* carried an article that was to set the scene across the whole of America. One journalist after another seemed to fall under the MX-5's spell: "The Miata's fuel-injected 116bhp dohc four (the only engine Mazda offers) keeps giving all the way up to its 7000rpm redline. Musically, the engine is a perfect tenor, serenading the driver lustily to 6200rpm, where the exhaust note begins to sour. This engine is mated exclusively (no automatic transmission offered) to a terrific five-speed manual with super-short throws and a precise feel."

The magazine managed a 0-60 time of 9.5 seconds (around a second slower than the Toyota MR2 or Honda's CRX Si), whilst top speed was recorded at 117mph (187kph), and the standing-quarter covered in 17.0 seconds (with a terminal speed of 81.5mph, or 130.4kph).

These figures were nothing more than respectable at the end of the day, but Mazda looked at all-round performance, not just 0-60 times. This policy is one that Porsche has always adhered to - making a complete package rather than a vehicle that is simply quick in a straight line. In other words, a car has to feel right, too.

In this respect, the Mazda team had succeeded. Like every magazine in America, the engineers were more than happy with the overall package. Compared to the competition, it was said "The Miata's four-wheel disc brakes don't seem to give it any relative stopping advantage, either. The brake feel is very good, however, with excellent communication between the pedal, brakes and tyres ...

"We even had the convertible top up one time to check on the headroom (we found plenty) ... The top's sealing against rain and wind noise was superb. With the top down, the swirling winds wafted freely through the driving compartment, but did so without buffeting the occupants to distraction or noisily ruining conversation. It is also important to point out that chassis flexing, a crucial consideration (and problem spot) on convertibles, was virtually non-existent in the Miata ..."

Hailing "the return of the honest sports car," *Car & Driver* was equally enthusiastic. "If the new Mazda MX-5 Miata was any more talented and tempting, buying one would be illegal ... The Miata delivers an overload of the kind of pure, unadulterated sports car pleasure that became all but extinct 20 years ago."

Although probably just a touch biased as a member of the MANA organisation, Bob Hall summed up feelings generally when he described his first drive home from the office: "The very first time I drove a Miata home was kind of an interesting experience. Normally my ride home is about 28 miles, and it takes me 35 to 40 minutes. I stretched it out just a little bit that evening - I think it went to about 137 or 138 miles!"

As for the bodywork, Mark Stehrenberger carried out an expert and in-depth styling analysis. Finding very few faults, he eventually declared: "It's a winner!"

Of the 263,000 Mazdas sold in the USA during 1989 (Mazda's record sales period in the States at that time), no less than 23,052 of them were Miatas, despite it arriving midway through the year. 1990 was a poor year for Mazda Stateside, but nonetheless, Miata sales still continued to rise, helped, no doubt by the introduction of silver paintwork and the option of automatic transmission, added to the line-up in March. Press reaction

The 1990 model year Miata with optional hard-top in place. In the USA, the hard-top was only available in red but, in the author's opinion at least, it was a very attractive package.

A 1990 model year Miata, which was the name given to the MX-5 for the American market. Note the optional seven-spoke alloys.

had been extremely favourable, and the MX-5 Miata was a far greater success than anyone had anticipated.

The home market
Car design was becoming more fashion-driven, especially in Japan, a country very receptive to trends.

Booms seem to come and go overnight, but when they do happen, they are extremely intense. The retro-boom seems to have

Memories of the 'Bubble Time' - eager buyers placing their orders for the new J58G Eunos Roadster. In terms of percentages, Japan's economic growth was running at 5.7 per cent - almost twice the national average of most other industrial nations during this period.

An advert dating from mid-1989, a couple of months before the Eunos sales channel (which also sold some of the Citroën range) became operational.

lingered longer than most, however. Starting in the early to mid-1980s, one of the first car manufacturers to cash in on this particular boom was Nissan, with the March (or Micra) providing the basis for the highly successful Be-1,

launched in 1985. After this there was the Figaro and then the Pau. The Figaro proved so popular that, in the end, Nissan had to hold a lottery to decide who could have one!

A number of firms followed

Nissan's lead. Even at the 1997 Tokyo Show, there were still dozens of exhibits displaying the retro-look. However, with the retro-boom in full swing in Japan when Mazda launched the MX-5, it meant that timing was not only good in

A double-page spread from a pre-launch Japanese brochure. Apart from the tail badges, which were obviously different due to the various names of the car around the world, the badge on the nose section was unique to the home market.

49

Interior of the Special Package model, shown here with optional air conditioning and CD player. Unlike America, in Japan, the detachable hard-top was available in either red or black.

America, but also Japan.

Having been officially announced on 3 July, deposits started being taken two days later, and the Eunos Roadster eventually went on sale in Japan on 1 September, sold exclusively through the Eunos sales channel. Oddly, the full four-day press launch wasn't held until 4 July, despite a number of magazines already covering the car beforehand. The launch took place in Hakone, with the Mazda design team present, along with 15 cars.

The home market had a standard 1.6 litre model (which started on chassis NA6CE-100021), and the so-called 1.6 litre Special Package version, the first of which carried chassis number NA6CE-100022. The basic model (priced at 1,748,000 yen) weighed in at just 940kg (2068lb) and was indeed basic. The Special Package added 10kg (22lb) and a further 150,000 yen. The Special Package included power-assisted steering, seven-spoke 5.5J x 14 alloy wheels, electric windows, and a Momo leather-rimmed steering wheel.

Major options included air conditioning (150,000 yen), a detachable hard-top (165,000 yen), a CD player (62,000 yen) and limited-slip differential. Other components mentioned at the launch included a wood-rimmed Nardi steering wheel with matching gearknob and handbrake handle (which unfortunately didn't appear for some time), a polished cam cover, chrome door mirrors, and an uprated suspension kit. The 5.5J alloys mentioned earlier were augmented by two types of 6J x 14 wheel - a Mazdaspeed five-spoke design, and a 17-spoke one from the SPA concern.

Minor items included polished treadplates with the 'Roadster' logo, a front airdam skirt (provided by

高回転型1600DOHC16バルブ+パワープラントフレーム。ダイレクトレスポンスの快感。

4輪ダブルウィッシュボーン+オープン専用・高剛性軽量ボディ。ダイレクトハンドリングの快感。

Another double-page spread showing the technical specifications for the home market, as well as the 1.6 litre four-cylinder engine and the LWS chassis. Note the PPF running down the centre, and the seven-spoke wheel design, chosen because seven spokes weigh less than the eight found on a traditional Minilite rim.

The Eunos Roadster with optional rear luggage rack, rear spoiler, and chrome door mirrors.

the factory in black), projector lamps (situated in the air intake), rear mudflaps, an alloy gearshift gaiter retainer, an alloy handbrake lever handle, and door edge mouldings. Besides Eunos clothing and luggage, perhaps the trendiest accessory was a TAG Heuer 2000 Series watch with the word 'Eunos' stamped into the security clip on the strap.

Reviewing the new Mazda in June 1989, Shigeharu Kumakura of *Car Graphic* thought it was a bit "tail happy" and that the engine could do with a little more refinement, but he immediately fell in love with the interior. The tester also commented on the lack of scuttle shake, the excellent soft-top (claiming there was no real need for a hard-top), and was pleased with the movement of air within the cockpit whilst the hood was down. Interestingly, the feel of the gearshift was highly commended, although the gear spacing between second and third and third to fourth was felt to be not close enough.

In its September 1989 edition, *Motor Fan* pointed out that there were two types of sports car - one that lets you enjoy the sensation of speed, the other the feel of control. The MX-5 fell into the category of driver enjoyment through control.

It was noted that the Eunos Roadster was not a fast car, but the overall mood was good. Little things were very pleasing: "the exhaust note under 4000rpm is very quiet, but over this it becomes musical. The delivery of torque is very smooth, and the whole car reacts to each movement of the accelerator." The tester was also happy with the classical sports car interior, but thought the seats needed to give the driver more support during hard cornering.

Japanese auto-makers always seem to strive for a sports car boot to have at least enough room for two golf bags. The new Mazda was no exception, although after the battery was moved from its original location behind the seats, providing this amount of space was no longer possible. A lack of luggage capacity was one of the few major problems identified by journalists and end users, but Mazda knew the problem existed and would go a long way towards solving it in the future.

It looked as if Mazda had timed the promotional build-up to perfection. Like America, virtually all forms of media seemed to feature the MX-5, and this completely overshadowed the launch of a serious competitor - the Suzuki Cappuccino, a lightweight two-seater powered by a 658cc turbocharged engine. First displayed at the 1989 Tokyo Show, it failed to grab the headlines after the Mazda stole all the glory. For this reason, it wasn't until November 1991 that it finally went on sale. At just 1,458,000 yen, it was very reasonable.

Automatic transmission was added to the Eunos Roadster options list in March 1990. Priced at just 40,000 yen extra, it did, however, add 30kg (66lb) to the overall weight of the vehicle. Factor in the slightly detuned engine (to bring in maximum torque at 4500rpm), and it was obvious that this combination would hardly place the little Mazda in the supercar league, but in a country where most cars have two pedals instead of three, it made a lot of sense to offer the option. A Special Package model was the first to receive the four-speed automatic gearbox (chassis NA6CE-113858), although it was also available on the standard version, the first car being NA6CE-114565.

Available in Classic Red, Crystal White, Silver Stone Metallic, or Mariner Blue, the Eunos Roadster was an immediate hit. From September 1989 to the end of that year, no less than 9307 were sold. In 1990, this figure nearly tripled, with over 25,000 Roadsters finding new homes in the Land of the Rising Sun.

Other markets in 1989
Apart from America and Japan, the only other markets to get the MX-5 in 1989 were Canada and Australia.

For many years, Canadian vehicles have usually complied quite closely with American specification models, and the MX-5 was no exception. Almost 3000 found their way to Canadian buyers in the first year of production, a figure that rose to nearer 4000 in 1990.

As for Australia, its models were very similiar to Japanese spec cars in that both had right-hand drive. By this time, emission regulations were becoming much the same across the world (all countries were stricter than they had been in the 1970s, following the lead of California), so this no longer meant special exhaust equipment for certain markets. In addition, Australia is quite close to Japan (at least compared with America or Europe), so shipping is much quicker.

Sales started in Australia in October 1989 (just one model was listed), and, by the end of the year, 621 had been sold. Naturally, with 1990 being a full year for sales, this figure increased - in fact, by no less than 233 per cent. Shortly after the launch, *Modern Motor* named the car in its 'Best Car Awards for 89/90', the MX-5 eventually scoring 257 points out of a possible 470 to easily take the title.

Reaction in New Zealand was also favourable. In fact, *New Zealand Car* actually bought an MX-5, citing its good points as "just about everything." However, with a distinct shortage of supplies and strong demand, at one point, as

many were being bought 'out of the box' on the 'second-hand' market as from the dealerships, as the thought of a 30 per cent premium tempted a lot of people to sell their car as soon as it was delivered.

The model's first taste of competition came in the Teddy Yip Race of Champions. The event was staged as part of the 1989 Macau Grand Prix weekend, and comprised 16 MX-5s driven by some of the greatest names in motor racing, past and present. Ironically, it was a Toyota Group C driver, Geoff Lees, who took the flag at the finish, narrowly beating Andy Rouse.

The new car in Europe
The MX-5 was making headlines in Europe, too. Writing for *Supercar Classics* in late 1989, Mark Gillies said: "When the Mazda MX-5 hits the showrooms, it should offer all of the [original Lotus] Elan's virtues allied to high (Japanese) build quality, modern (but similar) appearance, far greater refinement and rather more crash protection."

Even *Classic Cars* magazine was enthusiastic: "Here it is! A new popular sports car for the Nineties: the Japanese Mazda MX-5 combines modern engineering with the nostalgic spirit of Sixties sports car motoring, and it costs about the same in real terms as an MGB once did ... At £14,249 we have no doubt there will be a queue of prospective owners chasing the 2500 MX-5s destined for the UK

The enthusiast's dream realised.

The sports car is back! The new Mazda MX-5 is all set to become the experience of the 1990s, offering the ultimate in open-top driving; wind in the face and the nimble feel of a taut and eager roadster.

Designed with classic looks and superb performance, the MX-5 has already caught the imagination and won the admiration of enthusiasts throughout the world.

Its lightweight body, front engine and rear-wheel drive configuration, provide perfect balance and handling mixing nostalgia with the modern; it is an opportunity to again discover the pure joy and passion of driving.

Some of the world's top motoring publications have already described the Mazda MX-5 as:

"Nimble, precise, even, smooth - wonderful" – *Autoweek*

"With 1960s style allied to 1990s sophistication and reliability, the MX-5 looks like a winner" – *Autocar & Motor*

"Just born and already a star" – *Road & Track*

"We felt like cheering" – *Car & Driver*

From the very outset, the Mazda designers' aim was to produce a sports car that embodied the traditional spirit of the two-seater roadster of old. The result is a car that instantly evokes a feeling of sheer exhilaration with one objective in mind - pure fun!

A classic formula
The MX-5 has superb handling and performance that has been internationally acclaimed. With its engine situated behind the front axle line coupled to rear-wheel drive, it has near perfect 50:50 balance offering the ultimate in road-holding, handling and ride.

The traditional layout of the MX-5 reflects Mazda's belief that a superb sports car has to have superb balance. To obtain the ultimate in handling a number of components have been specially crafted to be as light as possible; for example the bonnet is made from aluminium and lightweight materials are used for the bumpers.

This all means the car weighs only 955 kilograms, enabling it to be a sparkling performer, but for all its

sports car attributes the MX-5 is also exceptionally safe. Its all steel bodyshell is immensely strong and designed for total passenger safety.

The MX-5 is a vehicle with a singular purpose – to be a sports car. Its classic styling, superb handling and performance have all been obtained without compromising comfort and space. In fact there is room

50:50

to accommodate two adults and their luggage.

The thrill is back
The entire concept behind the MX-5 is simplicity combined with fun. The styling reflects this thought; smooth flowing

contours that provide maximum aerodynamic efficiency, yet embody the thrill of the classic two-seater sports car.

Its snug, low-slung cockpit has a distinctly traditional look and feel, with a leather-trimmed steering-wheel, large round instrument dials and high bucket seats. Once you're behind the wheel you will find out why it is just so special.

For a start, the gear change is second to none. Its short gear shift is more reminiscent of a racing car gear change than a road car. And the pedals have been ideally spaced to give both a relaxed drive and a fast gear change.

The Mazda MX-5 is putting excitement back into motoring.

Part of the first British catalogue for the MX-5, printed in March 1990: "The enthusiast's dream realised."

THE NEW MAZDA MX5. IT'S SET MOTORING BACK 30 YEARS.

Remember the classic sports cars of the Sixties? Those growling, nippy two-seaters that you thought had gone for ever?

They're back in the new Mazda MX5. It's one of the most advanced cars on the road.

But you'd never guess as you step back three decades into the snug, low-slung cockpit.

The traditional leather-trimmed wheel and large round instrument dials are just as you remember them. As indeed is the stubby gear shift with the ultra short throw. (*Car and Driver* magazine compared it to a toggle switch.)

As you'd expect, the 1.6 litre fuel-injected 16 valve DOHC engine is mounted at the front. And supplies power to the rear with a throaty roar that's guaranteed to make you grin. As well it might. Mazda engineers listened to recordings of over 100 classic engine notes to perfect it.

The result even managed to move some hard-bitten motoring journalists. "Flat-out gorgeous" was the verdict of *What Car?* While *Road and Track* judged the MX5 to be one of the five best cars in the world. (Second only in fact to the Ferrari Testarossa).

Admittedly though, not every detail is authentic. The roof doesn't leak for a start. Nor will the car break down every week. (Like all Mazdas it's so reliable it comes with a 3 year warranty). And although the odd purist might object we've also included power steering, electric windows and a high quality car stereo. At under £14,500 it won't break the bank either.

We could go on and on. But there is a better way to appreciate the MX5. Have a word with your Mazda dealer and take a test drive down memory lane.

mazda
Building Excitement

Early advertising from the UK. It used much the same theme as that in the States, harking back to memories of the sixties - a golden era for sporting machines.

---

market in 1990."

But the author was a little more sceptical, predicting that the new Mazda was going to find life harder in Britain than it had in the States and Japan. This country has always been extremely slow in warming to

the qualities of Japanese cars ... As I wrote in the second volume on the Nissan Z-cars: "At the end of the day, British buyers want a badge, and often pass judgement on a car before they've even seen it, let alone driven it. They also have an image

of pricing relative to the marque. If it has the right badge, it's brilliant and excellent value for money - the wrong badge, it's an over-priced heap of junk! In that respect, it is sad to reflect on how little things have changed since the early 1970s."

British taxes on new and imported cars, which seem extortionate compared to America and Japan (and even some other parts of Europe), would negate much of the MX-5's price advantage - a Panther Kallista or four-cylinder Morgan could be had for similar money. The new Elan was expected to cost less than £20,000 (it eventually went on sale at £17,850), a TVR S2 was £16,645, the top-of-the-range Caterham was only £11,570, and the new Reliant Scimitar range started at under £10,000. Besides, the British weather makes the everyday use of convertibles questionable for all but the bravest of die-hard open car enthusiasts, and many would doubtless regard the Mazda as a cheeky impersonator.

In addition, if a drophead can only occasionally be used, why not buy a real old English sports car? The classic car boom was at its height, so spares were plentiful thanks to firms reproducing them, and magazines were packed full of cars for sale. A monthly from the time of the MX-5 launch was advertising a chrome bumper MGB Roadster, fully restored to "outstanding condition" for £9250,

53

while a garage had a Lotus Elan S3 Drophead for £14,000. Both would attract cheaper classic insurance, another consideration.

There was also the new Lotus Elan hovering in the background, which, naturally, got a lot of the limelight in the British press. However, in its guide to the 1989 Motorfair, *Autocar & Motor* said: "Mazda throws down the gauntlet to Lotus as the MX-5 makes an appearance in the UK for the first time. Due to go on sale here this February, the MX-5 will be a crowd-puller as a logical, cheaper rival to the Elan."

The Mazda MX-5 was actually launched on the 14 March 1990 (starting with chassis JMZNA18B200100001). It came with the familiar 1.6 litre twin-cam engine (which in UK spec developed 114bhp) and a five-speed gearbox. Features included power steering, 5.5J x 14 seven-spoke alloys, electric windows, a Momo leather-rimmed steering wheel, black cloth trim, and a Clarion CRH60 radio/cassette unit. It was available in four basic colours: Classic Red, Crystal White, Mariner Blue and Silver Stone Metallic - the same options as those for the home market.

William Kimberley reviewed the car for the April 1990 edition of *MotorSport*, and stated: "Considering that the car will cost £14,249 inclusive of tax and VAT, it is strange that the door mirrors have to be hand-adjusted from the outside, that a clock is not included and that the aerial does not fold down but has to be unscrewed to remove it. The windows, though, are electrically operated. These quibbles apart, the car itself is a charmer. The gearbox is superb, the engine responsive and the sheer *joie de vivre* of driving it exhilarating."

After recording a top speed of 114mph (182kph) and a 0-60 time of a fraction over nine seconds, *Autocar & Motor* was equally complimentary. It said: "The MX-5 is a total success. Mazda's single-minded determination to provide fun has produced a car of the rarest quality. Above all else it is its ability to involve the driver intimately in its every reaction and response that makes it a joy to drive. Few others, at any price, can offer so much."

The same magazine later carried out a test to find the best-handling car on sale in Britain. Gathering together ten sporting machines and a similar number of drivers (including ex-F1 man, Jonathon Palmer), the MX-5 came away a clear winner. It scored 23 points - eight more than the Porsche 944, and 13 more than the third-placed Ford Sierra Cosworth 4x4.

All of Mazda's attention to detail had obviously paid off and the press loved the car, but this enthusiasm was as nothing if people didn't go into Mazda dealerships (there were 185 in the UK at that time) and part with their money. Fortunately for Mazda, the author's scepticism was unfounded; the MX-5 seemed to create a new breed of enthusiast, one not deeply rooted in the classic car movement and only happy to wallow in nostalgia, but a breed that wanted the fun of an open car combined with trouble-free, reliable motoring.

The end of a perfect year
Hirai summed up the general feeling with: "Some people thought this simple idea was stupid, but the original RX-7 concept has gone too far upmarket. This level is now vacant. We may not make a big profit with this, compared with cars like the 929. There might not be so many of these customers, but they have very strong feelings. It is like seeing your former lover 30 years later."

By the end of 1989, the MX-5 had already picked up a large number of accolades. In the USA, *Auto Week* voted it 'The Most Fun Car', while *Road & Track* included it in its 'World's Best Cars' listing, where it finished second only to the Ferrari Testarossa; *Automotive News* called it the 'Hit of the Year'.

In its home country, *Sports Nippon News* hailed the Eunos Roadster as the 'Best Sporty Car'. Even *Autocar & Motor* in the UK voted it the 'Best Sports Car' in a review of 1990 models. As the months passed, the awards came thicker and faster, and from all points of the globe. It is doubtful whether a single model has ever had so much praise heaped upon it.

4

PRODUCTION HISTORY

After such a universally warm reception, it was fairly obvious that the MX-5 was destined for success. The popularity of the little roadster took everyone by surprise, and, by the end of 1990, over 140,000 had been built (cumulative production of all Mazda vehicles reached 25 million units at the same time). Forgetting the 12 produced in 1988 during the pilot build, this meant that, in just two years, the MX-5 had already outsold the Alfa Romeo Spider by quite some margin, despite the car from Milan having been introduced way back in 1966!

To the surprise of many people abroad, the Eunos wasn't awarded the Japanese 'Car of the Year' title. However, the model that clinched it - the Toyota Celsior (or Lexus LS400 outside Japan) - was an exceptional motor car and a worthy winner, even more so when one considers the market sector it took by storm. The new Nissan Skyline was another stunner, especially in GT-R guise, and took second place. The Eunos Roadster came third, which was quite an achievement given the competition - Nissan's 300ZX and Infiniti Q45, and the new Toyota MR2 included.

At the 1989 Tokyo Show, a car finished in British Racing Green and sporting a tan leather interior had been exhibited on the Mazda stand to gauge reaction. In July 1990, it joined the line-up in Japan - badged as the V Special - to

A rare shot of MX-5 production. The Mazda sports car was produced almost exclusively in Hiroshima, although for a brief spell during the boom of the early 1990s, it was built at Hofu in the Yamaguchi Prefecture. Once demand subsided, production shifted back to the Hiroshima Plant Complex.

オーセンティックな深い味わい、Vスペシャル。

心とからだ、ともに
V
SPECIAL.

EQUIPMENT

OPTIONS

The home market's V Special of July 1990. The automatic gearbox option (shown here labelled number 3) was introduced in Japan four months earlier. A polished cam cover, uprated suspension, and detachable hard-top (finished in body colour) made up the options list.

Studio shot of the V Special, introduced on the home market to celebrate the first anniversary of the Eunos Roadster (Japan's name for the MX-5). Finished in Neo Green, it featured a tan leather interior and a host of extras.

The tasteful interior of the V Special, with its gorgeous Nardi steering wheel.

celebrate the first anniversary of the Eunos Roadster. A variation on the Special Package model, a classic wood-rimmed, three-spoke Nardi steering wheel dominated the driver's view, and the natural theme was extended to the matching wooden gearknob and handbrake trim. A CD player was included as standard, as were polished treadplates with the 'Roadster' logo. Finished in Neo Green with a tan interior (including leather-trimmed seats) and hood cover, it was available with either manual or automatic transmission, and priced at 2,122,000 and 2,162,000 yen respectively.

By the end of 1990, a further 25,226 Eunos Roadsters had been sold, taking the home market total to 34,533 units. In the meantime, the M2 project had been founded in Japan, which brought together a group of engineers and planners to develop MX-5 specials (see Chapter Five).

The MX-5 in Britain

The 1990 British Motor Show was held at the NEC, opening at the end of September; Mazda occupied Stand 108 at the event. The show saw the world debut of the Gissya concept car - a futuristic MPV that perhaps predicted the forthcoming trend for this type of vehicle. Sadly, it stole quite a lot of the thunder that the MX-5 deserved. Mind you, with a lengthy waiting list only just starting to shorten, it probably didn't need any more promotion.

In the following month, a hard-top became available through the dealer network, having been announced a few weeks previously. Made from glassfibre, it sported a lined interior, heated rear screen, a courtesy light and through-flow ventilation. Priced at £1145, it was produced in conjunction with TWR (Tom Walkinshaw Racing) of Oxford, and was listed in Classic Red, Mariner Blue and Crystal White to match car body colours, or Black with a grained finish. There was also a trolley and cover available for owners to store the hard-top safely when not in use.

The official Mazda UK price list dated 5 September 1990 quoted £14,899 for the basic car, with metallic paint adding £175, and air conditioning (a rarely taken-up option in Britain) adding a further £1259 to the bill. At this time, the turbocharged RX-7 coupé was £22,599, while the Cabriolet was

Action from the final round of the 1990 Mazda MX-5 UK Cup, held at Silverstone. Patrick Watts (who was declared champion at the end of the series) is seen leading Mark Lemmer (runner-up in both the race and the series) and Robert Speak. A total of 27 competitors took part in the MX-5 UK Cup that year.

£24,999. The most expensive 323 was £13,279, with prices in that range starting at £8469, so the MX-5 wasn't exactly cheap.

Indeed, Roger Bell, writing for *Supercar Classics* at the time commented: "Here is a forward-to-the-past ragtop roadster that epitomises what fun-car motoring is all about. Apart from its indifferent performance, the standard MX-5 is hard to fault dynamically. Explicit steering is so sharp, so accurate that it faithfully obeys commands as if by telepathy. Fingertip delicacy is rewarded with composed balance and precision,

just as surely as clumsiness is punished by raggedness. It rewards the sympathetic driver with an intimacy that no other Japanese cars (and few European ones) possess. The neat hood (augmented now by an optional TWR-made hard-top) is even better than an Alfa Spider's. There's only one serious problem with the MX-5. It costs £14,250, which is surely far too much."

In fact, the price was even higher but, nonetheless, by the end of the year Mazda UK had sold 27,598 vehicles, of which, no less than 2246 were MX-5s. This was

actually quite an impressive figure, for the rest of Europe only managed 7021 sales, and Australia could do no better than 1446 units.

Inspired by the MX-5 race at the 1989 Macau Grand Prix, a one-make series was established in the UK. The 1990 Mazda MX-5 UK Cup was run over 12 rounds, taking in Britain's finest racing circuits along the way, with all the cars being slightly modified by Roger Dowson Engineering. Patrick Watts was declared champion after dominating the series; he finished on 116 points (32 ahead of his nearest rival). It is interesting to note that Watts was also champion of the Honda CRX one-make series that year, and when Mazda returned to the BTCC scene in 1992 (with the 323F), it was Watts who was chosen as its driver.

The MX-5 BBR Turbo
Although virtually all road test reports were complimentary, not everyone thought the MX-5 was faultless. In a *Classic & Sportscar* article comparing various sports cars, Julian Balme pointed out a number of gripes: "The God-awful positioning of the front number plate, the hideous wheels (if you're going to copy a Minilite, then do it properly), and the flip-up headlights are like surfboards when erect. The other two things I dislike about the car are the steering and the lack of excitement emanating from the exhaust system." To be fair, there were just as many aspects of the

The MX-5 BBR Turbo. Although the badging was very discreet, with 'BBR Turbo' added at the end of the existing 'Mazda MX-5' script on the tail (as well as the trailing edge of the front wings), the catalogue described it as "The Ultimate Sports Car of the Decade." The optional wheels were by OZ Racing.

vehicle the writer did like, especially when he compared the MX-5 to his first generation Lotus Elan.

In the same article, Mike McCarthy had few criticisms, but in the depths of an English winter found that "on slippery, icy surfaces, it was the most lethal of the lot, with zero grip. In any direction." When the final ratings were compiled, the order of merit was as follows: first, the AC Ace, then the Jaguar E-type, Alfa Romeo Spider, Lotus Elan, Mazda MX-5, Jaguar XK120, Chevrolet Corvette, MG TC, MGB, and finally the Fiat X1/9.

Once the honeymoon period was over, by far the most common complaint about the car in Britain was a shortage of horsepower. Mazda UK was quick to try and silence the critics, though, and a press release issued on 8 November 1990 described a new turbocharged version of the MX-5. It stated that the latest model, known as the BBR Turbo, "promises to be one of the most exciting sports cars of the decade." The release continued: "Mazda Cars (UK) Ltd, in conjuction with Brodie Brittain Racing, are proud to present the Mazda MX-5 BBR Turbo - a superbly-designed sports package that retains the handling characteristics of the standard car."

Brodie Brittain Racing of Brackley, Northamptonshire, was recognised as one of the country's leading specialists in the art of turbocharging, with years of experience in the field of motorsport. "The Mazda MX-5 BBR Turbo can accelerate from 0-60 in a blistering 6.8 seconds, and then on to a potential maximum top speed of 130mph [208kph]. Even more impressive is the huge increase in engine power and torque

The various components which made up the BBR turbo conversion.

Another view of the MX-5 BBR Turbo. Like the other BBR pictures seen here, this press photograph was actually sent out by the Mazda UK Press Office, confirming the official status of the project.

performance - BBR has raised the standard 114bhp to a potent 150bhp, and torque has been increased from 100lbft at 5500rpm to 154lbft at 5500rpm - giving a massive 50 per cent boost in mid-range power. The result is that the Mazda MX-5 BBR Turbo can truly claim to be *the* new high-performance sports car of the 1990s.

"Yet for all of its attributes, the BBR Turbo is also one of the most tractable turbocharged cars available, whether you're motoring in town, cruising on the motorway, or just enjoying its handling and performance through the country lanes on a summer's evening.

"Priced at £2700 (depending on dealer location), the Mazda MX-5 BBR Turbo conversion is available from Mazda dealers throughout the country and is supported by a full three-year Mazda Cars (UK) Ltd warranty."

The car was also offered with a special set of alloy wheels and Dunlop D40 M2 tyres (priced at £999.95) along with a limited-slip differential costing £620.98. However, Mazda was quick to point out that the package was more than just a case of bolting a turbocharger to the standard car - extensive testing in all conditions had ensured that reliability and economy didn't suffer. In addition to closed circuit testing, more than 6000 miles (roughly 10,000km) were covered on public roads, while the prototype turbo engine ran for

150 hours non-stop without missing a beat.

More than 140 separate parts were used in the BBR conversion, but naturally the most important component was the race-proven Garrett T25 turbocharger. A completely new exhaust manifold, cast in high temperature alloy, and a stainless steel heat shield and exhaust downpipe were fabricated, along with an air-to-air intercooler. Competition spec hoses were used throughout, and the engine management programmes were recalibrated. In fact, BBR actually designed an auxiliary engine management computer to control the fuel-injection, ignition and boost pressure.

The figures comparing a standard MX-5 to the BBR Turbo make interesting reading:

After the announcement of the BBR Turbo, *MotorSport* revealed that: "The brief from Mazda UK was not an easy one, not least because the inside of the engine had to be left well alone. That meant keeping the 9.4:1 compression ratio,

unusually high for a turbo engine, and also retaining the pistons, camshaft, etc. In fact, the conversion had to come in a kit form that could be sent to any one of 70 Mazda dealers ... To keep the Mazda warranty, 150bhp is the limit [but] BBR are working on what they describe as a Phase 2 conversion, that pushes out [over] 230bhp, although this comes without the Mazda sanction, and the work can only be done by BBR."

The same magazine also road tested the car, and had this to say: "There is little turbo lag and the engine retains its tractability. The delightful little MX-5 gearbox makes stirring the cogs about an absolute delight, but the engine has a broad enough spread of power to keep that a pleasure rather than a necessity. The 0-60 time is significantly reduced from 8.7 seconds to 6.8 seconds, and the top speed has become a genuine 130mph [208kph]; a 130mph that in this diminutive, firmly sprung sports car is quite fast enough.

"BBR independently turned

	Standard MX-5	MX-5 BBR Turbo
Power	114bhp @ 6500rpm	150bhp @ 6500rpm
Torque	100lbft @ 5500rpm	154lbft @ 5550rpm
0-60mph	8.7 seconds	6.8 seconds
Top speed	121mph (194kph)	130mph (208kph)

How the standard MX-5 compares with the MX-5 BBR Turbo.

The attractive cover of the 1991 model year Miata brochure. The same picture was also used in magazine advertising in the States; indeed, through the years, many Mazda catalogues have used retouched rather than new photographs to illustrate updates.

their attention to the suspension, and in conjunction with Koni developed some dampers specifically for the MX-5. They tried some four or five combinations before settling on the correct type. These are combined with BBR springs that have a progressive action like rising rate suspension in motorcycles. The first portion of the suspension travel is soft, but the resistance of the springs increases as the deflection increases, so that in quick cornering there is far less roll than on the standard car, but the ride comfort is not unduly sacrificed. There are also anti-roll bars in the BBR kit." The BBR suspension kit was priced at £495 plus fitting, incidentally.

An American update

During 1990, the Miata was named 'Automobile of the Year' by *Automobile* magazine. The car deposited with *Road & Track* had everyone in raptures, although it was noted that, whilst cold, the engine had a tendency to hesitate and the brakes were a little sharp on the first few applications. Also, after just 9000 miles (14,400km), the hood was starting to show signs of wear. However, there had been

The 1991 model year Miata in Mariner Blue. Standard colours at this time included this shade, Classic Red, Crystal White and Silver Stone Metallic. There was also a limited run Special Edition in British Racing Green.

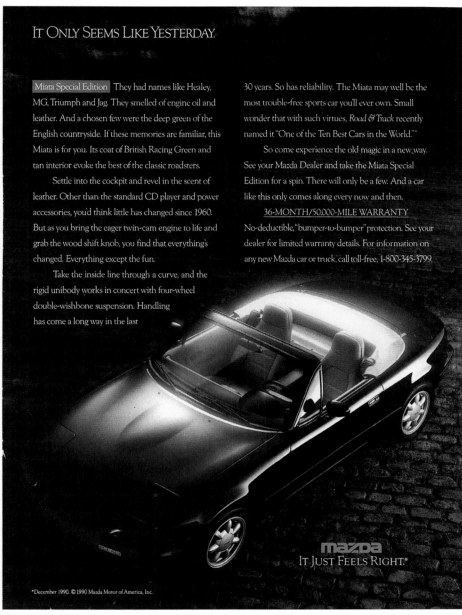

Tasteful advertising for the Miata Special Edition. Based on the Package B model, each car came with a personalized interior badge.

no unexpected bills, and only $70 worth of maintenance. Obviously, the title of 'most trouble-free' sports car in the 1990 JD Power Survey was well-deserved.

Despite a poor year for Mazda as a whole in the States, Miata sales were still very strong in 1990, and it seems that *Road & Track* went a long way to explaining why in a comparison test involving the RX-7, Nissan 300ZX, Porsche 944 and Toyota MR2. The journal stated: "For most of us, the job of a sports car is to take pavement - particularly winding pavement - and alchemize it into that elusive thing called fun. This the Miata does better than all the others ... A majority of the group said the Miata would be their first choice if they had to pick one car for the entire trip. A Feature Editor said, 'It has everything I want from a sports car - it's fun, light, quick, agile and it's the cheapest. What more could you ask?'"

The same magazine named the Miata 'One of the Ten Best Cars in the World', and *the* 'Best Sports/ GT' in the $13,000 to $21,000 bracket.

Interestingly, *Motor Trend* had found it hard to choose a winner when it compared the Miata to the second generation MR2 GT, declaring it an honourable draw, but in a similar test in the UK, *What Car?* thought the Toyota was best - just! However, while only 25,000 MR2s were exported worldwide in 1990, American Miata sales for the year added up to 35,944 units; people were definitely voting with their wallets in favour of the Mazda. By this time, the changes for the 1991 model year had been announced.

For the 1991 season, the Miata started at $14,300, and was now available with ABS braking as a $900 option. One magazine stated: "With that single addition, the Miata is just about perfect." Maybe Mazda thought so, too, for other than the new ABS system, mechanical specifications and options stayed pretty much the same as for the previous year.

However, March 1991 saw the launch of the high spec Special Edition. Basically - apart from a few subtle differences (such as the steering wheel) - it was the American equivalent of the home market's V Special. Ironically, the dark green

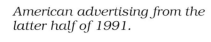
news by the end of the year, 31,240 sales - less than 15 per cent down on 1990's figures - was actually quite amazing. The Special Edition had obviously helped, but there was no denying that the Miata was still very popular.

The home market in 1991

In July 1991, a minor change was announced. It was found that a 'performance bar' - basically a brace that connected the lower control arm pivot points on both sides - was needed to stiffen the car and strengthen the rear suspension. Chassis NA6CE-150212, built in August, was the first vehicle to receive this modification. Naturally, export models produced after this date inherited the same bracing piece.

Sales of the revised cars began in August. The basic Eunos Roadster (now available in manual

Standard colours in Japan included Classic Red, Silver Stone Metallic, Crystal White and Mariner Blue (by this time, the detachable hard-top was available in all the shades). There were actually three other colours available in 1991 - the V Special could now be bought in Neo Green or Brilliant Black, and the J Limited came in Sunburst Yellow. All cars illustrated here have the Special Package equipment, except the Crystal White example, which is a basic model.

shade was known in the States as British Racing Green, but the Special Edition was undoubtedly an attractive package with tan interior and hood cover, leather-trimmed seats, CD player, polished treadplates, electric windows, a personalized brass plaque and real wood detailing (including a Nardi gearknob) all coming as standard; a matching hard-top was available

for $1400. Listed at a hefty $19,249, the automatic transmission option came slightly cheaper than usual, but demand for the BRG car pushed prices well above list in any case. In fact, all 4000 built were sold within just three months.

Looking at the bigger picture, demand waned slightly in 1991. But, considering the price increases and the fact that the Miata was old

A dramatic picture from the home market's catalogue of late 1991.

BODY COLORS

CRISTAL WHITE

CLASSIC RED

SILVER STONE METALLIC

MARINER BLUE

Well-appointed interior of the J Limited.

Beautiful publicity shot of the V Special from July 1991, seen here in its traditional green coachwork colour, and the new black option (nearest the camera).

manual car was now listed at 2,157,000 yen, while the automatic came in at 2,197,000 yen. The Neo Green paintwork was still a feature, but the V Special could now also be bought in Brilliant Black, thus becoming the first roadster on the home market to be offered with black coachwork. Polished kickplates around the door speakers were now a standard fitment on this top-of-the-range model.

At the same time, Japan's first limited edition example was announced: the 1.6 litre J Limited finished in a colour known as Sunburst Yellow. Based on the

guise only) was still listed but never particularly popular. With prices starting at 1,885,000 yen for the manual car (an automatic gearbox added 40,000 yen), the Special Package found a great deal more favour.

The V Special continued, albeit at a slightly higher price - the

The J Limited, Japan's first limited edition model.

Action from the third round of the 1991 Mazda MX-5 UK Cup. Robin Parsons (seen here leading the field into Druids) won the ten lap event at Brands Hatch.

Special Package, the manual car was priced at 1,900,000 yen, with the automatic being listed at 40,000 yen more. Features included the same Nardi steering wheel as that used on the V Special, a Nardi gearknob (on manual cars), wood trim on the handbrake, and stainless treadplates. A hard-top finished in the same colour as the body was listed as an option. The first J Limited carried the chassis number NA6CE-150211, and only 800 were ever built. Amazingly, they were all sold on the first day.

There was a rumour during this period, reported in Australia's *Modern Motor* magazine, that Mazda was testing a turbocharged two-litre version of the MX-5. Given the lengthy lead times associated with magazine articles, it's unlikely this car had anything to do with the recently-formed M2 team, but mention was made of semi-retractable headlamps, a feature later found on a number of M2 prototypes. Whatever, nothing more was heard of the project.

For the 1992 model year, side-impact bars were added to the specification (from chassis NA6CE-200000), and a remote bootlid release was placed alongside the fuel filler lever. A total of 63,434 MX-5s were built during the 1991 calendar year, taking the cumulative total to almost 205,000 units. Of these, 22,594 were sold on the home market.

As a matter of interest, the 1991 Tokyo Show saw the debut of

two more concept vehicles that would have competed directly with Mazda's Roadster - the Daihatsu X-021 and the Mitsubishi HSR-III. The Daihatsu was perhaps the closest to the MX-5 concept, but neither went into production. The Subaru Rioma was another worthy debutante, although, had it been given the green light, this high powered, four-wheel drive Targa-top model was intended for a slightly different sector of the market.

Britain in 1991

The MX-5 one-make series returned in 1991 (again over 12 rounds), with sponsorship coming from Clarion, Car Line, Dunlop and Castrol. At the start of the year, David Palmer, Marketing Director of Mazda Cars (UK) Ltd, said: "The introduction of the Mazda MX-5 UK Cup has been tremendously successful. Throughout 1990 we saw some very close and entertaining racing at every round. With some new competitors involved for 1991, I think the series should be even more spectacular. It promises to be another memorable year."

What Car? magazine voted the MX-5 'Sports Car of the Year 1991',

further adding to the model's bulging trophy case. Then, on 14 March 1991, Mazda UK announced the £18,249 MX-5 Limited Edition to celebrate the first anniversary of the car in Britain. A total of 250 were made available, 25 of which were reserved for tax-free sales or personal exports.

The model was basically another variation on the V Special theme, the British Racing Green paintwork set off by contrasting tan leather seats and a tan interior. Naturally, it came with a very high specification, and featured a wood-rimmed steering wheel, wooden gearknob and handbrake handle, unique 6.5J x 15 alloy wheels, central locking, four-speaker Clarion CRX111R radio/cassette, polished treadplates, a clock, and leather-trimmed overmats.

The press release read: "Each car will only be available in traditional British Racing Green and will come with a certificate of authenticity, stating that it is a Limited Edition MX-5, together with an individually numbered and engraved brass plaque mounted on the dashboard. To make each car even more personalized, a special leather owners' wallet bearing an identical plaque to the one fitted to the car is included, along with a specially embossed leather keyfob."

David Palmer stated: "Following the successful launch of the Mazda MX-5 last year and the tremendous reception it received, we felt that a Limited Edition would be a suitable way of marking the first anniversary of the MX-5. Although this new version is mechanically the same as the standard car, it boasts an outstanding equipment list which we believe makes it a very special car. We will only ever market 250

and anticipate that each one will fast become a collectors item."

Following Mazda's success at Le Mans, Mazda UK launched its second limited edition model of the year. Writing for *MotorSport* , Simon Arron said: "In celebration of the company's first-ever Le Mans victory this year, Mazda has built a limited edition eyesore. Looking like a cross between a stick of Blackpool rock and a jar of Swarfega, the MX-5 Le Mans is equipped with a BBR turbo kit (boosting power to 150bhp) and body addenda. It does not come with a free respray voucher, but that doesn't appear to have dissuaded potential customers, as all 24 have now been sold at £20,499 apiece."

Obviously, Mr Arron wasn't too

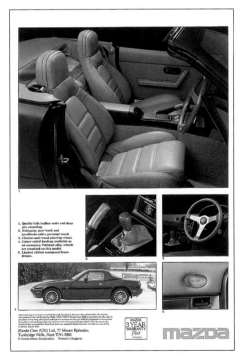

The sumptuous interior of the MX-5 Limited Edition, finished in tan leather. Only 250 of these models were built, each individually numbered.

An official publicity shot of the ultra rare MX-5 Le Mans.

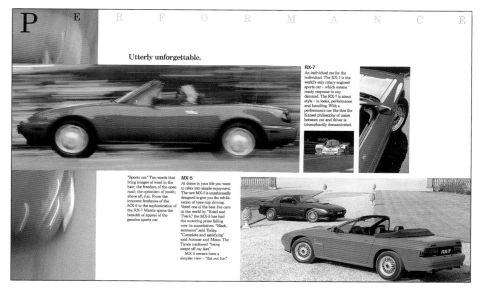

impressed with the colour scheme, which was essentially a facsimile of the bold design found on the winning Mazda - bright green, and even brighter orange, in a chequered pattern. At least two are known to have been resprayed black, whilst another was considerably toned down prior to sale.

The 1991 Earls Court Show saw the British debut of the MX-6. This elegant Grand Tourer (which eventually went on sale in the UK during February 1992) was joined on the Mazda stand by the recently launched MX-3 coupé (known in Japan as the Eunos Presso), the top version powered by the world's smallest V6 engine. The sporting theme was continued with the RX-7 Turbo Cabriolet and, of course,

the MX-5, two of which were exhibited. Apart from the usual 121, 323 and 626 models, the display was completed by the Mazdaspeed 787B which had won at Le Mans earlier in the year, and the Group A 323 rally car that Hannu Mikkola had campaigned during the 1991 WRC season.

At the end of 1991, Mazda UK calculated it had sold 22,416 vehicles during the year. Although sales had fallen slightly compared to the previous year's figures, in actual fact, the MX-5 (accounting for 1986 units) had taken a larger percentage of Mazda's market share, increasing from 8.1 per cent to 8.8 per cent. The 1991 annual sales total was a record as far as Europe was concerned; including the UK figures, more than 14,000 MX-5s were sold during the year.

1992 Stateside

Changes for the 1992 model year had been announced in October 1991. Of course, the suspension modifications brought about in Japan during the summer of 1991 were inherited by the American cars, but more specifically for 1992, a remote bootlid release was fitted across the Miata range, and the Package B option now included an electric aerial; the optional hard-top (priced at $1500) at last came with a heated rear screen.

The base model had a $14,800 sticker price, with Package A adding $1370, and Package B putting $2040 on the invoice. Individual

Italian advertising from the summer of 1991.

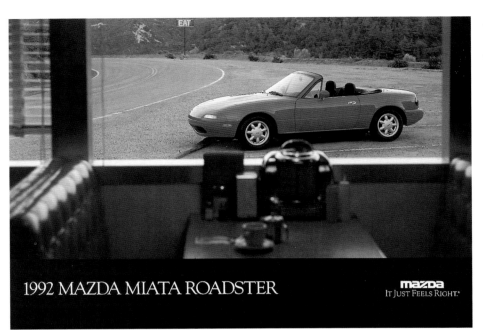

1992 MAZDA MIATA ROADSTER

mazda
IT JUST FEELS RIGHT.

American advertising for the 1992 model year Miata, seen here in postcard form.

options included air conditioning (at $830), automatic transmission ($750), ABS brakes ($900), a limited-slip differential ($250), CD player ($600), floormats ($65), and the aforementioned hard-top.

In March 1992, the Silver Stone Metallic body colour was discontinued and two new hues joined the line-up: Sunburst Yellow and Brilliant Black. The Sunburst Yellow shade was only available with the Package A upgrade, although air conditioning, an automatic gearbox, an lsd and a hardtop could be bought as options. Like the J Limited in Japan, which was finished in the same bright colour, production was restricted, and just 1500 cars were allocated for the States.

The Brilliant Black model was not a limited edition, but had a higher specification than that of the run-of-the-mill Miata. Tan leather trim came as standard, and the hood was finished in the same colour to give a classy contrast with the coachwork. It came with alloy wheels, power steering, a radio/cassette unit, and electric windows included in the $17,050 price. For a further $1400, the black

car could be specified with the newly-introduced Package C, including alloy wheels by BBS, a Nardi wooden gearknob, wooden handbrake trim, stainless treadplates, cruise control, an electric aerial, and headrest speakers. Over 7000 Brilliant Black Miatas were sold, prompting Mazda to rethink the Package C option for the 1993 season.

In March, *Road & Track* carried out a test comparing ten of the best handling cars available in America at that time. Of the Sunburst Yellow Miata (complete with yellow hard-top), racer Danny Sullivan said: "Well, it's a fun little car that's comfortable and easy to drive fast. The steering is responsive, but not too quick, and in the high speed corners the Miata feels very stable. Braking is very good; I was getting deeper and deeper into each corner and I never sensed any fade. It puts the power down well, and you'd get a slightly tail-out attitude on the fast stuff, but it was not bad overall. It's a little underpowered, but that's to be expected."

It was interesting comparing notes made by Roger Bell in the UK with those made by Danny Sullivan

in the States, and reminded the author of a comment made by Maurice Ford, an old friend who used to race in the 1960s, regarding our mutual love of old Alfas. He observed that "You're never really going that fast, it just feels like you are!" The MX-5 had been cleverly engineered to feel the same way. Relatively narrow tyres (at least by modern sports car standards) combined with just enough power to excite, kept the limits low enough for people not to get into too much trouble; nothing will happen too quickly or suddenly as it might in a very high powered machine, or one with wider, grippier rubber. While someone like Bell or Sullivan could extract the best from the vehicle, it was designed to flatter any driver.

In a *Motor Trend* survey, an amazing 97.7 per cent of owners thought the fun-to-drive capabilities of the Miata were excellent; in fact, the car excelled in virtually every performance and creature comfort category, although it was perhaps significant that most bought the car initially on the grounds of styling. With 17 per cent saying they desired more power, handling was highlighted as a specific area that most owners liked and, with a fine reliability record, 73.6 per cent said they would be happy to buy another. All this press coverage and the various special editions helped keep sales at a high level, and allowed Mazda to divert some of its advertising budget to other vehicles in the

The MX-5 SE of April 1992.

range. Of the 52,712 MX-5s built in 1992 (which represents a figure 30 per cent higher than yearly expectations declared at the launch), no less than 24,964 of them found homes in the States.

Although rarely seen in IMSA events, the Miata could often be found competing in SCCA (Sports Car Club of America) meetings. Indeed, the Miata took SCCA Showroom Stock C honours for the first time in 1992, a category ideally suited to the little Mazda. On this occasion, it was Randy Pobst who took the victor's laurels, winning his heat by a fraction of a second!

The UK market in 1992

Features for the 1992 season included a remote bootlid release in the centre cubby box, security window etching, front number plate holders, and the use of a 'Finish Line 540' radio/cassette in place of the Clarion-badged unit. Standard colours included shades of red, white, blue and silver.

Following the success of the previous Limited Edition model, Mazda UK decided to offer the MX-5 Special Equipment. As the press release declared, it was "offered exclusively in black with a contrasting leather tan interior, together with a high specification list that includes anti-lock braking and an electric aerial. The MX-5 SE model goes on sale to the UK public on Monday 6 April and will be

MX-5 Special Equipment

Part of the MX-5 SE brochure showing salient points of the top model.

available throughout the Mazda Cars (UK) Ltd national dealer network priced at £17,788 (including car tax and VAT)."

Marketing Director, David Palmer, said: "The Mazda MX-5 has proved to be a universally popular car throughout the world. In the UK we have launched a series of special edition models to cater for people who want to own an MX-5 that is a little different from the rest. We believe that the Mazda MX-5 SE will be another success for us. It has all the attributes of the standard car coupled to a very extensive equipment list."

The Mazda MX-5 SE model was the first cosmetic upgrade to be offered in unlimited numbers in the British Isles, and featured Brilliant Black paintwork, tan leather seats and interior trim, a wood-rimmed steering wheel, wooden gearknob and handbrake handle, ABS braking, ten-spoke 7J x 15 polished alloys with locking wheelnuts, 'SE' badging (next to the MX-5 badge on the top left-hand side of the rear panel), chrome treadplates, an electric aerial, and an analogue clock. Interestingly, it was one of the first UK models to be built in the Hofu plant, although production would return to Hiroshima by the end of the year.

Whilst reviewing the MX-5 SE in its September 1992 issue, *MotorSport* also mentioned that Lotus had stopped building the new Elan: "Both received widespread press acclaim, but Japan's more cost-effective mass-production techniques have meant that the MX-5 is still being turned out - and sold - in high numbers, while the more expensive Lotus has recently been axed for financial reasons." Regarding the car itself, it was stated: "Designed as a convertible from the outset, the MX-5 is devoid of the rattles and body flex that often beset cabriolets that have been adapted from coupé originals. Build quality is first rate ... Whether or not one requires the SE pack is purely a question of taste and, perhaps, of budget. The bottom line is that the MX-5 remains a joy to drive, however you care to dress it up."

Mazda UK sold 1017 MX-5s in 1992. The total for the rest of Europe came to 5614 units during the same period, taking the figure to 6631 for the year.

The S Special & S Limited

Although the recession which followed the boom of the late 1980s naturally hurt the Japanese car manufacturers, it was a change in the local taxation laws and unfavourable exchange rates that did the real damage.

It was the exchange rates that were holding Mazda back; a luxury car division (called Amati) was planned to compete with the Lexus, Infiniti and Acura organisations but, in view of the economic situation, the idea was binned. Yoshihiro Wada, Mazda's President since December 1991, didn't seem overly worried in public, although it came as no surprise to followers of the industry that Ford's involvement with the company became ever stronger.

However, Mazda was determined to celebrate the third anniversary of the Eunos Roadster in style and, in July, announced the S Special. Production began in the following month so that it could take advantage of a scheduled minor change - side impact bars, and the option of an airbag (fitted in what for Japan was a unique four-spoke steering wheel, but basically the same as the one found in the States) - and sales started in September.

The S Special was a distinctly sporty version of the Eunos Roadster. Available in Classic Red or Brilliant Black, it came with manual transmission only and was priced at 2,030,000 yen. It featured an uprated suspension with Bilstein shock absorbers, a front strut brace, 6J x 14 BBS alloy wheels fitted with 185/60 tyres, a Nardi three-spoke leather-trimmed steering wheel, Nardi leather gearknob, stainless treadplates and speaker grilles, and a rear spoiler. The only luxury item was the optional Mazda Sensory Sound System (a complicated Pioneer 130W stereo system that included a CD player), which was priced at 220,000 yen.

In December 1992, Mazda announced the S Limited - a run of

The S Special of 1992 vintage, seen here in both of the colour finishes available on this sporty model. The car nearest the camera is fitted with the Sensory Sound System.

coloured BBS alloys, and the aforementioned Sensory Sound System.

All told, 18,657 Eunos Roadsters were sold in Japan during 1992, almost three times as many as were sold in the whole of Europe. Incidentally, the 250,000th MX-5 (built at Hiroshima on 9 November 1992) went to Australia, and is now an exhibit at the Australian National Motor Museum.

The US market for 1993

For 1993, the car's suspension was refined to give "improved ride qualities without sacrificing handling," but the thing that most noticed was the new badge on the nose (leading to the deletion of the 'Mazda' decal on the front bumper

In December 1992, Mazda announced the S Limited. Finished in Brilliant Black, it came with a red leather interior, attractive gold coloured BBS alloys, and the Sensory Sound System.

1000 cars based on the S Special. Sales began in January 1993 (the first car was chassis NA6CE-209203), with the price being set at 2,350,000 yen. Finished in Brilliant Black, the model came with a red leather interior, attractive gold-

Interior of the S Limited.

- even though some retouched catalogue pictures left them on!) and the centre caps on the alloy wheel option. In addition, the steering wheel boss now had 'SRS Airbag' in place of the previous 'Mazda' script.

An AM/FM stereo radio/cassette with integral digital clock became standard, having previously been part of the Package A option, and Brilliant Black was added as a standard colour; the base Miata was now priced at $15,300.

The option packages were rearranged for the 1993 model year and included the following items: Option Package A ($1300) added

---

CONCEPT

THE ROADSTER RETURNS.

It has long been felt that the perfect driving experience was one that provided a direct connection between the road, the wind, the car, and the sky. Only one type of car could do it: the classic roadster. But in recent years, that kind of car disappeared. The driving enthusiasts at Mazda asked, "Why?" and set out to give the world a modern car that recreated the special feeling and pleasure of classic sports car driving. That car is the Mazda MX-5 Miata, a car that becomes a part of you, and responds, not just to your command, but almost to your thought. In short, a car with heart and soul.

Picture yourself on the most perfect two-lane country road you know of, your closest friend in the passenger's seat and the music from the throaty Miata exhaust making you forget all about those CDs you brought along. And suddenly you come to that sharp curve you've always wondered about.

But then, quickly, it's gone. Shifting, braking, steering, and accelerating are all so quick, so direct and natural, that you're out

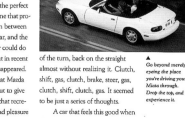

of the turn, back on the straight almost without realizing it. Clutch, shift, gas, clutch, brake, steer, gas, clutch, shift, clutch, gas. It seemed to be just a series of thoughts.

A car that feels this good when driven this enthusiastically isn't something that just happens. Like every car we make, the Miata was designed using Kansei Engineering, our deeply held philosophy demanding that a car must go beyond merely performing right; it must also feel right. Using Kansei Engineering we learn things we could never learn from a computer. Things like how much "road feel" the driver gets through the steering wheel; if the

We have accurate reconstructions of 20 different road surfaces from all around the world at the Global Road Circuit on our Miyoshi Proving Ground in Japan. Our engineers use it to fine-tune our vehicles for any type of driving you might encounter.

▲
Go beyond merely eyeing the place you're driving your Miata through. Drop the top, and experience it.

The past, present, and future of automobile design combine perfectly in an organic, sensuous form.
▼

exhaust sounds just right when downshifting; even how a driver feels when resting an elbow on the window sill. This devotion to designing vehicles based on the needs and emotions of the people driving them, leads Mazda to solve problems in unique ways.

When our research showed us, for example, that the Miata would feel right only if it had perfect, 50/50 front/rear weight distribution, we did critical design work with the car suspended from its exact center on a single steel cable. This permitted ideas effecting weight distribution to be immediately seen and evaluated. Among other things, this resulted in giving the Miata a light, but strong, aluminum hood, and mounting the low-weight battery in the trunk.

The optional hardtop turns your roadster into a gorgeous coupe. Its glass window with defroster makes the Miata a four-season delight.
▼

When our engineers and designers were done, the classic roadster was back. But with modern technology and reliability, and a special feeling behind the wheel that could only have come from Mazda. Drop the top and let the wind blow through your hair. These are the good old days.

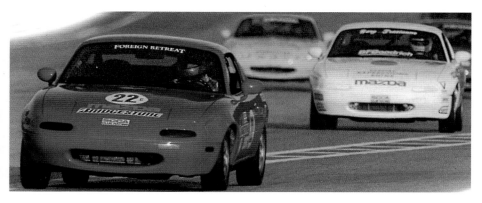

The Miata seen competing in SCCA racing, where it soon acquired an excellent reputation. It took the Showroom Stock C title on several occasions.

power-assisted steering, a leather-wrapped steering wheel, electrically-adjustable mirrors, alloy wheels and headrest speakers to the basic model. Package B ($2000) included everything in Package A, plus cruise control, electric windows, and an automatic electric aerial. The new Package C ($2700) had all the items in Package B, plus a tan-coloured interior with leather seat facings, and a tan vinyl top. This was available on all paintwork options with the exception of cars finished in Mariner Blue, which could be supplied with the standard black trim only.

Mazda's Sensory Sound System (MSSS) could be bought as a separate option, as could ABS braking (with Package B or C), automatic transmission, a limited-slip differential (for manual cars), a hard-top, and air conditioning.

Midway through the year, the Miata Limited Edition made its entrance. The American cousin of the S Limited, it was finished in Brilliant Black with a red leather interior (a red vinyl tonneau cover was also included), and came with the usual luxury touches - air conditioning, a leather-trimmed steering wheel, a Nardi leather gearknob, cruise control, the MSSS stereo system, power windows and

Opposite: Two pages from the 1993 model year Miata catalogue, complete with retouched photographs to depict the new badging.

mirrors, stainless treadplates and speaker grilles, a special keyfob, and even a Miata book. However, power-assisted steering, ABS, a limited-slip differential, 14-inch BBS alloy wheels fitted with 185/60 tyres, an uprated suspension with Bilstein shock absorbers, and front and rear spoilers were also included in the $22,000 list price. Only 1500 examples were ever built but, as *Sports Car International* pointed out, with the horsepower output unchanged, "the engine is not enough to warrant such a harsh suspension."

The Miata was the SCCA Showroom Stock C class winner again (this time courtesy of Michael Galati, in a race dominated by the little roadsters), although it wasn't the only car in the Mazda range to acquire an important title, as the new RX-7 received the 1993 'Import Car of the Year' award from *Motor Trend* magazine.

Sales in America were still falling, but 21,588 units was a more than respectable figure for the year; across the border, Canada took another 1501 (Canadian sales had been falling steadily by around 25 per cent year-on-year since their peak in 1990). Added together, this accounted for the bulk of exports during 1993, as European sales fell to an all-time low.

The 1993 model year in Britain

The Mazda stand at the 1992 British Motor Show (held at the NEC between 24 October and 1 November), had the new RX-7 as its star attraction. As the press release stated: "One of the highlights of the stand will be the Mazda RX-7 Turbo. This stunning new sports [model] created a sensation at its international debut in Tokyo at the end of 1991. The RX-7 has just gone on sale in the UK, but with just 120 cars available this year, it is set to be a very exclusive sports car." Known in Japan as the Anfini RX-7 (and sold through the Anfini sales channel, established in 1991), the 237bhp machine was capable of covering 0-60 in just 5.3 seconds, before powering on towards a top speed of 150mph (240kph).

The RX-7 joined a distinctly sporting line-up, including the MX-3, MX-5 and MX-6, as well as the 323, 626, and luxury Xedos 6 range. To reinforce Mazda's desired sporty image, the 323F used by Patrick Watts in the 1992 British Touring Car Championship was also on display.

From 4 January 1993, a number of Mazdas were subjected to price increases. The Mazda MX-3 1.8i now cost £15,729, the standard MX-5 was £15,780, while the MX-6 started at £18,519. However, the recently launched RX-7 remained at £32,536.

On 5 May, Mazda UK announced the second MX-5 SE. This latest MX-5 SE was basically the same as the original, although the alloy wheels were different on

MAZDA CARS (UK) LTD
BRITISH INTERNATIONAL MOTOR SHOW '92

Some of the cars on display at the 1992 Motor Show held at the NEC on the outskirts of Birmingham. Nearest the camera and to the left is the Xedos 6, while the new, third generation RX-7 can be seen next to it. A 626 is behind the RX-7, with the elegant MX-6 making up the foursome.

volumes for the popularity and attraction of the car ... The 1993 Mazda MX-5 SE owners can be sure that they will be driving a very exclusive car indeed."

By July, a number of changes had started to filter through for the

The MX-5 SE of May 1993.

this edition (6.5J x 15), and the stereo unit was also changed. The press release noted: "A new 1993 special version of the Mazda MX-5 will go on sale on Tuesday 1 June, available only in Brilliant Black with an extensive standard equipment list.

"The Mazda MX-5 SE, priced at £18,686, is offered in black and comes with contrasting tan leather interior with extensive use of wooden mahogany trim. The specification list is impressive and includes an anti-lock braking system, electrical aerial, and seven-spoke chrome-plated alloy wheels."

Jan Smith, the new Marketing Director of Mazda UK, said: "The Mazda MX-5 has proved to be one of the most successful and sought-after cars currently available. The fact that production worldwide has now exceeded 250,000 speaks

A 1993 MX-5 in standard UK trim, just before European models adopted the new corporate badge on the nose panel and wheel centres.

Patrick Watts with the Xedos 6 developed by RD Motorsport for the 1993 BTCC season. Watts, who won the 1990 Mazda MX-5 UK Cup, had driven a two-litre 323F in the previous year, but with little success. During 1993, he claimed the fastest lap on one occasion, along with a pole position. David Leslie drove the Xedos 6 in 1994, but Mazda finished the season early, pulling out from the series in July.

next season. An electric aerial was declared standard, as was the Clarion CRX52 radio/cassette unit, whilst on the safety front, the MX-5 now came with side-impact door protection beams. The new corporate chrome badge appeared on the nose, replacing the old 'Mazda' decal applied to the lower left-hand side of the bumper (a handy identifying feature when trying to date vehicles).

During 1993, Mazda UK sold a total of 18,944 vehicles, but only 910 of these were MX-5s - less than 5 per cent of Mazda's market share in the British Isles. MX-5 sales for the rest of Europe added up to

Dashboard of the French 1993 model year MX-5. Most pictures used in catalogues were the same across Europe (including the UK), and were simply reversed and retouched as necessary for left- and right-hand drive cars; only the dashboard shots had to be specially taken. For the 1995 model year worldwide, the traditional style calibrations on the oil pressure gauge were replaced by 'idiot-proof' 'L' and 'H' markings at each extremity.

Italian advertising from the summer of 1993, this piece showing the entire Mazda range for the European market.

THE REINCARNATION
OF THE CLASSIC SPORTS CAR.

Mazda MX-5. Legendary form re-created and combined with visionary technology. Acclaimed throughout the world. A testament to Mazda's total commitment to designing cars with imagination. Cars of an unrivalled quality that are a pure pleasure to drive. ◇ The inspired Mazda MX-5. Not simply a sporty convertible, but a true hot-blooded thoroughbred sports car. Simply magnificent. An open-air driving experience that will take you all the way back to the future. ◇ Designed without compromise the MX-5 is an open 2-seater, front engine, rear wheel drive sports car experience. Its exciting spirit is an extension of your own. Performance exhilarating. Response and control exceptional. Driver feedback keeping you in touch with car and road. If ever a car integrated driver and machine, this is it.

3914 units for the year.

News from the Antipodes

After a high of 1446 sales in 1990, the Australian market was becoming something of a disappointment; only 746 sales were recorded in 1991, and 1992's figures fell again to just 502 units. The press was still behind the car, but, ultimately, it was the public that had to buy it. In an attempt to try and make the convertible more tempting, Mazda launched the $39,990 MX-5 Classic.

Finished in red with a tan leather interior, the package included BBS alloys, a CD player, a Nardi gearknob with matching handbrake trim, and even a signed picture of Toshihiko Hirai (he left the company shortly after to become a university lecturer).

Limited to 100 units (this was Australia's fourth limited edition, incidentally - the first was a Neo Green model launched at the end of 1990 and restricted to 300 examples; there were 55 produced in Malibu Gold during 1992, and another 300 in Neo Green later that year), it sold out almost immediately, despite competition from the vastly improved Ford Capri, which was built in Australia and was some $11,000 cheaper. However, including the Classic, total Australian sales for 1993 still added up to only 453 cars.

All change in Japan

Kenichi Yamamoto, one of the main

Interior of the Australian specification car. The handbrake remained in this position on all cars for all markets, regardless of whether they were left- or right-hand drive.

Another view of the model for the Australian market. Sales were strong in the Antipodes during 1989 and 1990, but dropped off rapidly thereafter.

The B6-ZE (RS) engine. It should be noted that, on this 1.6 litre unit, the maker's name and 'DOHC 16-VALVE' is cast into the metal; soon these would become a useful identifying feature.

supporters of the LWS project, retired in the early part of 1993. Voted RJC 'Man of the Year' in 1991 (the RX-7 was voted RJC 'Car of the Year' at the same time,

それは、バランスの探究。

ユーノスロードスターならではの「人馬一体感」。その楽しさに満ちた世界が、いまあらたな進化を遂げた。目指したのは、運動性、安全性、快適性など、これからのライトウェイトスポーツが問うべき、すべての能力の高次元バランス。DOHCエンジンの排気量アップ、ボディとサスペンションの剛性アップ、さらに、ブレーキ性能のアップとオートマチックのリニューアル…、すべては、ライトウェイトスポーツ本来の人馬一体感と、すぐれた危険回避能力に代表される安全性、そして、日常的な扱いやすさを同時に進化させるための施策である。新しいロードスターに託した開発陣の思い。それは、ステアリングを一度でも握れば、たちどころに知ることができる。

ユーノスロードスターは、あらたに自然吸気1800DOHCエンジンを搭載した、最高出力130ps/6500rpm(ネット※1)、最大トルク16.0kg-m/4500rpm。高速タイプのバルブタイミング、軽量コンロッド、新たに採用したホットワイヤー式のエアフロメーターをはじめとする吸気抵抗の軽減などにより、レッドゾーンまで一気に吹き上がる高回転特性とともに、ぶ厚い低中速トルクを獲得。ドライバーの意志にリニアに応えるアクセルレスポンスをさらに研ぎ澄ましました。5段マニュアルトランスミッションには、確実で滑らかなギアシフトをサポートするため、セカンド・ギアにダブルコーンシンクロを搭載しました。また、採用した電子制御式4段オートマチック[C-AT※2]は、よりスムーズな走行フィールを実現、パワーとノーマルモードを自動的に切り替えるオートパワー制御も備える。また、1/2/3速を任意に固定できるホールドモードが、ダイレクト&シャープな走りを王道する。そして、トランスミッションとデフを剛結合するアルミ製P.P.F.(パワー・プラント・フレーム)、エンジントルクのダイレクトな伝達とシフトフィールの高剛性感を実現する、FRのユーノスロードスターならではのアイテムも。5段マニュアル車にはレスポンスにすぐれたトルク感応型リミテッドスリップデフ、"トルセン"LSD※3(Torque Sensing Limited Slip Differential)を装備。オイルの粘性を利用して差動を制御するビスカスLSDに対して、両軸のトルク差を感知しながら適切なトルク配分を行なうことで安定したトラクションがよりダイレクトに得られる。これにより、アクセルワークで車体姿勢を積極的にコントロールすることも可能にしている。排気システムは、排気マニホールドからテールパイプに至るまですべてステンレスパイプ製、高周波音をカットし、抜けがよく低音のきいたエグゾーストサウンドとしている。

1800DOHCの冴え。

A double-page spread from the Japanese catalogue of August 1993 showing the new 1.8 litre engine (note the raised details on the cam covers), the Torsen differential, and electronically-controlled automatic transmission.

incidentally), he had witnessed enormous changes within Mazda and could be justifiably proud of the role he had played in the company's development.

Things were happening on the Eunos Roadster front as well. In February 1993, the V Special adopted the Sensory Sound System as standard but, more importantly, in July, Mazda announced the first major facelift of the MX-5. With Hirai declaring his wish to leave the company (he finally left in March 1993), Shiro Yoshioka was put in charge of the project.

Complying with forthcoming regulation changes meant a sizeable weight gain for the car. Mazda concluded that the only way to keep the vehicle's performance at its current level was to increase engine capacity. Initial thoughts were to retain the 1.6 litre four and introduce a new two-litre unit to augment it. Instead, the 1.8 litre BP-type engine from the Familia

The new 1800 series in all its glory. Again, the Japanese market range was very extensive.

The V Special II made its debut with the announcement of the 1800 series.

Interior of the late-1993 V Special.

GT was chosen, largely because it was a good compromise: some of the Roadster's edge on economy would have been lost with a two-litre lump (and meant higher insurance, too), while the 1.6 would have struggled to remain sporty with the heavier body, especially when combined with an automatic transmission. Modified to give 130bhp at 6500rpm, the 1839cc unit was given the BP-ZE designation.

The body was strengthened in anticipation of the new engine, with 'performance rods' added up front and in a U-shaped configuration at the back to enhance torsional rigidity. In addition, a cockpit brace bar was introduced, joining the seatbelt anchor towers to further enhance shell rigidity.

The suspension settings were revised to suit, while the brake discs increased in diameter from 235mm (9.2in.) to 255mm (10.0in.) at the front, and from 231mm (9.1in.) to 251mm (9.9in.) at the rear. A Torsen limited-slip differential came with the five-speed cars, and the optional alloy wheels were completely restyled. Interestingly, despite the rim width

The 1.8 litre Special Package model, seen here finished in Classic Red.

Interior of the latest Eunos Roadster (this is a Special Package model), clearly showing the Momo steering wheel and the cockpit brace bar fitted behind the seats.

increasing to 6J (from 5.5J), each wheel was around 1kg (2lb) lighter than the original design, representing quite a saving overall.

Although the manual gearbox ratios were untouched, the final-drive ratio was changed from 4.3:1 to 4.1:1. The optional four-speed automatic transmission was now an electronically controlled unit with slightly different ratios, but the final-drive was actually the same as the manual cars at 4.1:1 (instead of 4.444:1 as used on the 1.6 litre automatics), signifying another important change.

The 1.6 litre cars had carried the NA6CE chassis designation, whereas the new 1.8 litre models were given the NA8C code (production began in August on chassis NA8C-100016). A useful identifying feature at the rear of the car was the 'Roadster' badge, the script now red instead of the original black. Other distinguishing features included a different number plate holder, standard rear mudflaps, and the addition of large elasticated door pockets. On the base models, Classic Red, Silver Stone Metallic and Chaste White became the extent of the standard colour range, signifying the end of Crystal White and Mariner Blue.

Announced in July, sales of the 1.8 range started in September. At 1,791,000 yen, the manual only 1.8 litre Series I standard model served as an entry level Eunos Roadster, but the Special Package version (available with either manual or automatic transmission) again made up the bulk of sales. Weighing in at 990kg (2178lb) in manual form (10kg, or 22lb, more than the basic car), it was priced at 1,966,000 yen, whilst the automatic gearbox added 30kg (66lb) and 50,000 yen.

The V Special was continued (2,336,000 yen in manual form, or 2,386,000 yen with an automatic gearbox), but there was now also

Another view of the Special Package model, this time with the optional hard-top in place.

inch BBS alloy wheels, polished treadplates and kickplates (which surrounded the door speakers), and a Nardi steering wheel. Incidentally, prices were around 36,000 yen less in Tokyo due to lower delivery charges.

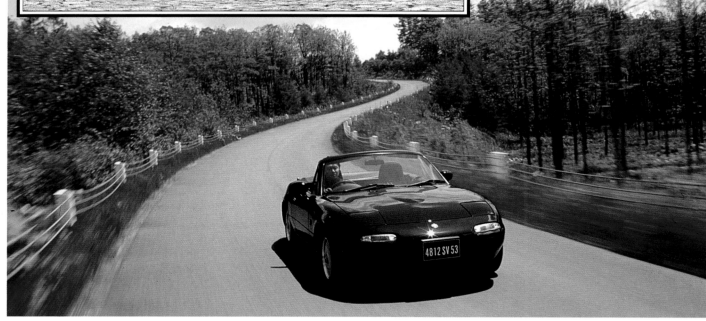

The S Special at speed in the ideal sports car arena.

the V Special Type II. The extra 100,000 yen needed to secure one added a highly polished finish to the seven-spoke alloy wheels, chrome door mirrors, and a tan coloured soft-top.

The line-up was completed by the manual only S Special, priced at 2,111,000 yen. Based on the Special Package model, it came in either Laguna Blue Metallic or Brilliant Black, and featured an array of tempting items: an uprated suspension with Bilstein shocks and thicker anti-roll bars, a front tower brace, rear body brace, 14-

A few months later, in November, Mazda released a limited edition of just 40 cars finished in Brilliant Black with a tan hood. Known as the Tokyo Limited, this employed a number of interior parts used from the M2-1002 run (see Chapter Five). The cream leather

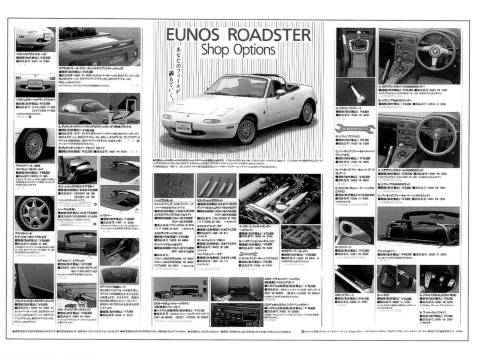

The options available for the Eunos Roadster. Many of these items eventually found their way onto Japan's various limited edition models.

The J Limited II with its distinctive Sunburst Yellow coachwork. The wheels, being the latest seven-spoke design, were obviously different to the original J Limited, but the black windscreen surround was another useful distinguishing feature.

yen, seemed cheap compared with the 3,000,000 asked for the M2-1002.

In December, according to the Mazda Yearbook, "Mazda and Ford entered into a long-term strategic relationship to enhance their competitive strength" and, in the same month, another limited edition Eunos Roadster was announced - the J Limited II. Based on the Special Package model, the J Limited II was finished in Sunburst Yellow, just like the original J Limited. However, the windscreen surround was finished in black on this occasion. Bucket seats with independent headrests were used, a CD player was a standard fitment, and Pirelli P700-Z tyres were mounted on the familiar 6 J x 14 seven-spoke alloys.

trim was beautiful, and the added detailing fully justified the 2,458,000 yen price tag - even the automatic version, at 2,508,000

Interior of the J Limited II.

The opening pages of the first British catalogue to feature the 1.8 litre models.

The true modern classic

The Mazda MX-5 first appeared in the UK in 1990 like a refreshing breeze from the past. Turning heads. Stirring passions. And persuading enthusiasts everywhere that in terms of sheer fun and exhilaration, there is still nothing to compare with an open top sports car.

The excitement the Mazda MX-5 generated is hardly surprising. For it embraced special values that many feared had vanished for good. And in doing so symbolises Mazda's uncompromising belief in what a sports car should be: affordable fun.

The original Mazda MX-5 concept was based on a single thought: that the ideal man/machine relationship should be similar to that between a horse and rider; instinctive, immediate; tactile; moving together as one.

To maintain this driving enjoyment, every aspect of the new Mazda MX-5 1.8i and 1.8iS has been judged in terms of how it would enhance the driving experience. For this lightweight sports car, a front engine rear-wheel drive layout was still the natural choice and true to the sports car tradition, there's not an ounce of excess weight on either model.

Although the new Mazda MX-5 1.8i and 1.8iS models embody the classic formula for driving fun, there's nothing "retro" about the technology that has gone into them.

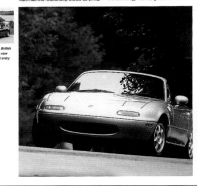

Featured here in British racing green the new Mazda MX-5 1.8i entry level model.

From the spirited 16 valve 1.8-litre fuel-injected DOHC engine to the ultra-rigid monocoque chassis, modern technology plays a major role. Enhancing safety and reliability. And making the driving experience all the more satisfying.

Wrapped in sensuous bodywork, and wearing a new style of ultra-light aluminium wheels, there's no mistaking the new Mazda MX-5 1.8iS for anything other than what it is: a purpose-built modern sports car that is designed to provide excitement from the moment you turn the key.

The traditional British climate doesn't put a damper on the fun. The strong weather-proof convertible top can be raised and secured quickly and easily by either driver or passenger.

The spirit of the classic lightweight sports car lives on in the new Mazda MX-5 1.8i and 1.8iS models, and continues to evolve in a natural way. There is no other car to challenge its claim as the true modern classic as it takes its place in the hearts of today's sports car enthusiasts everywhere.

The sleek profile of the new Mazda MX-5 1.8i model will appeal to sports car lovers everywhere.

Limited to just 800 examples, prices started at 2,030,000 yen for the five-speed version, with the optional automatic transmission adding a further 50,000 yen. Roadster sales in Japan added up to a total of 16,789 units for the year, by the way.

1994 model year in the UK

Although the SE continued to be listed at £18,686 (its original launch price), by now the cost of a standard 1.6i model had risen to a hefty £16,490. However, on 18 April, Mazda UK announced two new models to supercede them - the MX-5 1.8i and 1.8iS.

The main difference compared with earlier models was obviously the increase in engine size (to 1839cc), raising power from a modest 114bhp to 130bhp, and boosting maximum torque output to 112lbft. However, the new models also benefited from an uprated suspension and a stiffer body (through the use of the additional bracing described earlier) to give a better ride and improve handling. Inside, the old high backed seats were replaced with a new type (like those found on the J Limited II) incorporating an adjustable headrest. At the same time, door armrests were deleted, with door pockets taking their place.

The top 1.8iS model had all the previous 1.6i features, but added ABS, a driver's side airbag, new (and lighter) 6J x 14 seven-spoke alloy wheels, a rheostat for the panel lights, electric mirrors, an electric aerial, and a Clarion CRX87R detachable radio/cassette unit.

The 1.8i was the basic model, coming with 5.5J x 14 steel wheels, a urethane steering wheel, and a generally lower level of equipment. The base model was sold without power-assisted steering, the ABS system, airbag, electric windows, internal bootlid release, and radio/cassette unit. However, to keep insurance companies happy, both models were fitted with an immobiliser as standard.

Going on sale from 2 May, Laguna Blue Metallic and Chaste White replaced the Mariner Blue and Crystal White shades, whilst British Racing Green and Brilliant Black became available as standard colour options. Classic Red and Silver Stone Metallic made up the six colour range.

Complete Car tested a basic 1.8i in its August 1994 issue, and gave the Design & Quality, Going & Stopping, Handling & Grip and Value & Economy categories four out of five stars each, with only Comfort & Equipment falling behind with three stars. After outlining the key points in the development of the LWS model, the magazine continued: "As the years rolled by, a few changes began to detract from the concept. First, the car started to creep upmarket in trim levels and price. Then there was the compulsory catalytic converter, which robbed the engine of much of its pep.

"Mazda has corrected both these faults in the latest revision. The car now comes in two guises, with a cheaper, stripped-down version, tested here, for people who want to get back to basics. Unlike the pricier 1.8iS, the 1.8i has no power steering, no anti-lock brakes, no airbag, manual windows, steel wheels rather than alloys, and a plastic rather than leather steering wheel. But at £14,495, it's £2900 cheaper than the iS and around £2000 cheaper than the old 1.6.

"The engine has a low speed urge that was never present on the 1.6, but it still has the rorty exhaust note that the company worked hard to achieve with the original car. It

Power to stir your emotions

From your first encounter, you'll remember the sound of the new Mazda MX-5 1800cc fuel-injected 16-valve DOHC engine.

This new engine unit provides quick throttle response thanks to a race-bred induction system, distributorless ignition, and a lightweight flywheel. Furthermore, it offers a smooth, linear power delivery all the way to the 6500rpm redline at the wheels as well as ample low-to-mid-range torque. Pentroof combustion chambers and hollow camshafts are just a few of the technical

Torque curves that translate into smooth acceleration and linear power all the way to the vehicle's redline.

The 1800cc DOHC engine features electronic fuel injection and tuned stainless steel "headers".

enhancements concealed under the cross-flow aluminium cylinder head.

Helping the engine to breathe deeply is a tuned exhaust system with stainless steel "headers".

Harnessing the power of this spirited engine is a special 5-speed, close ratio manual transmission. The compact gear stick linkage has quick, easy movements to allow you to move through the gears with clockwork precision.

To lock the Mazda MX-5's drivetrain in rigid alignment, Mazda created an ingenious, aluminium structure called a Power Plant Frame (PPF). This is an evolutionary development of the classic front-engine rear-wheel drive layout, only used in the world's most exotic cars. During hard acceleration or braking, the PPF minimises vibration and driveline shudder and slack.

After driving the new Mazda MX-5 you'll never forget the way it feels.

The Power Plant Frame (PPF) locks the engine, transmission, and differential into a single rigid unit to ensure a complete feeling of togetherness and a noticeable lack of drivetrain shock and vibration.

Safer for your peace of mind

Although Mazda intended to make the new Mazda MX-5 1.8i and 1.8iS models incredibly fun cars to drive, we didn't overlook the aspect of safety. In fact, we believe that safety features enhance driving pleasure by providing you and your passenger with greater peace of mind.

Exhaustive simulation tests were conducted in the event of a collision. Data collected was fed back to the body engineering group. In the end, they created a body that not only looks beautiful, but functions well if required to do so.

The same highly rigid structure that contributes to the excellent new Mazda MX-5 handling and steering response, also serves to protect the occupants. Stress-carrying members of the monocoque body were made as rigid as possible. The deep cross-sections of the side sills and the large central tunnel provide critical reinforcement around the cockpit. Even the floor panel is designed to function as a stress-bearing component. In the event of a collision, the force of impact is distributed through the

frame of the body and crushable front and rear sections of the car.

Energy-absorbing bumpers on both ends of the vehicle help minimise body deformation in the event of a front or rear collision. To provide an added measure of protection, the doors have been reinforced with high-tensile steel side door beams.

Flame retardant materials are used in the upholstery and trim. And the Mazda MX-5 1.8iS model standard equipment includes a full size driver's side SRS airbag.

The new Mazda MX-5 1.8iS is equipped as standard with a full size driver SRS airbag that emerges from the centre of the steering wheel to cushion the driver's upper body in the event of a serious frontal collision.

Impact-absorbing "crushable zones" combined with strong reinforcement around the cockpit to enhance occupant safety. (1.8i and 1.8iS).

High-tensile steel side door beams provide added cockpit protection (1.8i and 1.8iS).

Both the new Mazda MX-5 1.8i and 1.8iS models include a vehicle immobiliser system as standard equipment.

The new Mazda MX-5 standard immobiliser system is passive armed. To disarm before driving, touch the touch key against the dash mounted receptacle pad.

Another spread from the British catalogue, highlighting the improvements, not only in power (for the 1.8 litre machine) but safety as well. The PPF was retained on the new series.

has perhaps lost a little of its smoothness at high revs, but it performs well - and smoothness is not the ultimate aim in this sort of machine. The gearbox still works with beautiful click-click precision and tiny movements ... The new MX-5 also has substantially better roadholding than the old model, particularly at the rear. The handling is better, too."

Despite little change in the overall power-to-weight ratio, the now defunct monthly recorded a 0-60 time of 8.6 seconds, and a top speed of 119mph (190kph). During the test, 29.3mpg was returned overall, with 40.9mpg being possible at a steady 56mph (90kph).

In the same month, *MotorSport* tried the 1.8iS. It was noted: "Until this spring, such changes as there had been were more cosmetic than technical. Now, however, the original 1.6 engine (which was actually quite perky, though made to sound more so by a trick exhaust) has been superseded by a 1.8 unit derived from that in the 323, albeit lightened. Power has accordingly risen 15 per cent, to 130bhp - on a par with the MX-5 UK Cup racers

that provided the basis for a one-make series in 1990/91. The car is heavier, though (by 50 or 70kg [110lb or 154lb], according to which model you choose), and doesn't feel substantially nippier. Indeed, top speed is little changed, at a claimed 123mph [197kph] (up from 121), and 0-62mph [0-100kph] will take an estimated 8.6 seconds (another fractional gain).

"In parallel with engine development, the chassis has also been modified. Although the original was a paragon of balance, and torsional rigidity, further bracing has been added, and the suspension has been tuned to cope with the extra weight. Mazda says that its intention was to 'suppress roll during the initial stages of cornering and improve the overall ride comfort while maximising the handling.'"

In September, *Complete Car* published a comparison test. After the results came in, the MX-5 1.8i was declared "the best all-rounder. This will suit the sports car enthusiast just as much as the image-conscious looking for a fashion statement. It looks great

and chic but is extremely enjoyable to drive, and still offers traditionally excellent Mazda build quality and generous warranty into the bargain. In this cheaper, stripped-down version, it is actually a pleasant change to find features such as manual window winders and steel wheels. This is the car which, at a push, could most easily be used as an only car."

The £14,495 Mazda was awarded eight out of ten points, while the £16,600 Caterham 7 K-series took seven points. The Suzuki Cappuccino, the cheapest of the bunch at just over £12,000, got six, the same as the Reliant Scimitar Sabre, which was slightly cheaper than the MX-5 at £13,995.

At the end of 1994, Mazda UK calculated that a total of 18,047 vehicles had been sold, 1250 of which were MX-5s - the rest of Europe only achieved 3769 sales during the same period. This was naturally a vast improvement on the previous year, but how long could it last?

Australian update

Interestingly, the December 1994 issue of the Australian *Wheels* magazine, which looked back on the staff's favourite cars of the year, said: "How do you explain other manufacturers' reluctance to tackle the MX-5? [It] still holds the monopoly on user-friendly, two-seater sports cars - a fact weighing ever more heavily in its $40K price tag."

While the covers on the 1992 and 1993 issues had not been the most exciting ever, the cover of the 1994 model year Miata brochure was particularly attractive. The little Mazda entered the Guinness Book of Records *in 1994 when the Miata Club of America managed to get 242 cars running together at Indianapolis.*

In Australia, although it was a fraction more expensive than the Honda CRX, the MX-5 was cheaper than a Toyota MR2 and about the same as a front-wheel drive Celica. Australia had two 1.8 litre models - the standard MX-5 1.8 and the Clubman - but the competition, armed with convertibles from various corners of Europe, was preparing to muscle in on some of the Mazda's action.

Australian sales for 1994 amounted to 404 units, but dropped to just 196 in the following year.

America in 1994 and 1995

Of course, the biggest change for the 1994 model year (announced in October 1993), was adoption of the 1.8 litre engine. In US guise, the power output was listed at 128bhp at 6500rpm (a gain of 12bhp), with maximum torque quoted at 110lbft. Not only was this an increase of 10lbft, it was also more useable, coming in 500rpm lower down the rev range than before.

The American market naturally gained all the body modifications associated with the 1.8 litre machine (namely performance rods front and rear, and a vinyl-covered brace bar connecting the seatbelt anchor towers), as well as the Torsen differential and restyled alloys (both in the Package A option), uprated suspension and larger brakes, all introduced with the bigger engined Eunos Roadster in Japan. In addition, for the US,

dual airbags were made a standard fitment.

Mariner Blue was replaced by the new Laguna Blue Metallic shade, and the 'Miata' script on the rear badge was now in red instead of black. At the start of the 1994 model year, the Miata's base price was just $16,450 but, in reality, few cars were sold without one of the option packages. The popular Package A, priced at $1710, included power steering, alloy wheels, a leather-trimmed steering wheel, electric door mirrors, headrest speakers and (with manual transmission models) a Torsen differential. Package B had all the items in Package A plus cruise control, electric windows and an electric aerial. Package C came with everything in Package B plus a tan leather interior and matching soft-top. Separate options included air conditioning (at $830), ABS brakes, the latest electronically controlled, four-speed automatic gearbox, a body coloured hard-top, the Mazda Sensory Sound System with CD player, and floormats at just $65.

At the Chicago Auto Show, where the Mazda stand carried a couple of interesting alternative fuel MX-5s brought over from Japan, two new special Miatas were announced - the M Edition and the R Package. The M Edition was a luxury Miata finished in Montego Blue Mica ("a colour best described as twenty fathoms deep" according to Mazda's advertising material),

with a tan leather interior and tan hood. Features included highly polished, seven-spoke alloys, a wooden gearknob and handbrake handle, electric windows and mirrors, central locking, and a special keyfob. Weighing in at 1073kg (2360lb), it cost $21,675 - $4250 more than the base model at that time.

The R Package option was available on the basic car, priced at $1500. Stiffer springs, bushings, and harder shock absorbers (sourced from Bilstein) gave the Miata R notably sharper handling, but a somewhat choppier ride. With its alloy wheels, Torsen limited-slip differential and front and rear spoilers, the R was a pure sports car. Items such as power-assisted steering and ABS were not available - in fact, a stripe (designed by Mark Jordan and listed at $230) and air conditioning were the only options.

Car & Driver found the R quicker off the line, but, more importantly, it was much better in manoeuvrability and slalom tests.

A 1994 model year Miata in White. America listed Classic Red, Laguna Blue Metallic, White and Brilliant Black for 1994; the tan leather trim that came with the Package C option was available on all four colours.

The R Package. Although officially announced at the 1994 Chicago Show, its sporty specification had been mentioned in the 1994 model year catalogue.

It also recorded 0.86g on the skidpan against 0.83 for the M Edition. The magazine summed up the R with the comment: "The suspension glows on the track."

US sales for 1994 were almost the same as they had been in 1993 - at 21,400 units, there was a shortfall of only 188 cars on the previous year.

In competition, 1994 was the first year that the Sports Car Club of America moved its annual run-offs to Mid-Ohio (they had been held at Road Atlanta since 1970). The Miata duly took the SCCA Showroom Stock C title for the third year in a row (Michael Galati in car number 9 taking the flag), while Terry McCarthy (car number 23) claimed the E-Production crown. Incidentally, the new 1.8 litre cars were placed in the Showroom Stock D category.

For the 1995 model year, it was decided to combine Package A and B to create a new option known as the Popular Equipment Package; Package C became known as the Leather Package, although the R Package (still for manual Miatas only) remained unchanged. The optional ABS braking system was now lighter than before, and Montego Blue Mica could be specified on all cars in the range unless they were fitted with the R Package.

Midway through 1995, Mazda

A
First, the Mazda Miata burned up the track to become the SCCA Showroom Stock C Champion.

roadster
Now it's ready to burn up the road. Presenting the new Miata R Package. A lightweight racer with

so racy we
128 horsepower, new sport suspension and a Torsen® limited-slip differential. Plus, special features

gave it an
like a front air dam and rear spoiler. The 1994 Miata R Package. The only car that's racier is rated RX.

R rating.

mazda
IT JUST FEELS RIGHT.®

The Mazda MX-5 Miata has been an *Automobile Magazine* "All Star" for 5 consecutive years and is backed by a best-in-class, 36-month/50,000-mile, no-deductible, "bumper-to-bumper" limited basic warranty. See your Mazda Dealer for details. For a free brochure, call 1-800-639-1000. © 1994 Mazda Motor of America, Inc.

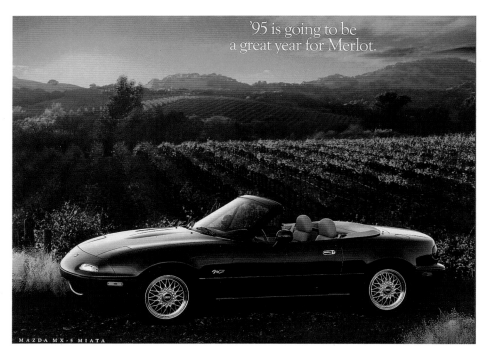

'95 is going to be
a great year for Merlot.

MAZDA MX-5 MIATA

The 1995.5 model year Miata M Edition, the second in the M Edition run. This particular version was finished in Merlot Mica, whereas the first series had been painted in Montego Blue Mica. The colour would change for each season.

introduced another special Miata M Edition. Finished in a striking Merlot Mica (a purple metallic shade), it was priced at $23,530. For that, the buyer got leather trim, 6J x 15 BBS alloys fitted with 195/55 tyres, ABS brakes, a limited-slip differential, Nardi wooden gearknob and handbrake trim, polished treadplates, M Edition floormats, a CD player, and unique badging. A nice touch was the M Edition keyfob and lapel pin.

While sales in Canada were down to three figures, American sales for 1995 remained fairly constant, with just over 20,000 units being recorded for the year (of which, around 3500 of these were M Edition models).

Japan's Limited Editions
Having seen how successful short run cars with various unique features could be in promoting sales for very little outlay, Mazda announced the 500-off RS Limited in July 1994. With sales starting in September, the 2,215,000 yen RS Limited was based on the S Special and finished in Montego Blue Mica.

Interesting features included a lightened flywheel, a 4.3:1 final-drive ratio, Bridgestone Potenza RE010 tyres mounted on BBS 6J x 15 alloys, Recaro bucket seats, RS decals on the front wings, and a Nardi leather-trimmed, three-spoke steering wheel. However, despite Mazda's best efforts, sales fell again in Japan, 1994's total failing to break the 11,000 mark.

Undeterred, sales of the M Package-based G Limited began in January 1995. Priced at just under 1,900,000 yen in manual guise (an automatic was available on this model), only 1500 were built, all finished in Satellite Blue Mica with a dark blue hood. Low-back bucket seats, like those used in the J Limited II, were fitted, along with a new style Momo leather-covered steering wheel, seven-spoke alloy wheels, and an uprated sound system.

In the following month, the R Limited was introduced at 2,175,000 yen. Based on the S Special, the R Limited came in Satellite Blue Mica or Chaste White (of the 1000 built, the blue shade

accounted for 894 sales) with a red leather interior. Like the RS Limited, it featured a lightened flywheel, 4.3:1 final-drive, BBS alloys and Potenza tyres, but this time had a wooden three-spoke Nardi steering wheel and gearknob, as well as wood trim on the handbrake lever.

By this time, Brilliant Black had joined the basic colour line-up, so buyers no longer had to order a limited edition or the V Special for the privilege of black coachwork; it became available from January '95. In addition, the S Special could be bought in Chaste White, thus giving three colour

This is the G Limited, a run of 1500 vehicles based on the M Package.

The home market's RS Limited of 1994 vintage, restricted to just 500 examples.

Interior of the RS Limited, complete with its chunky yet lightweight Recaro seats.

choices on that model instead of the previous two.

Britain in 1995

On 14 March, the California Limited Edition was launched at the Design Centre in London to celebrate the MX-5's fifth anniversary, although sales didn't start until 27 May. Based on the 1.8i model, all cars had Sunburst Yellow paintwork, power steering, 7J x 15 five-spoke alloy wheels, and a Clarion CRX601R radio/cassette unit. Only 300 of the £15,795 cars were made, all carrying a numbered plaque on the fascia and a 'California' badge mounted on the rear panel.

Ironically, with people complaining of a lack of power on the old 1.6 litre car, just as many campaigned for the return of the 1.6i, not least the marketing people at Mazda UK. Higher insurance rates and the escalation of list prices weren't exactly hurting sales (one would expect them to fall after an initial boom, and 1994's figures were actually an improvement on those from the previous two years),

The S Special-based R Limited. Almost 900 were produced in this dark blue shade, with the rest finished in white, to bring the total to 1000 units.

A rare publicity shot of the R Limited, dating from February 1995.

but the competition was starting to get its act together, particularly the Rover Group with its new MGF. A cheaper car in the line-up would certainly help the MX-5 maintain its market share.

On 12 April 1995, the 1.6i was re-introduced as the entry level model to complement the £14,495 1.8i and £17,395 1.8iS. The detuned 1598cc B6 engine produced only 88bhp but, priced at just £12,995, few complained. Naturally, the specification was pretty basic: 5.5J x 14 steel wheels, no power steering, manual windows, no radio/cassette, plus the suspension modifications and body-bracing found on the 1.8 litre models was omitted.

Oddly, the brake discs were reduced in diameter by 20mm (0.78in) all-round compared to the 1.8 litre cars (the 1.6i's discs were, in effect, brought back down to the original dimensions), and it was initially only available in three colours: Classic Red, Brilliant Black and Chaste White. However, an immobiliser was included as standard.

Shortly afterwards, *Complete Car* stated: "Mazda has cut the price of its cheapest MX-5 by nearly £1500 in a bid to beat competition from the new MGF. The MX-5, the biggest-selling open sports car in the world, is now available from £12,995 for the 1.6i - cheaper than the original MX-5 launched five years ago in Britain.

"Commenting on the launch of

The Mazdaspeed catalogue from mid-1995. A combination of the Mazdaspeed front spoiler and side skirts gave a drop in drag of around 7 per cent. Note the rather hefty Mazdaspeed anti-draft device behind the seats, fitted in conjunction with a rollbar.

The California Limited Edition. Note the windscreen surround in body colour - the second version of the home market's J Limited had appeared with a black frame.

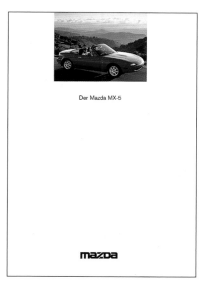

Der Mazda MX-5

Although much of the photography had been seen before (and quite a lot of it was shared within Europe), at least each country had a unique mix and highlighted different features. From left to right we can see the UK, Dutch and German brochures from 1995. The German edition (printed in May) carried details on the 1.6 litre model, but the British and Dutch catalogues - although printed around the same time - left it out for the time being as it was not available until the end of the year. Occasionally, similar-looking brochures would appear in the Far East; Singapore listed the 1.8 with a five-speed manual or four-speed automatic transmission while, for a time, Hong Kong received the automatic only.

the Rover MGF, Mazda Cars UK boss David Heslop said he believed its arrival would expand the market for all sports cars. 'We're biased, but we think the MX-5 is a prettier car,' he added. 'And our research shows that real enthusiasts like the traditional formula of front engine and rear-wheel drive.'"

The sparring continued in a quality newspaper, with Rover bosses knocking the MX-5 by saying it had no pedigree and therefore the MG was better. As a historian, I find it hard to believe that anyone could say Mazda is lacking in pedigree. The marque has achieved some excellent results in the American and European motorsport arenas (the RX-7 has notched up more IMSA wins than any other car in the history of the series), and the author witnessed the Hiroshima company's victory at the Le Mans 24-hour race in 1991. So many companies have established themselves with good results at the famous Sarthe track,

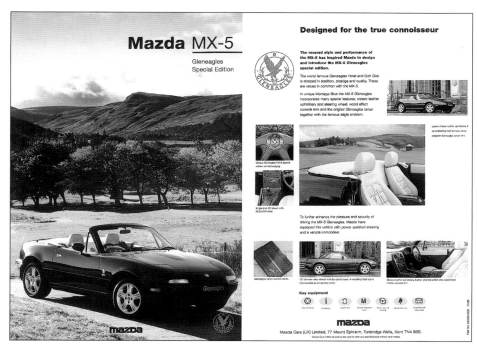

Britain's luxurious Gleneagles model (named after the world-famous golf course) was launched at the 1995 Earls Court Motor Show. One example was donated by Mazda UK in a bid to raise funds to help send Scottish athletes to the 1996 Olympics.

Another shot of the MX-5 Gleneagles.

and some are still selling cars on the back of this reputation to this day. At the time, I was not an MX-5 fan, but I couldn't help asking myself if the MG marque had ever won outright at Le Mans!

The argument could go on forever, but there was no doubt that Mazda had a strong competitor in the MGF, which was due to be launched in August to coincide with the issue of the new registration letter.

In fact, despite all the column inches on the smaller engined car, the 1.6i wasn't available until November (by which time it cost £500 more). Official figures on the 1.6i quoted 0-62mph (100kph) in 10.6 seconds and a top speed of 109mph (174kph). In the meantime, in mid-1995, the 1.8iS received a restyled steering wheel (complete with airbag); in addition, another limited edition car was on its way.

At the 1995 Earls Court Motor Show, Mazda UK launched the 1.8

litre Gleneagles. Based on the 1.8i, the Gleneagles was finished in Montego Blue and, although the hood itself was black, it came with a champagne coloured hood cover to match the interior. Priced at £16,465, it had power-assisted steering, leather seats, attractive 15-inch five-spoke alloys, a Momo leather-trimmed steering wheel (with the Gleneagles emblem on the boss), a wood effect console, a CD player, Gleneagles tartan trim on the gearlever gaiter, and, of course, special 'Gleneagles' badging.

Mazda UK Ltd later donated a Gleneagles model to the British Olympic Appeal to help send Scottish athletes to the 1996 Atlanta Olympics. It was hoped that £250,000 could be raised through the sale of lottery tickets - was this the most expensive MX-5 ever?

The November 1995 issue of *Complete Car* pitted the MX-5 1.8iS against the new front-wheel drive Alfa Romeo Spider (eventually

launched in the UK in spring 1996, at £22,000), the £15,995 1.8 litre fuel-injected MGF, and Fiat's recently announced Barchetta, priced at £13,995. Tony Dron, a classic car enthusiast and ex-BTCC Champion, noted that the MX-5 "looks a little dated now, but [it is] still a yardstick by which to judge these new sports cars."

The article went on to say that "driven fast, the Mazda does not roll excessively: it turns into corners well, understeering mildly at normal speeds. Push it a little harder and it's quite easy to provoke a mild and easily controlled tail slide which requires simple throttle control. Overdo it and you might spin but it is relatively easy to drive the Mazda in this entertaining fashion."

The Mazda was the lightest of the bunch (by over 40kg, or 88lb), but it was the slowest and only the Alfa was worse on overall fuel consumption. Despite a number of compliments for the Hiroshima-built machine, in the end it was

August 1995 saw the introduction of the Series II cars, powered by an uprated version of the 1.8 litre engine that had been adopted across the range two years earlier. This is the Japanese Special Package model.

placed third, the MG taking the spoils with the Fiat runner-up.

In its September 1995 issue, *Car & Driver* compared the MX-5 (in Italian specification) with the Alfa Romeo Spider and Fiat Barchetta on home ground. The general concensus was that the Mazda was starting to show its age against the Italian newcomers, "but it's still a performer, and a beauty in profile." Perhaps the competition was starting to catch up?

One thing the *Complete Car* article highlighted was how little the MX-5 weighed. The 1.6i was naturally the lightest car in the range, tipping the scales at just 965kg (2123lb). The 1.8i was 25kg (55lb) heavier, while the 1.8iS weighed just over a ton, at 1018kg (2240lb). All were extremely light by the day's standards.

By the end of the year, the changes for 1996 were already filtering through. Armrests came back in preference to the unpopular door pockets, instruments lost their chrome ring surrounds, and the 1.8iS radio/cassette unit was changed. Laguna Blue was deleted from the colour charts, leaving Classic Red, British Racing Green, Silver Stone Metallic, Brilliant Black and Chaste White, although the BRG and silver shades were still not available on the 1.6i model.

Amazingly, MX-5 mania seemed to gather pace again. In 1995, Mazda UK sold 17,775 vehicles (only a few short of the total for 1994), but MX-5 sales almost doubled - no less than 2495 found homes during the year. These were the best results in the UK to date, although most other markets recorded a fall in sales; the rest of Europe could only muster 5221 sales in 1995.

More changes in Japan

August 1995 saw the introduction of the 133bhp Series II 1.8 litre engine. Although the BP-ZE (RS) designation was retained, the Series II version featured a 16-bit ECU (Electronic Control Unit) and a lightweight flywheel to enable the engine to rev more freely. The 4.3:1 final-drive ratio was brought back on five-speed cars, although automatic models stayed at 4.1:1.

An airbag was now standard on all Roadsters, the original, low mounted interior lights were replaced by a single unit by the rearview mirror, the chrome dial surrounds were deleted, the sunvisors became a simple one-piece affair, door pockets were reduced in size (and not fitted at all on the basic car, or those with the polished speaker surround plates), trim materials were changed, and the colour of the 'Roadster' script found on the rear panel was changed from red to green.

Production of the Series II cars started on chassis NA8C-400007 and, as usual in Japan, the line-up was an extensive one. The standard model remained in manual guise only, becoming even more basic (even the hood cover was optional),

but it was available in the full range of colours: Classic Red, Chaste White, Silver Stone Metallic, Brilliant Black and Neo Green.

The Special Package model remained the most popular, with prices starting at 1,930,000 yen for the manual version or 1,980,000 yen for the automatic. The Special Package came with alloy wheels, power steering, Torsen differential (manual cars), a new stereo radio/cassette unit, electrically adjustable door mirrors, electric windows, and a new leather-trimmed, three-spoke steering wheel, complete with airbag, of course.

In between the base model and the Special Package, there was now the 1,790,000 yen M Package. At 100,000 yen more than the basic Roadster, it had steel wheels and the basic three-spoke steering wheel, but featured power-assisted steering, electric windows and a decent stereo system.

The V Special grade was retained (starting at 2,300,000 yen), as was the V Special Type II with its unique features (again, it was 100,000 yen more). Colour options were restricted to just Brilliant Black, Neo Green and Chaste White on these models, and they came with a new three-spoke, wood-rimmed steering wheel from Nardi.

The manual only S Special was also continued at 1,995,000 yen,

The 1800 Series II range in Japan and its leading features.

その楽しさは、アクセルを踏んだ瞬間、
きっと誰にでも直感できる

A delightful publicity shot from autumn 1995 featuring the Special Package model.

at 2,080,000 yen and limited to 700 cars) was finished in wine red with a tan coloured soft-top and matching leather-trimmed interior; an aluminium alloy gearknob, shift plate and handbrake lever were used for the first time. The Combination B was the same price, but limited to 800 examples, and

The V Special Type II from the same era.

but there was now an S Special Type II at 190,000 yen more. The extra money gave Potenza RE010 tyres mounted on 6J x 15 BBS alloy wheels (the run-of-the-mill Type I had the usual 14-inch, seven-spoke alloys, which Kijima-san thought was the best combination). Incidentally, the S Special cars were available in either Montego Blue Mica, Brilliant Black, Chaste White or Classic Red.

At the end of the year, Mazda announced the VR Limited Combination A and Combination B models; sales of these interesting variations - both based on the S Special Type I - started in January 1996. The Combination A (priced

The S Special Type II of late 1995 vintage.

The wine red VR Limited Combination A. Just 700 of these S Special Type I-based cars were produced, with sales starting in January 1996.

Finished in dark green, this is the VR Limited Combination B. Launched alongside the Combination A model, 800 examples were built.

came in a shade known as Excellent Green Mica. This model had a dark green soft-top, black leather interior, and the same alloy gearknob, shift plate and handbrake. Although based on the Type I, both cars had five-spoke 6J x 15 alloys instead of the familiar seven-spoke items.

Despite the many changes in the range - and the special editions

- sales continued to decline rapidly in Japan. In fact, only 7178 Mazda roadsters were sold on the home market during 1995. This meant that, for the first time, European sales figures had exceeded those of Japan.

America in 1996

The 1996 model year line-up was announced in October 1995.

Engine power increased to 133bhp, but the main changes centred on meeting new regulations - namely, the 1997 Federal side impact requirements and OBD-II emissions. Other, more minor, changes included relocation of the interior lights and the addition of a small light in the boot.

The three option packages from 1995 were available again (the

93

An advert for the home market VR Limited Combination A and Combination B models. The wheels were later adopted as standard on the UK specification 1998 model year 1.8iS.

Popular Equipment Package, the Leather Package and the R Package), but there was now also a Power Steering Package that added just power-assisted steering and wheel trim rings to the basic car; it was priced at a very reasonable $300, while the base model came in at $18,750.

To recap, the $2090 Popular Equipment Package included alloy wheels, power-assisted steering, a leather-wrapped steering wheel, cruise control, power windows and mirrors, headrest spreakers, an electric aerial, and a limited-slip

The 1996.5 model year Miata M Edition (the third in the series), finished in Starlight Mica.

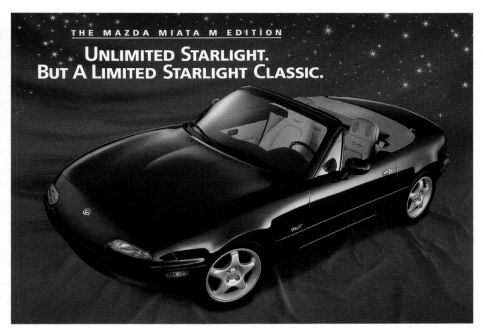

THE MAZDA MIATA M EDITION

**UNLIMITED STARLIGHT.
BUT A LIMITED STARLIGHT CLASSIC.**

Another view of the 1996.5 model year Miata M Edition. The interior featured tan leather trim, along with a wooden gearknob and handbrake garnish, and a leather-wrapped steering wheel.

differential on cars with a manual transmission (those with an automatic gearbox had to do without the lsd, but the PEP option came $390 cheaper).

The $2985 Leather Package included a tan interior with leather seat facings and a matching tan hood, while the $1500 R Package featured alloy wheels, a Torsen lsd, uprated suspension components (including Bilstein dampers), front and rear skirts, and a rear spoiler.

As for individual options, air conditioning was listed at $900, as were ABS brakes, the hard-top was $1500, and an automatic gearbox cost $850. The $875 MSSS was now augmented by the Mazda Premium Sound System which, at $675, boasted a CD player and uprated speakers. Floormats rounded off the options list, priced at $80.

Only four colours were listed as standard: Classic Red, Brilliant Black, White and Montego Blue Mica. These were available across the range, with the exception of the blue shade, which couldn't be specified with the R Package.

Road & Track observed: "Now approaching its sixth birthday, the

Mazda Miata hasn't lost a bit of the shine it possessed when it rolled into our hands and hearts in the late 1980s. Lightweight, front-engine/rear-drive roadsters with looks to charm and personality to spare, new Miatas are still affordable and used ones are bargains (and well looked after by their loving owners). If you can't have fun in this car, maybe you belong somewhere in a Dickens novel."

Midway through 1996, the $24,760 Miata M Edition appeared in Starlight Mica, an attractive dark blue metallic shade found on the Millennia saloon. Trimmed in tan leather with a matching tan coloured hood and hood cover, the high spec package included such niceties as 15-inch five-spoke alloys (fitted with 195/50 tyres), a limited-slip differential, ABS brakes, air conditioning, a top stereo unit with CD player, headrest speakers and an electric aerial, cruise control, a Nardi wooden gearknob and handbrake handle, a leather-trimmed steering wheel, power windows and mirrors, a remote keyless entry system, and an alarm. The only options were automatic

transmission and a hard-top, as virtually everything else seemed to be fitted anyway.

The USA took another 18,408 Miatas during 1996 (the M Edition accounted for 2968 of these). This meant the running total for American sales now stood at a massive 196,770 units, a figure which represented some 48 per cent of production at that time.

The Land of the Rising Sun in 1996
Mazda built a total of 1,197,872 vehicles in 1987, of which over two-thirds were passenger cars. Production figures rose to a peak of 1,422,624 in 1990 before falling back to just over one million in 1993.

After that, production continued to fall, with only 773,567 vehicles being built in 1996 (around 600,000 were passenger cars, with well over half of them being exported). The MX-5 accounted for less than 1 per cent of this figure but, by the end of the year, cumulative production of the MX-5 had reached more than 400,000 units (the 400,000th vehicle was built on 2 November 1996). The RX-7 had already surpassed 1,000,000 units by this time, although it had been on sale since 1978, of course.

In 1996, the Eunos sales outlets were integrated into the Mazda Anfini, Mazda or Ford dealerships, the Eunos Roadster being sold through the Mazda Anfini sales

Introduced in December 1996, the B2 Limited was based on the M Package model. Restricted to 1000 examples, the B2 designation stood for Blue & Bright.

Announced at the same time as the B2 Limited, the R2 Limited was based on the S Special Type I. R2 stood for Racy & Red (the red referring to the car's interior); production was limited to only 500 units.

Racy and red interior of the R2 Limited.

channel, lining up alongside the RX-7, MS8, MPV and Eunos Presso. The Anfini network boasted 87 dealers with a total of 633 outlets across Japan, but annual sales figures were still dismal, with less than 4500 cars finding homes during the year.

At the end of 1996, in December, all models adopted a new Momo four-spoke steering wheel (with airbag), and two more limited edition Eunos Roadsters came along: the B2 Limited at 1,898,000 yen (or 1,993,000 with automatic transmission) and the manual only R2 Limited at 2,098,000 yen.

Based on the M Package, B2 apparently stood for Blue & Bright, although the Twilight Blue Mica shade chosen for the vehicle was hardly the brightest in the Mazda range and the black interior was rather austere to say the least. Anyway, limited to 1000 examples, the main features included a dark blue soft-top, highly-polished 14-inch seven-spoke alloys, chrome door mirrors, moquette-trimmed bucket seats, chrome dial surrounds, and a combined CD/cassette/radio unit. Air conditioning was available as an option.

The 500-off R2 Limited (which was based on the S Special Type I) came in Chaste White, despite the R2 appellation standing for Racy & Red! This was actually a reference to the red and black interior, which included red leather seats.

A British spec 1.8i model dating from the early part of 1996. This car is painted in Classic Red; other colours included Brilliant Black, Chaste White, Silver Stone Metallic and British Racing Green, although the last two mentioned were not available on the 1.6i. Note the standard steel wheels.

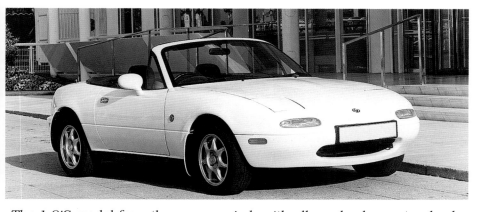

The 1.8iS model from the same period, with alloy wheels as standard.

The Merlot (right) was launched in the UK in mid-1996 alongside the smaller engined Monaco. It came with a luxurious grey leather trim, wood finish to the dashboard, and a leather-wrapped steering wheel; a CD player also came as standard. Although both models had five-spoke alloy wheels, they were actually slightly different in design.

Bridgestone Potenza tyres came on 6J x 15 five-spoke alloys, while the aluminium alloy gearknob, shift plate and handbrake lever were revived, along with the chrome dial surrounds found on the B2 version.

The British market in 1996

A Mazda UK press release described the salient features of the MX-5 as follows: "The race-bred induction system, distributor-less ignition and lightweight flywheel ensure a quick, lively throttle response ... The drivetrain is locked in rigid alignment by means of an ingenious aluminium powerplant frame. Suspension is all-independent, using double-wishbones and anti-roll bars, while a brace bar and performance rods increase body rigidity on 1.8i models for enhanced chassis control.

"The rack-and-pinion steering has just 3.3 turns lock-to-lock and with power assistance on the 1.8iS this is reduced to 2.8. Braking is by discs all-round, ventilated at the front, solid at the back, and reinforced by ABS on the 1.8iS.

"For security, all models are fitted with an engine immobiliser, security-coded window etching, lockable glovebox and central storage box, and remote fuel flap releases.

"The plastic nose section is designed to resist stone chips and incorporates pop-up halogen headlamps. Everything is set up for a sporty experience: the tightly grouped pedals and dials, leather steering wheel on the 1.8iS, the driver's left foot rest.

"But safety is built in, too, from the side impact door beams and energy absorbing bumpers to the flame retardant trim and upholstery. A driver's side airbag and anti-lock braking are standard on the 1.8iS, which offers additional luxury with its detachable RDS

MX-5
1.8 LTR LIMITED EDITION
- Neo Green
- Tan leather seats
- Tan soft top tonneau cover
- CD player and tweeter speakers

The Australian market's 1.8 Limited Edition, restricted to just 75 units. Launched in January 1996, it was finished in Neo Green with a tan leather interior and tan hood cover; the wheels were the familiar seven-spoke production items. Sadly, despite the introduction of a number of special versions over the years, sales in Australia remained low.

radio/cassette, alloy wheels, electric windows and door mirrors, and remote boot opening."

On 12 June 1996, Mazda UK announced two new limited edition models - the MX-5 1.6 Monaco and the MX-5 1.8 Merlot. From the press release, it was obvious that these latest additions were aimed squarely at a certain Rover Group product: "The Mazda MX-5 Monaco costs £13,750 - which is £2645 below the price of the cheapest MGF - while the high specification MX-5 Merlot costs nearly £2500 less than the MGF VVC, at £16,350.

"Finished in British Racing Green and fitted with a tan hood, the Monaco is mechanically identical to the MX-5 1.6i. Special features of this limited edition roadster include alloy wheels and a radio/cassette player. The MX-5 Monaco has a top speed of 109mph [174kph] and accelerates from 0-62mph [100kph] in 10.6 seconds. It achieves 42.2mpg at a steady 56mph [90kph].

"The luxurious Merlot - which has a special deep lustrous red body colour called Vin Rouge - has [light grey] leather upholstery, quality wood trim, a CD sound system, alloy wheels and power-assisted steering, [along with a Momo leather-trimmed steering wheel]. The 1.8-litre, 16v engine develops 131bhp to give acceleration from 0-62mph [100kph] in 8.6 seconds plus a top speed of 123mph [197kph]. It returns more than 40mpg in the steady 56mph [90kph] test."

Although Australian sales picked up very slightly (241 units for the year, taking the running total for that country to 4609), Europe was the only market to show a notable improvement. In Britain, MX-5 sales continued to strengthen. During 1996, Mazda UK had a bumper year, selling no fewer than 3855 examples of the popular convertible. The European mainland recorded 5730 sales, bringing the total for the whole of Europe to a healthy 9585 units (more than twice the figure for the home market during the same period).

The American scene
In 1997, the MX-5 Miata was included in the American *Automobile* magazine's 'All Stars' listing for the seventh consecutive year, although the $19,675 price tag (including delivery charges) was a far cry from that advertised at the start of the decade. 1997's colour schemes remained the same as for the 1996 model year, but the options were revised once again.

The Power Steering Package included power-assisted steering and wheel trim rings, while the new Touring Package listed power steering, a leather-wrapped steering wheel, electric windows, electrically adjustable door mirrors, alloy wheels and door pockets. The latest Popular Equipment Package had everything in the Touring Package, plus a Torsen limited-slip differential (for manual cars), the rear subframe performance rods, speakers in the headrests, cruise control and an electric aerial. The Leather Package built on the Popular Equipment Package with a tan leather interior and tan vinyl top. The R Package (for manual cars only) incorporated uprated suspension with Bilstein shock absorbers, rear subframe performance rods, a Torsen lsd, front and rear spoilers, a rear skirt, and alloy wheels with locking wheelnuts.

Separate options included a detachable hard-top, air conditioning, four-sensor, three-channel ABS brakes, the 160w Mazda Premium Sound System, and a four-speed automatic

IN OUR
NEWEST GREEN,
YOU'LL DETECT
SHADES OF
THE PAST.

MAZDA MIATA
1997 M EDITION.

transmission with 'Hold' facility. Accessories, such as polished alloys, stainless treadplates, racing stripes, a boot-mounted luggage rack, rear spoiler, aero parts kit, tonneau cover, front 'bra', foglights and a CD changer, were also offered by dealerships.

The M Edition for the 1997 model year was finished in a shade known as Marina Green Mica on this occasion, an attractive dark green colour set off by the contrasting tan leather trim and hood. Other features included highly polished, 15-inch, six-spoke alloy wheels, stainless treadplates, special floormats, Nardi wooden gearknob and handbrake trim, a CD player, and air conditioning.

A press release dated 1 July described the latest American special edition - the $22,520 STO Edition. It read: "Arriving just in

The M Edition for 1997, the fourth in the series, was finished in Marina Green Mica. The first had been painted in Montego Blue Mica, while those that followed came in Merlot Mica and Starlight Mica, respectively.

time to make the most of warm summer nights throughout the country, Mazda has announced the addition of a new limited production version of the company's classic roadster - the 1997.5 MX-5 Miata STO Edition. The STO stands for Special Touring Option, a combination of popular options that embodies the true lightweight,

Two views of the well equipped Miata STO Edition which was announced in July 1997. STO stood for Special Touring Option, by the way.

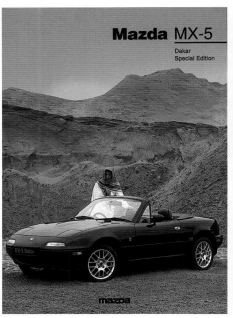

affordable sports car spirit of the Miata ... Only 1500 of the Miata STO Edition [models] will be produced.

"Highlighting the 1997.5 STO Edition is Twilight Blue Mica paint, topped off by a tan leather interior and tan vinyl top. In addition to the unique paint scheme, the STO Edition features special Enkei 15-inch wheels and low-profile 50-series tyres; rear lip spoiler; STO Edition logos on the floormats; Nardi leather shift knob (manual transmission only); stainless steel scuff plates; an STO Edition sequentially numbered dash plaque, and certificate of authenticity.

"The car is also equipped with a full complement of luxury features, including headrest speakers, leather-wrapped steering wheel, power mirrors, power windows and a CD player. The only options are air conditioning and a four-speed automatic transmission."

Just over 17,000 Miatas were sold in the States during 1997 (although only 11,950 were officially exported to America that year, along with a further 618 for Canada), while in SCCA racing, the Miata resumed its winning ways after a couple of lean years - Pratt Cole took the E-Production title and Michael Galati claimed Showroom Stock B honours.

The situation in the UK

By this time, the Mazda had a whole string of competitors to contend with. The BMW Z3 was another newcomer (albeit a more expensive one), but, comparing it to the MX-5, Gavin Conway of *Autocar* said: "The Z3 has more cabin space, better performance, more mature yet still enjoyable handling, and a much bigger dose of badge pride."

In January 1997, the 400-off Dakar Limited Edition was announced. Priced at £17,210 on the road, it was finished in Twilight Blue Metallic, with the interior in mid-grey leather with dark blue piping. Other features included unique 15-inch, 16-spoke alloy wheels, burr walnut trim, a chrome rear brace bar, chrome treadplates, a Momo leather-trimmed steering wheel, Dakar floormats in grey with dark blue edging, a radio/cassette unit, and power-assisted steering. Each vehicle had a numbered plaque and 'Dakar' badging.

By spring 1997, a high level brake light had found its way onto the bootlid; the interior light was now incorporated into a new rearview mirror, and the 1.8i now had the same boot release arrangement as that found on the 1.8iS.

On 16 May 1997, Mazda UK announced the special edition MX-5 Monza. Named after the famous

Italian racing circuit, the Monza was finished in British Racing Green and priced at £14,595. Limited to just 800 examples, it featured 14-inch, five-spoke alloy wheels with locking wheelnuts, an uprated sound system and exclusive Monza badging, in addition to the standard equipment of the 1.6i upon which it was based.

A fortnight later, on 29 May, this was followed by the MX-5 Harvard. Based on the MX-5 1.8i in Silver Stone Metallic, it was equipped with power steering, 15-inch, five-spoke alloy wheels, burgundy leather upholstery with grey piping, a CD player, immobiliser, chrome brace bar, wood trim, a Momo leather-wrapped steering wheel, high level stop lamp,

The 1.6 litre Monza reached the UK market in May 1997. Finished in British Racing Green, this particular model was limited to 800 examples.

One of the last 1.8iS models to wear the now-familiar seven-spoke alloys. In October (for the 1998 model year in effect), the new five-spoke alloy wheels were adopted. The eagle-eyed will notice the fatter base on the door mirrors for cars with electrically adjustable mirrors.

Mazda UK's third special edition model of 1997 - the 1.8 litre Harvard.

locking wheelnuts, polished treadplates, and special floormats with the Harvard logo.

The Harvard was priced at £17,495. To put this into perspective, the July price list quoted £14,410 for the 1.6i, the 1.8i was exactly £1000 more, while the 1.8iS was £18,510. Mica and metallic paint finishes cost £250 extra, leather trim added £923 to the list price, and air conditioning (available on the 1.8 litre cars only) was a hefty £1395.

In October 1997, the final changes were made to take the car into 1998 until the new model's

The MX-5 Classic, launched in the UK in October 1997.

Mazda MX-5 Berkeley

Japan's SR Limited - the last special edition model for the home market. This example is shown in Sparkle Green Metallic but Chaste White was also available. In all, only 700 cars were built, with the white shade being the most popular colour.

The 400-off Berkeley was announced in January 1998, and was the UK's final version of the first generation MX-5. Finished in Sparkle Green Metallic and with a black and grey leather interior, it was priced at £17,600, and was basically very similar to Japan's SR Limited model.

The SR Limited in Chaste White.

introduction. Both the 1.6i and 1.8i received power steering as standard, and the 1.8iS wheels were changed to 6J x 15 five-spoke alloys - almost the same design as those found on the Harvard but with dished centres.

At the same time, the 1.8i-based MX-5 Classic was launched. Finished in Brilliant Black, it featured black leather seat facings with red stitching, 15-inch, five-spoke alloy wheels with locking wheelnuts, wood trim, a stainless steel rear brace bar, polished treadplates, a Momo leather-trimmed steering wheel, floormats in black with red edging, 'Classic' badging, and an RDS radio/cassette unit. It was priced at £17,495 on the road.

Sales throughout the British Isles continued to rise at a staggering rate. Accounting for almost exactly half of Europe's sales during 1997, Mazda UK sold 4956 MX-5s, bringing the running total to an impressive 18,715 units.

The final version of the first generation MX-5 was announced in January 1998 - the limited edition Berkeley, finished in Sparkle Green Metallic. Only 400 were produced, and the leading features were a black leather interior with contrasting light grey on the seat facings and door panels, 15-inch, five-spoke alloy wheels with locking wheelnuts, a chrome boot rack, a stainless steel rear brace bar, stainless treadplates, dark burr wood trim, a Momo leather-wrapped steering wheel, black leather gearlever and handbrake gaiter, a CD player, and black floormats edged in grey. A numbered plaque was mounted on the centre console, and 'Berkeley' badges were fitted just below the side repeater indicators on the front wings. The Berkeley was priced at a very reasonable £17,600.

The home market
The range for the 1997 model year was unchanged from that which resulted from the reshuffle in the latter half of 1995; standard colour schemes were also unaltered. Prices had risen slightly over the last couple of years, but not by a great deal compared with those of the

The family tree of the first generation Roadster for the home market.

export markets. For instance, the basic model was 1,770,000 yen in Chiba (the author's home town in Japan, near to Tokyo) in December 1996, while, at the other end of the scale, the V Special Type II started at 2,470,000 yen.

In August 1997, the SR Limited was announced to celebrate the eighth anniversary of the Eunos Roadster in Japan. Based on the M Package, the manual version (with Torsen limited-slip differential) weighed exactly 1000kg (2200lb) and was priced at 1,898,000 yen; the automatic weighed 30kg (66lb) more and cost 1,978,000 yen.

Two colour options were available: Sparkle Green Metallic (the same colour as that seen on the British Berkeley) and Chaste White (of the 700 examples produced, white was the most popular shade, accounting for 384 sales). The standard Momo steering wheel with airbag was employed (shortly after the launch of the SR Limited, dual airbags became an option), but it had highly polished, seven-spoke alloys, black leather seats with light grey nubuck type inserts, chrome door mirrors, chrome dial surrounds, a CD/

tuner, and a Nardi leather gearknob to distinguish it from the rest of the line-up.

By this time, more than enough cars had been sold on the home market to ascertain the various trends. The Special Package was the most popular model, accounting for roughly 40 per cent of sales. Japanese buyers usually prefer automatics, although only around 15 per cent of the Eunos Roadsters sold featured an automatic transmission. The most popular colour, however, would not surprise anyone who has lived in Japan - it was white. Next in line was green, followed by black.

Japanese sales figures released for December 1997 confirmed the growing popularity of utility vehicles and MPVs in preference to sports cars and coupés. The best-seller in the sporting sector was the Toyota Corolla Levin with 722 units for the month; the Celica managed 464 sales, while the Supra clocked up just 145 - the MR2 recorded a disappointing 91 sales. Mazda was also struggling, with sales of 206 Eunos Roadsters and 202 RX-7s. The Nissan 300ZX and the rest of the Fairlady Z range found just 40

customers, although this was still quite a lot compared to sales of Honda's NSX supercar, which amounted to only 13 units.

By comparison, Honda sold 4230 of its CR-V and no less than 11,123 of its StepWgn people mover. In the smaller MPV class, Suzuki sold over 16,000 Wagon R models. Even executive cars were outselling sporting machines at a rate of almost ten to one! As the world's most dedicated followers of fashion, the Japanese were clearly telling the manufacturers that the sports car era was well and truly over unless they were offered something new: Eunos Roadster sales for the year added up to just 3537 units.

Fortunately, Mazda had a new model. The second generation MX-5 was eagerly awaited and, at the 1997 Tokyo Show, the car everyone wanted to see was finally unveiled.

However, the original MX-5 had started a roadster renaissance. It also left a lasting impression, making it into the final cut of 100 cars put forward for the 'Car of the Century' title - one of only seven Japanese models (the Lexus LS400, Honda NSX, and the first generation of Toyota Corolla, Honda Civic, Datsun Z and Mazda RX-7 made up the total) left in with a chance. The Mini was ultimately declared the winner, a choice which the author finds very hard to understand ...

5

SPECIALS

This chapter concerns itself with the official MX-5-based specials, such as the various show cars that have been exhibited over the years, the vehicles powered by alternative fuels, and machines which came about because of the M2 project. Modified and tuned vehicles, including those by Mazdaspeed, are covered in the next chapter.

Club Racer

In addition to the production models, Mazda decided to show a Miata-based car it called the 'Club Racer' at the 1989 Chicago Show. MRA (nee MANA) stylist, Mark Jordan, was credited with the sporty design.

The respected American journal, *Road & Track*, described the vehicle in its May 1989 edition: "In eyeball-splattering canary yellow, it featured fat Yokohama tyres (205/50 ZR15 front, 255/45 ZR15 rear) faired into sweetly Coke-bottled sheet metal, a plastic rear cowl cover, six-inch spoiler and teensy headlights under plastic covers. Shocks were Bilsteins, body coloured wheels were real/fake Minilites by Panasport. Dee-lish."

The interior was also modified, including leather trim, high back seats (with the Miata logo and racing harnesses) and a Momo steering wheel. In effect, the aftermarket industry started on the very day the car was launched!

The M2-1001

The M2 project was established in November 1990, with the M2-1001 the first offering. All of the staff involved (about 30 people) were Mazda workers, and included Masakatsu Kato (the man behind numerous Mazda concept cars), Hirotaka Tachibana (the development engineer who had been of great importance on the first generation MX-5 project) and Masanori Mizuochi, now Chairman of the Roadster Club of Japan (RCOJ). The main objective of the project was to be a direct contact between the company and the car's users, as well as building MX-5 specials for show purposes and test marketing.

The M2-1001 was announced on 1 December 1991 (by which time the M2 team had settled down in its new headquarters in Setagaya, Tokyo), but delivery didn't start until March 1992. The car featured a 130bhp engine linked to a five-speed manual transmission, a stiffened chassis, modified suspension, and wider 195/50 tyres mounted on 15-inch, eight-spoke alloy wheels. Finished in dark blue paint, the whole package weighed in at 960kg (2112lb).

From the outset, it was stated that only 300 were being built, and this fact contributed greatly to tempting buyers to part with a hefty 3,400,000 yen. For this kind of money, it was possible to buy a basic Nissan 300ZX, or a high spec Toyota Supra in Japan. Nevertheless, the M2-1001 was heavily over-subscribed. In the end,

The Club Racer was displayed alongside the production models at the Miata launch in Chicago. Apart from the obvious body changes, the Club Racer also featured a modified exhaust system.

Rear three-quarter view of the so-called Club Racer.

a lottery system was used to determine who would get one, resulting in many disappointed enthusiasts; Mazda could quite easily have sold at least 600 more!

M2-1002

After the phenomenal success of the M2-1001, you'd be forgiven for believing that the 1002 couldn't fail. It was a similar scenario: 300 cars would be built - again, finished in dark blue, but with a tan hood. The 1.6 litre engine was left as standard on this occasion (with a five-speed gearbox), as were the chassis details.

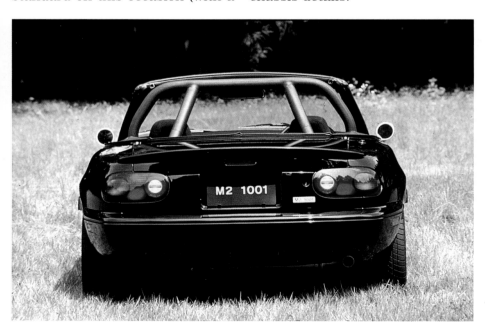

It was the cockpit that was the main feature on the 1002. Wood trim came from Yamaha, and ivory leather was used almost everywhere. Even the top roll on the fascia was leather, but this time in a dark blue. Without a doubt, the interior was truly beautiful, and would have made any Italian coachbuilder proud. All this added an extra 10kg (22lb) to

The M2-1001 was the first product to be developed by the M2 organisation, Tachibana's brainchild, established in November 1990. Announced in December 1991, the 1001 was obviously more muscular around the front end, but there were also a number of delightful touches, such as the racing-style alloy fuel filler cap and door mirrors. Cars were numbered from 001 to 300.

Interior of the M2-1001 - Tachibana's favourite M2 vehicle.

Sadly, the M2-1002 (seen in the foreground in this shot) was not as successful as the 1001, pictured in the background. All M2 cars had unique tail badges and a numbered plate by the nearside door mirror. M2 numbers ran consecutively, so the 1002 series was ultimately allocated 301 to 400.

Left: Another view of the M2-1002, with, above, a close-up of its stylish interior.

explaining the 1002's disappointing sales.

M2-1003 also concentrated on interior appointments (it also had a Rod Millen rear deck aero cover and BBS alloys), but, after the poor response to 1002, the project was shelved before seeing the light of day.

The MX-5 and alternative fuels

Development of the electric MX-5 had started in January 1992 and was scheduled to continue for two years. The project was set up with the objective of exploring alternative fuels, as environmental concerns were paramount in virtually every country around the world, not least in Japan, which has had quite a strict policy since the 1970s.

the weight of its predecessor, despite the lack of power steering (something which 1001 had).

Announced at the end of 1992, delivery started in February 1993. However, by the end of May when it was discontinued, only 100 of the 3,000,000 yen machines had been sold; some of the interior parts were later used on the Tokyo Limited of late 1993.

The failure of 1002 was almost certainly down to a question of timing. It's relevant to remember

that the MX-5 was launched at the height of an economic boom when people - especially in Japan - had plenty of money to spare for luxury items. The 1001 seemed to catch the mood of the moment; by the time the 1002 was launched, the economy had slowed down somewhat ... the bubble had burst. It is hard to imagine Japan struggling but, by all accounts, people were selling cars rather than buying them during this period, and this goes a long way towards

One of three electric MX-5s built to test the potential of alternative fuels. Mazda also built a hydrogen powered version, which proved the more practical of the two in everyday situations. However, the M2 organisation offered a course in early 1995 giving guidance on how to convert an MX-5 to electric power.

The hydrogen powered MX-5.

In February 1993, Mazda UK released the following statement: "Still very much a prototype project, as only three have been built, the battery powered Mazda MX-5 was designed in conjunction with the Chugoku Electric Power Company and will be used by the company to run practicality tests for using electric cars on a daily basis.

"In testing, the electric Mazda MX-5 has achieved performance figures compatible with a petrol driven 1.5 litre automatic. Powered by an electric AC motor, the energy source is taken from 16 nickel cadmium batteries situated in the engine bay. With a top speed of 80mph [128kph], acceleration of 0-25mph [40kph] in just 4.2 seconds and a range of up to 111 miles [178km], an electrically powered MX-5 is being considered as a viable alternative for the future."

Weight was the biggest problem. With power-assisted steering and air conditioning, the electric MX-5 weighed in at a hefty 1410kg (3102lb) in an unladen state. This was due to the four batteries up front and another 12 in the boot. In reality, only lighter, more compact batteries would ever make electric power a viable option in a car of this type.

Hydrogen power deserved more careful consideration. It emits no hydrocarbons or carbon dioxide when it burns; it has high potential energy, and can be used in all types of engines.

In Japan, the Ministry of International Trade & Industry (MITI) was aiming to use hydrogen to gradually replace other energy sources. Mazda was called in to help with the project and conducted a year-long monitoring test in conjunction with the Nippon Steel Corporation's Hirohata works located near Kobe. R&D head, Seiji Tanaka, said: "Our first objective is to use available fuels more efficiently by producing better engines. At present we are researching the Miller-cycle and developing lean-burn technology. Our second objective is to investigate alternative fuels such as natural gas and methanol and electric cars. But this will not cut pollution. Hydrogen offers many advantages over all these, especially electric cars, and with the rotary engine fuelled by hydrogen, performance is very close to the petrol engine."

The hydrogen was stored in metal hydride powder, made up predominantly of titanium and iron. When the gas is cooled under pressure, the powder will absorb the atoms, allowing safe storage of a litre of gas in just one cubic centimetre of powder. Heating the powder releases the gas. The only problem with this method is that the boot is filled with aluminium canisters.

The hydrogen powered car had a rotary engine from the normally aspirated RX-7, but externally (apart from the obvious script down the sides of the vehicles), there was nothing to tell it apart from an MX-5 straight out of the showroom. It was the same story inside, the only exception being a more appropriate fuel gauge.

The electric car also looked surprisingly standard. Again, the fuel gauge was replaced, this time with a charge meter. The electric MX-5 was very quiet but, as noted earlier, not particularly quick. In fact, 0-62mph (100kph) took 21.5 seconds - a figure that doesn't really stack up against 9.4 seconds for a

M2 Inc. advertising from mid-1993, featuring the M2-1008 coupé.

petrol driven machine. The hydrogen model, however, could cover the same yardstick in just 13.0 seconds, which is much more acceptable. It could also reach 93mph (149kph) with a five-speed manual transmission, but we shall have to wait and see whether or not hydrogen power has a future.

An M2 finale

Despite the lack of a new model, the M2 team had been keeping itself busy since the debut of the M2-1002. In addition to the 1003, many interesting projects had been carried out on various Mazda vehicles, but none were thought suitable for production for one reason or another. In the process, two particularly stunning Eunos Roadster-based machines were unfortunately allowed to slip through the net - M2-1006 and M2-1008.

M2-1006 came about in mid-1992, and featured wider bodywork, RX-7 suspension pieces and a 220bhp three-litre V6 engine from the Sentia (929). Naturally, with this much power, it was quite a handful. To keep the car in check, 225/50 VR16 tyres were fitted at the front, with 245/50s at the back.

The M2-1008 was an attractive coupé, with a Club Racer-type nose (complete with faired-in headlights) and a tail styled along the lines of the Ferrari Daytona - even the round rear lights seemed to pay tribute to the Pininfarina design, although single lamps were used on the Mazda instead of two on each side, as on the Italian car.

Before closing down the M2 operation in April 1995 ("due to the faltering business situation within

The M2-1028 finished in Chaste White and Dark Blue - the two shades available on this model. As well as a number of modifications to make the bodyshell stronger, the 1028 had an aluminium bootlid, lighter wheels, and glassfibre seats to save weight. The engine featured a higher compression ratio, lightened flywheel, tuned ECU, and a free-flow exhaust system. With 140bhp on tap, this was the most powerful M2 engine released to the public. M2-1028 numbers ran from 401 to 700.

The Miata M-Speedster made its debut at the 1995 Chicago Auto Show. Designed by Wu-Huang Chin of MRA, it featured a 1.8 litre supercharged engine that developed a healthy 200bhp.

Stunning interior of the M-Speedster.

Mazda itself"), the team managed to get a third and final Eunos Roadster-based car into production - the M2-1028. Announced in February 1994 at a price of 2,800,000 yen (delivery began in March), the 1028 was based on the five-speed, 1.8 litre model, but had a stronger - yet lighter - body (helped by a front strut brace and an aluminium roll-over bar) and a highly tuned engine.

Tipping the scales at 960kg (2112lb), it had 30 per cent better torsional rigidity; in fact, it was easily as strong as most closed cars. This, in addition to newly developed Bridgestone tyres and a harder suspension set-up, allowed an impressive improvement in handling (0.93g has been measured on the skidpan).

The 1028 was available in either Dark Blue or Chaste White, although a hood was not supplied - at the end of the day, the car was intended to be more at home on the track than commuting to work on a daily basis! However, a lightweight custom hard-top was part of the package. Of the 300 built, 185 were sold in white (the most popular colour for cars in Japan), leaving 115 finished in the blue shade. At least the M2 project went out on a high note, as the M2-1028 sold out within a couple of months.

The M-Speedster
The Miata M-Speedster made its debut at the 1995 Chicago Auto Show. It was designed by Wu-Huang Chin of MRA, and featured a supercharged 1.8 litre engine. To keep the 200 horses in check, 215/50 ZR15 tyres were employed, mounted on five-spoke alloy wheels. The suspension and braking system was also uprated, with 250mm (9.8in.) ventilated discs at the front and 225mm (8.8in.) solid discs at the rear.

Complete Car was quite confident that this vehicle gave an insight into the future, despite Tom Matano saying: "We have no intention of building it." Perhaps the magazine thought it was being used as a tool to gauge reaction, as at the end of the article, it said: "If US buyers give the thumbs up, it will form the blueprint for a revamp in Europe." Sadly, although there was almost universal praise for the machine, it turned out to be nothing

The aggresive lines of the M-Speedster, built on the so-called 'Mi-ari' - a one-off car produced by the Irvine team to honour Ferrari at Monterey in 1994. Twin round lamps were hidden under each headlight cover, and a pair of matching helmets nestled under the fairings behind the seats. Many thought that the M-Speedster would form the basis for the second generation MX-5.

The M-Coupé was first shown at the 1996 New York Show. The roof on this model was made from fibreglass but, had it gone into production, steel would have been used instead. Unlike the coupé developed by the M2 team, the rear lights on the MRA machine were standard Miata fare.

more than a concept car.

The M-Coupé

The M-Coupé was the third Miata-based concept car by MRA, making its debut at the New York International Auto Show in April 1996. It resembled the M2-1008 above the waistline, but was much closer to standard below it.

There were differences, of course: twin round headlights hid under each pop-up cover (which looked very attractive), and there was a feature line running from the sill to just behind the door. The lines of the fibreglass roof panel merged beautifully with the rest of the body - the design was a credit to Tom Matano and his team.

This elegant coupé was powered by the stock B6-ZE engine linked to a five-speed gearbox; 205/45 R16 Dunlop SP8000 tyres were employed, mounted on lightweight five-spoke alloy wheels. An interesting feature was the increased luggage space, created by moving the spare wheel to an underfloor position.

Again, Matano stressed that the M-Coupé was only ever meant to be a styling exercise, but the favourable reaction it received from the public fuelled rumours it might go into production. However, six years later, there's still no sign of a closed version of the MX-5.

6

THE MX-5 INDUSTRY

Only a few months after the MX-5 was announced, *Road & Track* was predicting a boom for custom parts. In the July 1989 edition, the magazine said: "Mazda has set up the stock Miata for comfort more than handling. The ride is comfortably soft with more body roll than we would have expected. All of this is not to say that the Miata, with its light weight and short wheelbase, isn't quick and responsive; it's both. But it could be quicker and even more responsive. Already it is easy to see the aftermarket explosion this car is going to cause."

This observation was very astute. Today, as well as a thriving custom scene, there's no shortage of companies around the world which supply enthusiasts with accessories. This chapter looks briefly at what can only be described as the MX-5 'industry'.

Parts & accessories

In Japan, the choice of parts and accessories is huge. During 1994, Mazdaspeed, TRD (of Toyota fame) and Nismo (Nissan Motorsports International), joined forces to organise the Tokyo Auto Salon, an alternative motor show that caters purely for tuning and performance companies. In 1997, Mitsubishi Ralliart added its weight to the alliance, which duly adopted the 'Works Tuning' banner.

Apart from promoting the tuning business, Works Tuning also organises motorsport events in

VeilSide of Tsukuba offers a wide range of conversions on various popular Japanese sports cars. This is the company's stunning Roadster Combat Model.

which owners can drive their cars at speed in controlled conditions. After all, if a person fits high quality performance parts, it follows that he or she is going to want to try them out! The worthy objective behind the track days is to enhance the experience of responsible drivers and persuade the likes of *Zero-Yon* road racers (who illegally speed on public roads) to adopt a more suitable arena in which to enjoy their vehicles.

The brochure from KG Works of Yokohama. The M-Coupé-style, twin headlight conversion (priced at 128,000 yen) is very elegant. Japan is full of companies like this offering body kits, cosmetic parts and tuning components. To list them all would take a book in itself!

The author went to the 1997 Tokyo Auto Salon and was amazed at how big the event was. With around 900 cars on display, it attracted almost as many visitors as the Tokyo Show! The range of body kits, tuning parts and complete conversions was staggering; some of the modifications are quite tasteful, others totally over-the-top.

As well as Mazdaspeed, some of the better known concerns dealing with the Hiroshima marque included VeilSide, HKS, Racing Sports Active, KG Works, Hayashi, Manatee, Garage Vary, Yours Sports, Dave Crockett and RE Amemiya Cars, but the list was practically endless. Indeed, *Hyper Rev* managed to put together a book listing and describing the Eunos tuning scene in Japan which amounted to over 200 pages!

Trust of Chiba developed a turbo kit, and a company called Cockpit even offered an MX-5 fitted with a 400bhp rotary engine. Knight Sports, well known for its work on the RX-7, was also involved in supplying performance parts for the Roadster.

The owners' clubs also got involved. One club, known as Barchetta, designed and marketed its own parts. A front fibreglass

Advertising from the HKS concern. The car seen in the bottom left-hand corner is the T-003.

half-spoiler and bumper cover was available for 60,000 yen, while the attractive rear bumper was 100,000 yen. Smaller items were also listed, such as a gearshift gate box at just 6000 yen.

HKS offered a full T-003 conversion, and Pit Crew Racing's modifications made the Eunos look like an early TVR. Zoom designed a fairly convincing Lotus Elan lookalike, while others offered nose panels that were shaped to resemble different vehicles, ranging from the Ferrari Daytona through to the Nissan 300ZX. One concern even built a nose that reminded the author of a cross between the Daimler SP250 and Austin-Healey Sprite.

Of course, the full custom scene is much stronger in Japan where the cars are so much cheaper to buy. In Britain, the purchase price and high residual value on the second-hand car market puts most people off the idea of modifying their car too much, as it would affect the price when they came to sell it.

However, subtle modifications

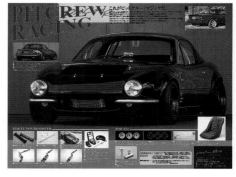

The Pit Crew Racing company of Suzuka offered this interesting conversion.

are commonplace. The industry supplying somewhat more restrained aftermarket components has blossomed, and the variety already rivals that for some of the more established 'classics' for range. For instance, the catalogue issued by Moss International Ltd (ironically, a company better known for supplying parts for classic British marques such as MG and Triumph!) lists items like stainless steel exhaust systems and replacement catalytic converters, high performance air filters,

Zoom Engineering of Tokyo produced this Lotus Elan lookalike.

Pages from Mazda UK's official accessories catalogue of 1996.

sparkplugs and leads, silicone hoses and a gel cell battery. Naturally, these are joined by uprated suspension and braking components, including strut tower and chassis braces.

For the interior, there are leather seats, real or fake wood trim kits, various gearknobs and steering wheels, and leather gaiters for the gearlever and handbrake. Kits are also available for interior lighting, electric windows, central and remote keyless locking, and an electronic boot release. There are also floor mats, stainless steel trim pieces for the sill tops, face vents and speakers, and an aluminium pedal set. The catalogue also lists replacement soft-tops, a hard-top, wind deflector, boot spoiler, various luggage racks and boot trim components, including a hydraulic lift kit. Auxilliary lighting, a protective front grille, roll-over bar, car cover, Minilite-style alloys, and a 7.5J x 16 wheel and tyre package make up the selection on offer.

Of course, the Moss catalogue is only one of many: Mazda lists the Finish Line range of accessories, which includes items such as a

detachable hard-top, alloy wheels, stereo upgrades, a rear spoiler, deck rack, polished treadplates, and so on.

American magazines regularly feature the Miata Mania Accessories Catalog, "jam packed with products designed to improve and personalize your car." Run down the classified ads, and you'll find Motorsport of California, Racing Beat (which was heavily involved in the success of the RX-7 in competition), Pacific Auto Accessories, Road Show International, and goodness knows how many others. Performance Techniques and Cartech International have both produced a turbocharger installation; Downing Atlanta and Nelson Superchargers of Los Angeles have gone down the supercharger route; and then there are the cars and accessories produced by Rod Millen and Mazdasports. For something a little more adventurous, Performance Car Kraft of New Jersey offered Ford V8 conversion kits with uprated braking systems to suit.

In Germany, Samurai Tuning of Essen was quick to produce the Samurai MX-5. With subtle modifications to the lower coachwork, a nice faired-in hood cover, rear spoiler and 225/50 ZR16 tyres on wide alloy wheels, it was quite a tasteful package.

Mazdaspeed

Mazdaspeed, the factory's racing

subsidiary, lists shock absorbers with four different settings, harder springs that also lower the car by 30mm (1.2in.), thicker anti-roll bars and strut braces, plus harder shock mountings and lower arm bushes.

Four pages from the Mazdaspeed brochure for the A-Spec aero kits. B-Spec modifications concentrated on the engine, with various states of tune being available.

It also stocks harder engine mountings, uprated brake pads for both front and rear, and uprated clutch components. Special exhaust systems, pistons, camshafts, lightened flywheels, an oil cooler, a modified gearchange, high performance air filters, and various viscous limited-slip differential units (plus a harder differential mounting rubber) round off the mechanical parts.

A number of engine tuning options are available, known as B-Spec modifications. Stage I takes a 1.6 litre engine to 130bhp, or a 1.8 to 145bhp. Stage II increases this to 144bhp on the 1.6, or 170 on the 1.8. There is also a supercharger kit, which boosts the 1.6 engine's power to 170bhp, and the 1.8 litre unit to 180bhp.

On the more cosmetic side, the list offers sportier sounding exhaust tailpipes, replacement dashboards, steering wheels, alloy wheels, gearknobs (with matching handbrake trim), various aerodynamic components, and a bucket seat. There's even a roll-over bar, which can also be specified with something Mazdaspeed calls an 'Aeroboard' - a device to cut buffeting in the cockpit.

For some time, Mazdaspeed has listed the A-Spec Aero Kit Type I and Type II alongside the B-Spec engine tuning menu, but, from April 1998, delivery of the Tokyo-based company's most adventurous project began: its first complete car for public sale. Known as the Roadster C-Spec, only 30 were ever built, but it was very significant nonetheless. Billed as "the final evolution," it featured some rather stunning coachwork modifications, plus a 200bhp two-litre Mazdaspeed Stage III engine. The basic version cost 4,350,000 yen, while the leather-trimmed Special was priced at 5,300,000 yen.

Delivery of Mazdaspeed's first complete car for public consumption - the C-Spec - started in April 1998. Only 30 of these 200bhp machines were ever produced, but at 4,350,000 to 5,300,000 yen, they were mighty expensive. The leather-trimmed model cost about the same as the Nissan Skyline GT-R V Spec.

FUNCTIONAL PARTS

Modified packages in the USA

It's not surprising to learn that the Miata was soon the subject of a number of transformations in the States, some of which were done from a styling point of view, others from a performance angle. Occasionally, complete packages would be offered, a few of which are mentioned.

Rod Millen, the New Zealander who has done so much to promote Japanese cars through his exploits in motorsport (he's represented Mazda, Toyota and Nissan at top level), was quick to spot the potential in the Miata. Rod Millen Motorsport, operating from California, offered a turbocharged machine known as the Turbo MX-5 Miata.

As Richard Homan explained in a 1989 *Road & Track* special: "On the engine side of things, the team was able to draw heavily from its experience with a similar 1.6 litre dohc 16v fuel-injected powerplant of Mazda origin - that of the turbocharged 323 GTX, a longtime bread-and-butter Millen

The Racing Beat body kit. So many bolt-on kits destroy the lines of the original vehicle, but one can still clearly see the distinctive MX-5 profile showing through on this restrained offering.

rally car ... Millen Motorsport raided the 323 GTX's engine, pirating the car's camshafts, pistons (thus lowering the Miata's compression ratio from 9.4:1 to 7.2:1), radiator, turbocharger and intercooler. The turbo implant is the golden nugget of the Millen Miata's performance upgrade. Tucked tightly into the engine bay, the little turbo is mounted stage left up against a Millen Motorsport-designed, stainless steel exhaust manifold ..."

Power was put in the region of 230bhp but, despite this, the standard gearbox was retained. A heavier clutch and a Millen limited-slip differential were used, however, as was an uprated suspension and braking package, the latter sourced from the RX-7 Turbo parts bin.

"Slung lower and filled out by the special 7J x 15 Rod Millen Motorsport directional aero wheels with 205/50 VR15 Bridgestone Potenza RE71R tyres, the Miata was beginning to look tougher; it was getting an attitude," noted Homan.

Thus, every aspect of the Miata's performance was improved. 0-60 was covered in 6.4 seconds instead of the standard car's 9.5, and the standing quarter was timed at 14.7 seconds (with a 95.5mph, or 153kph, terminal speed) - a full

Rod Millen's Club Sport aero cover. Millen has also successfully marketed a whole string of complete conversions based around Japanese sports cars.

2.3 seconds less. The top speed was now quoted as 126mph (202kph).

As for handling, the moderate understeer usually found in the stock Miata was reduced, helping the Millen car go through the slalom test quicker and pull 0.90g on the skidpan (against 0.83 for a showroom model). At the same time, braking distances were reduced to 85 per cent of those recorded with a standard car.

Of course, everything comes at a price, and, whereas the standard Miata cost $13,800, the fully loaded Millen car was roughly $25,600. This included the turbocharger ($650), intercooler and plumbing ($2200), modified camshafts ($300), pistons ($120), fuel management system ($1100), stainless exhaust manifold ($550), stainless exhaust system ($330), Centreforce clutch ($425), uprated brakes ($2240), limited-slip differential ($750), larger anti-roll bars ($350), spring set ($200), strut brace ($225), Panasport 7J x 15 alloys ($740), exhaust temperature gauge ($350), boost gauge ($32), Momo steering wheel ($210), rear spoiler ($195), and rear deck aero cover ($195).

The package was sold in Australia under the Racing Dynamics name. Yokohama 195/50 ZR15 tyres were fitted on Venette five-spoke alloys, but otherwise it was very similar to the car in the States. Some thought the price was a little high, but *Modern Motor* correctly pointed out that people happily paid a premium when the car was in short supply. The same Aussie magazine noted: "Improving on a design so widely commended was a difficult task, but the modified car does the trick."

Another company that transformed the standard Miata was Mazdasports of California, a newly established arm of Oscar Jackson Racing (of Honda fame), founded to exploit the potential of the Miata. Douglas Kott tried the car for *Road & Track* and was very impressed. He said: "The well-scuffed Yokohama A008Rs adhered to the 200 foot-diameter skidpad with a vengeance to generate 0.89g - 7 per cent more grip than the stock Miata on the same surface. At the cornering limit, its balance was commendable; a drop-throttle stunt that would have had the driver of the stock car cranking in lots of countersteer required only a minor steering correction in the Mazdasports Miata to keep

everything tidy and under control."

Racing Beat built a number of so-called 'California Miatas' to promote its aftermarket body panels. The full conversions included a new nose section, side skirts, a 'Streamline' rear deck cover, rear spoiler, and a restyled rear bumper.

Dave Hops of Monster Motorsports in California started modifying the Miata early in 1992. The 'Monster Miata' conversion basically involved swapping the four-cylinder Mazda engine for a 225bhp five-litre V8 from the Ford Mustang (complete with transmission), and then uprating suspension and braking components to suit. The brochure stated it was "Where the Far East meets the Wild West!"

Styling changes were amazingly subtle, resulting in the car looking like an M2 project, but performance freaks are usually more interested in figures: 0-60 in under five seconds was impressive enough to get the attention of most people! More than 70 were built during the first four years, but, in the

meantime, Hops introduced the 'Mega Monster'.

The Mega Monster, styled by Terry Choy, could be bought with a supercharged five-litre unit giving 400bhp, or a 5.6 litre lump producing an incredible 460bhp! Strangely, because the Mazda 1.8 litre four-cylinder engine is not particularly light, the Mega Monster conversion added only 120kg (264lb) to the weight of the car. Thus, even the 400bhp machine was capable of 0-60mph (96kph) in less than four seconds, and would happily go on to a claimed maximum of 160mph (256kph). Those not put off by its brute power would probably flinch at the $50,000 price tag. Not surprisingly, the Mega Monster is a fairly rare beast. However, Hops was also working on the Miata FXR - a turbo conversion boosting the 1.8 litre engine's output to a more reasonable 195bhp.

Another professional conversion was carried out by Dave Lemon of Mazdatrix, another Californian company more readily associated with the rotary engine. It therefore came as little surprise when Lemon - an ex-racing driver - used an RX-7 Turbo power unit to improve the performance of the Miata. With around 260bhp on tap, 0-60 came up in just 6.6 seconds, so the suspension and braking were suitably uprated to keep the car in check. The detailing was beautiful ...

In early 1995, *Car & Driver*

carried an article on the PFS Miata SC. PFS stood for Peter Farrell Supercars, a Virginia-based company run by Farrell, an ex-racer who became heavily involved with Mazda's competition success in the States. Apart from selling the occasional 360bhp RX-7, Farrell also commissioned Craig Neff (who built rock group ZZ Top's famous Cad-zilla) to build the supercharged Miata SC. With 185 horses under the bonnet, the 0-60 time came down to 6.9 seconds, while the top speed was now around 130mph (208kph). Naturally, the suspension was uprated, and the Miata SC actually pulled a full 1.0g on a 300 foot skidpan. Production models were priced at $30,000.

Buying hints & tips
There's no doubt that the MX-5 has caught the imagination of the motoring public. In March 1996, *Auto Express* said: "This roadster is guaranteed to put a smile on your face. It looks great and provides the sort of driving pleasure few cars can match."

However, popularity like this always breeds plenty of opportunities for making money. While the vast majority of people dealing in the MX-5 and its aftermarket add-ons are as straight as the day is long, the same journal highlighted a new problem that every potential buyer should be aware of - secondhand cars imported from Japan which have either been damaged, or are no

longer able to pass the strict tests carried out in that country after a car reaches its third birthday.

In mid-1997, *Auto Express* found that a large number of cars were coming into Britain with service histories in Japanese, and several had previously been involved in accidents. The engine management systems are different, and all home market vehicles are fitted with kph speedometers, giving an ideal opportunity to alter the mileage once it is replaced with an mph speedo. More recently, it has been uncovered that many of the cars stolen in Japan end up in Britain. Buyer beware!

Despite the flood of 'grey imports', the MX-5 will hold its value pretty well, regardless of whether or not it's a limited edition model. In fact, Mazda UK issued a press release which referred to an in-depth study to find the lowest depreciating cars in the UK carried out by *What Car?* magazine. The release read as follows: "The *What Car?* survey, in the July 1991 issue, was conducted to advise its readers which new cars would suffer from the smallest amount of depreciation within the first 12 months of ownership. A total of 20 vehicles were assessed, with the Mazda marque taking three places.

"The Mazda MX-5, currently *What Car?* magazine's 'Sports Car of the Year', was judged overall winner with the judges commenting: 'It's appealing on the road for all the right reasons -

steering accuracy, delightful gearchange quality, great handling ability and carefree wind-in-the-hair motoring.' The *What Car?* panel determined that the Mazda MX-5 would depreciate by just 15 per cent in the first 12 months."

Placed in the under £17,500 category, the MX-5 was followed home by Toyota's MR2 (17 per cent) and the BMW 318i at 20 per cent; the Hiroshima machine received the *What Car?* award again in 1997.

The moral of the story is there's rarely a true bargain. If an MX-5 is cheap, be careful. On the other hand, don't pay too much for a car that's not worth it. Ask plenty of questions, insist on seeing its service history, and have the car inspected by a professional body. If the car has been modified, make sure it has been done properly.

Running an MX-5
The best advice one can offer here is join an owners' club. Unlike most car clubs, which only come into being once a model attains 'classic' status (usually based on age, examples becoming scarcer and parts more difficult to source), the MX-5 had organisations popping up all over the world the minute it was launched. In America, Norman Garrett (who, as you will have learnt from reading the earlier sections of the book, was heavily involved with the car while he was with MANA), founded the Miata Club of America. By the end of 1989, it was estimated to have almost 5000 members, and

The Mazda MX-5 Enthusiast's Shop Manual (seen here in American Miata guise) - a great investment for owners of 1.6 and 1.8 litre cars.

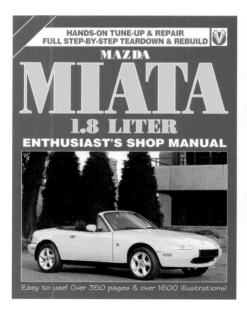

today that figure hovers around the 25,000 mark. With Chapters (branches) all over the country, the combined experiences of the membership will mean that someone, somewhere will have had a similar problem and, more importantly, found a way of overcoming it. There is even a UK Chapter (the MX-5 Owners' Club), with Hamish McLean currently holding the post of Chairman. Paul Grogan, ex-Chairman and co-founder of the club, kindly helped with some of the information for this book.

In Japan, as one would expect, there are numerous clubs. The biggest was founded by ex-M2 project man, Masanori Mizuochi, who is now the affable Chairman of the Roadster Club of Japan. The RCOJ came about in 1996 when a large number of smaller organisations decided to group together.

Rod Grainger of Veloce Publishing wrote and produced the *Mazda MX-5 Enthusiast's Workshop Manual* (known in America as the *Miata Enthusiast's Shop Manual*) to help owners complete DIY jobs on their car. It is probably the most useful investment an owner can make; there's helpful advice on every aspect of ownership. There is a manual for the original 1.6 litre models, and a separate one for the newer 1.8 litre cars.

The MX-5 is not a complicated car to work on, which is a good thing as the engine oil and air cleaner should be changed on a very regular basis if the car is to be kept in optimum condition. It's also recommended that the gearbox oil be renewed more often than the service schedules specify.

It's worth remembering that - with the exception of basic service items - MX-5 parts are quite (and sometimes very) expensive, but mechanical components have so far proven very reliable if the car is properly maintained. Refer to Rod's manual for the best possible advice, but other than the kind of wear and tear one would expect as mileage increases, there isn't really that much to look out for. Apart from badly repaired crash damage, there shouldn't be much of a problem with the body either, but it's worth checking under the wheelarches just in case. One important point: the original hood's rear screen is very susceptible to scratching and damage, and is far from easy to replace.

Seeing as we started this chapter with modifications, please note that the type of work involved in tuning and upgrading cars often requires someone qualified to do it. Even something as simple as putting wider wheels and tyres on the car may interfere with the geometry (and the body) unless the rolling diameter and offset are right. Before attempting anything, it may be worth asking if someone in your local club has tried a similar operation, or if the club can recommend a specialist. Also, always remember to inform your insurance company of any changes, however minor they may seem to you.

7

THE SECOND GENERATION

Mazda had obviously found a winning formula with the MX-5 series - sales well in excess of 400,000 units in such a short space of time is testimony to that fact - but it was inevitable that, sooner or later, the popular sports car was going to need a facelift.

Although sales were still strong in parts of Europe (the UK especially), they were gently falling off in America, and quite rapidly in Japan. The first generation (or M1) model could have carried on at these levels, but it was obvious that the older car wouldn't pass the stricter crash regulations planned for 1999.

Mazda, therefore, called upon its Technical Research Centres in Japan (both in Hiroshima and at the Yokohama branch, completed in mid-1987), America (the MRA team in California) and Germany (the European R&D centre, known by the initials MRE, which was completed in May 1990, situated in Oberusel on the outskirts of Frankfurt), to put forward their ideas. The brief was to update the car, enabling it to meet forthcoming regulations, but keeping its character intact.

Speaking in 1990, John Ebenezer (Mazda UK's Chairman at the time) said: "Few people are aware of Mazda's total commitment to producing more than just pedestrian cars and the Technical Research Centres are essential weapons in achieving this ambition. What makes them so unique and particularly exciting is that the Japanese have insisted upon a high level of local ideas and input. The result is that while most of the personnel in the Hiroshima and Yokohama centres are obviously Japanese, the Irvine and Frankfurt centres are more than 80 per cent staffed by Americans and Europeans, respectively. What is particularly pleasing for me as a Briton is the fact that four of the department heads in Frankfurt are British, who have all, incidentally, been recruited from Porsche ..."

Mazda is quite unusual for a Japanese company in that, of the top 35 positions at the end of 1997, eight were held by foreigners, due mainly to Ford's involvement. One of them, Henry Wallace, joined the Mazda board in 1993, along with two other Ford executives, and became President three years later. He was thus the first *gaijin* (or foreigner) to hold the presidency of a Japanese car company.

It is interesting to note that Ford (which had increased its share in the Japanese company to 33.4 per cent on 12 April 1996, thereby achieving a controlling interest), left the Mazda team alone during the car's development, asking only that the project be "speeded along." It's also interesting that, although sports car sales were in a downward spiral compared to those of RVs and MPVs, Ford still backed the M2 Roadster project, despite 1997 being a bad year financially (share values dropped almost 8 per cent).

Again, Mazda drew on the talent spread throughout its various design studios around the world in a bid to find the desired shape for the second generation MX-5 (J07E). The Frankfurt office submitted some stunning sketches, although they weren't developed further.

It was actually a far braver decision to support the M2 than the first generation ever was - there were far more competitors vying for the business of less customers. However, compared to the situation in Korea at that time, the Japanese company had little to worry about ...

A fresh face

Unlike the competition held as part of the OGG project (which ultimately led to the first generation MX-5), there were to be no winners or losers with the second generation; Mazda simply wanted ideas from its various design centres. The whole project was overseen by Martin Leach. Each design centre was given the same brief: keep the car's character intact. Tom Matano gave an interesting example of how the new car should be designed: "Looking from 100 metres away, a person should recognise the vehicle is a Miata. From 50 metres, it will still appear to be a Miata, but as it gets closer still, they will realize it is the new model."

The amazing thing is that all of the designs were very similar, although, as everyone started from the same point, it's perhaps not so surprising. From sketches, each centre (except the Frankfurt studio) produced full-sized clays which were presented for inspection at a meeting in Hiroshima. The proposal from the Yokohama office fell by the wayside quite quickly, leaving just the Irvine and Hiroshima offerings to choose from. After much

deliberation, the MRA design (credited to Ken Saward - an ex-Chrysler man) was the one chosen for further development.

Lower left and above: This series of drawings came from the Hiroshima studio. Covered headlights were investigated, but the consensus of opinion was to go with the exposed lights. Incidentally, the back looked like a Jaguar XK8 on the pink-coloured sketch, which was later used as the basis for Hiroshima's full-size clay.

The first clay produced to represent Hiroshima's proposal. The headlights, it has to be said, looked a little strange on this model, but the front spoiler detailing was very dramatic. The rear lights were quite big, but there were some very delicate lines in the styling; the top of the rear wing was particularly attractive. Note the door lines, which were very similar to those of the first generation model.

One of the design sketches submitted by the Yokohama office. The front three-quarter view of the same proposal showed that the Yokohama staff wanted to keep the pop-up headlight arrangement.

Two views of the clay made to represent the Yokohama design. The author feels that this was an exceptionally pretty car, which, sadly, was rejected.

A front and rear view of Irvine's design. With shades of the original remaining, Irvine's design was nonetheless far more muscular; already strong second generation (M2) features were showing through.

The modellers hard at work in California transforming a two-dimensional drawing into a three-dimensional clay.

Above and right: The finished clay built using the Ken Saward drawings as the basis. When the three full-sized models, from MRA (Irvine), MRY (Yokohama) and MC (Hiroshima) were reviewed at the start of 1995, this one, and the one from Hiroshima, were chosen for further development.

Left and below: The second full-size clay from the Hiroshima team, developed from a one-fifth scale model, and given the 'Theme A' moniker. The air intake and front spoiler were integrated now, and the door lines were made to look more interesting. In addition, the rear combination lights became more elegant, and this, combined with a different bumper shape, made the tail-end appear more substantial.

123

Clay of the MRA - or 'Theme B' - model.

The finished second clay from the California team. The headlights were made fractionally longer to incorporate the front indicators, which in turn led to adoption of separate side repeaters. The sill, or rocker panel, was given a beefier look, and the bootlid developed a lip spoiler.

Above and opposite top: Hiroshima's Theme A model was later refined, with a new air intake and lights, a slightly revised front wing line, a modified trailing edge to the door, and new tail graphics. It was eventually produced in glassfibre (the red car in this batch of pictures), and presented to the Mazda board for evaluation in August 1995.

Middle left: Work-in-progress at the Irvine facility, leading to the production of the final clay model seen here in this series of photographs.

Evolution, not revolution

Tentative development work on the 'full model change' had started in spring 1994, but it wasn't until November 1995 that the project began in earnest, by which time the first batch of mechanical mules was already undergoing extensive testing.

Takao Kijima had been appointed Chief Engineer of the MX-5 in July 1995, meaning that responsibility for the second generation fell on his shoulders. Kijima, who had been with Mazda since 1967, was an important member of the team which developed the first MX-5, and was also highly respected for his work through the years on the RX-7. Incidentally, his predecessor, Yoshioka, became Chief Chassis Engineer in the Development Centre. Koichi Hayashi, who had worked on the first generation body alongside Matano, was given the job of Chief Designer. Kijima found that the 1.8 litre engine hooked up to an F1-style steering wheel shift was on the cards for the next generation, but he quickly dismissed the idea as unsuitable for a car like the Miata. A new line of development was instigated ...

In May 1997, the excellent Japanese magazine, *Car Graphic*, published an interview with Takao Kijima. A lot of clues were given about what to expect from the new MX-5; for instance, it would definitely continue to have a front engine, rear-wheel drive (FR) layout, and the wheelbase and suspension set-up would stay much the same. The standard use of dual airbags, and the need to meet stricter safety and emissions regulations, was obviously going to increase the car's weight. In fact, at one point it was thought that up to 60kg (132lb) would be added. However, a light package was crucial; according to Kijima it was "hard work to find the balance between strength and weight, but to make an all-aluminium chassis like the [Lotus] Elise would make the car too expensive."

Kijima also wrote an essay outlining the aims of the design team. It read as follows: "In the eight years since the Rebirth of the Lightweight Sports Roadster in the form of the Mazda MX-5, more than 430,000 agile and friendly roadsters have been delivered to the world's enthusiasts, rekindling a powerful flame among them for exhilarating open-air motoring and imparting the joy of 'Oneness between the Car and Driver.'

"We at Mazda are firm believers in continuous improvement. A sports car must be thoroughly contemporary and up to date, incorporating the latest technological developments. To rest on your laurels is to stagnate and fall behind. The original MX-5 has thus been constantly refined, including two major updates and numerous improvements, to answer our customers' expectations and requirements.

"The last decade of the century has seen giant leaps in technology, particularly in electronics, but also in the design, development and manufacture of the automobile. At the same time, society's concern about safety and environmental issues has become more acute. We decided that the MX-5 must progress to meet the challenges of the 21st century. We will accomplish this by further enhancing the lightweight open sports car's dynamics and meeting all social requirements.

"There was one fundamental principle guiding Mazda's design and engineering team for the new MX-5's personality: 'We must value and assert the MX-5's inborn Soul, and train, strengthen and refine the Body.' The new car required no conceptual revision. Enhance the virtue of the compact, lightweight, two-seat open sports car, and offer a sports car unparalleled in ownership delight and driving pleasure, to people of all walks of life, young and young at heart. We pursued new dimensions in open-air motoring, fun-to-drive and styling.

"With the objectives clearly established, we pursued three key areas of development:

1) Joy of open-air motoring, in comfort and ease: The new MX-5 is

The MRA glassfibre model that was selected for further development to ultimately become the second generation MX-5. It is seen here in Hiroshima awaiting the attentions of Hayashi and his team. Note the appearance of flush door handles.

to be enjoyed primarily as an open sports car at all speeds and even in winter, barring extremely inclement weather. We were able to accomplish this goal with innovative design and features.

2) True sports car driving fun: 'Oneness of the Car and Driver' enables the driver to fully exploit the new MX-5's exciting, natural and safe performance potential. The development team's aim of instinctive 'drive-by-wish' precision was realized. Sounds are important ingredients in sports car driving. Thus, the new MX-5's engine and exhaust are tuned to delight the ears of the driver, passenger and onlookers.

3) Thoroughly modern yet unmistakable MX-5 styling: The instantly recognisable exterior design carries the lineage of the original MX-5 in a balanced, masculine manner, and the interior stimulates enthusiasm the instant you climb behind the wheel.

"The car's everyday practicality has also been improved, including a larger and more usable luggage compartment. Safety has been greatly enhanced by incorporating a highly rigid body structure and a standard dual SRS airbag system for all models.

"With this new model, we believe that we have extended the enjoyment of the fun of the lightweight sports car to a much larger audience.

"We fully utilized the latest Mazda Digital Innovation system (MDI), to incorporate numerous technological advancements into the design, to aid development, and to further improve build quality. The creation of an automobile is ultimately the work of people. And our team dedicated all its effort to ensuring that the sporting Soul of the original MX-5 now dwells within the safe and strong new Body."

Kijima felt it was important to further improve the car's best points and not allow the areas in which it was weak to lose ground against the competition. He had actually consulted Hirai on a number of aspects concerning the project, and also tested all the vehicles from competitors that had come onto the market since the introduction of the Eunos Roadster, noting their strengths and shortcomings. In essence, he wanted to enhance the Mazda's performance, handling, sound and driving sensations,

The engine specifications, as seen in the UK catalogue.

Cutaway drawings of the 1.8 litre BP-ZE (RS) power unit.

Engine

Kijima's interview in *Car Graphic* promised a 1.8 litre engine with a lightened flywheel (the 1.8 litre gave a better match for cars with automatic transmission), while a 1.6 litre unit would be available in Europe, giving the benefit of lower insurance premiums. The exhaust note had again been tuned (noise limits caused a few problems here), and there was also a hint of a six-speed manual gearbox.

With a number of revisions, it was hoped that the existing 1839cc BP-ZE (RS) unit would produce 145bhp at 6500rpm, while the 1597cc B6-ZE (RS) engine was given a target of 125bhp at the same revs. This latter figure represented about 10 per cent more power than before, if the original 1.6 litre specification is taken as the starting point.

After the intake and exhaust system was refined (the Variable Intake Control System - or VICS - was employed) under the direction of Yoshiaki Dairaku, and different pistons (to give a higher compression ratio), camshaft profiles and a remapped ECU were adopted, the Japanese catalogue confirmed that these targets had been met.

European specifications, however, suggested a shortfall of 5bhp on the 1.8, and no less than 15bhp on the smaller engine. In the American market, the 1.8 litre four-cylinder unit's maximum power output was quoted at 140bhp at 6500rpm, with 119lbft of torque at 5500rpm.

Once again, the exhaust note was tuned to give the new model a sporting bark, although, because of noise regulations, European versions were made substantially quieter than their Japanese and American counterparts.

Drivetrain

Kijima's hint at a six-speed gearbox became reality but, sadly, only for the 1.8 litre cars for the home market. (There was talk of the possibility of a six-speed for the year 2000 in the US, perhaps even with an uprated engine, but it was not a foregone conclusion.) As the press release noted: "The type BP 1.8 litre engine is equipped with a new six-speed manual transmission. The sixth gear performs as an overdrive, contributing to sportier driving with optimum performance including revving and acceleration at higher speeds.

"Both six-speed and five-speed manual transmissions use the short-stroke type stick-shift and promise quick shifting with a flick of the wrist. The transmission achieves higher rigidity from the improved internal synchronized system, producing quick, yet precise, handling even during severe shifting."

The six-speed gearbox (designated type Y16M-D, and jointly developed with the Aisin concern) brought the gears closer, of course, which would silence the critics who thought the difference in revs from second to third - and third to fourth, in particular - was too great on the original car, considering how high up the rev range peak torque came in. The six-speed unit came with a single dry plate 215mm (8.5in.) diameter hydraulically operated clutch.

The five-speed manual gearbox was of the M15M-D type,

A cutaway drawing showing the layout of the second generation model.

The front suspension.

The rear suspension.

	Japan 1.6	Japan 1.8	USA 1.8	Europe 1.6	Europe 1.8
1st	3.136	3.760	3.136	3.136	3.136
2nd	1.888	2.269	1.888	1.888	1.888
3rd	1.330	1.645	1.330	1.330	1.330
4th	1.000	1.257	1.000	1.000	1.000
5th	0.814	1.000	0.814	0.814	0.814
6th	-	0.843	-	-	-
f/d	4.30:1	3.91:1	4.30:1	4.10:1	4.10:1

Different gear ratios and final drive specifications.

incidentally, and was linked to a 200mm (7.9in.) clutch. While a single piece propshaft was used to take power to the back axle in all cases, gear ratios and final-drive specifications were different for the various markets.

Naturally, the electronically controlled, four-speed automatic gearbox (type SB4A-EL) had different ratios again, but it should be noted that, in Japan, the 1.6 litre cars had a 4.30:1 final-drive, while the 1.8s had a 4.10:1 unit. The 4.10:1 ratio was also used in America, but the automatic option was not listed for Europe. A semi-automatic transmission was apparently not even considered; although quite fashionable, it was deemed not pure enough for a back-to-basics sports car.

A Torsen limited-slip differential came on the manual 1.6 litre Special Package and manual 1.8 litre cars in Japan, and as part of the Popular Equipment Package in the States. In Europe, it came on the higher grade 1.8 litre machines as standard. The PPF transmission and drivetrain brace

was carried over from the first generation.

Chassis

Koji Tsuji was put in charge of the chassis, and to quote from the Tokyo Show press release: "The front engine, rear-drive layout is maintained, achieving an ideal front and rear weight distribution and optimum enjoyment of control. The engine is mounted midship behind the front axle. The battery and [spare] tyre are placed under the trunk floor. This provides a lower centre of gravity and increased trunk space. Decreasing the front overhang weight and placing all the heaviness as close to the vehicle centre as possible, allowed us to achieve superb yaw inertia moment and ideal 50:50 weight distribution.

"The new Roadster adopts a further refined double-wishbone suspension, which was well-known on the first generation. The carefully tuned suspension geometry was completely reviewed to optimize driving pleasure ... while adding to the vehicle's driving stability. The new damper and coil spring units

Takao Kijima - Chief Engineer for the second generation MX-5. During the vehicle's development, he tested the Fiat Barchetta, MGF and the new Alfa Spider, but stated that he failed to feel the desired "oneness between car and driver" that he wanted.

are individually off-set mounted to minimize transmission of road noise to the body.

"The four-wheel disc brake system is ventilated in front and solid at the rear. The brake system provides precise braking performance.

"The vehicle has rack-and-pinion steering. With the lock-to-lock 2.6 turns, it creates a direct yet quick handling feel. The overlapping effects of the re-adjusted suspension settings and reduced yaw inertia moment achieve extraordinary manoeuverability."

One or two points need further explanation. The new suspension settings made the car understeer less, making it much easier to drift through corners. Standard anti-roll bar diameters were 22mm (0.87in.) at the front, 11mm (0.43in.) at the rear. However, Japanese spec 1.6 litre models had a 19mm (0.75in.) bar up front, while the US Sports Package and home market RS grade had 12mm (0.47in.) bars at the back to compliment the stiffer set-up adopted on those vehicles.

As for the brakes, diameters (at 255mm, or 10.0in., up front and 251mm, or 9.9in., at the back) were the same as those found on the last of the first generation cars, while four-sensor, three-channel ABS was available but rarely standard (see the next chapter).

Power-assisted steering came on most cars (again, the next chapter outlines the various specifications), American models were listed with 3.2 turns lock-to-lock on the standard rack, or 2.7 with the speed sensitive power steering.

The wheels were revised yet again, with pressed steel or light alloy options available. The five-spoke alloy wheels came in either 14- or 15-inch guise, but both designs looked very similar. The details of those supplied to the various markets are covered in the following chapter.

Body

Hayashi was basically given a free hand, but he said: "Before full-fledged development began, we tried out different approaches with a view to changing the image during designer training programmes, and on several other occasions. But we decided that the lightweight sports spirit of the original model should not and could not be changed. After much debate, we reached the conclusion that we should simply polish up the spirit of the first generation to create the next generation roadster. Ultimately, all of the proposals submitted by our design centres carried over the image of the original model with a more dynamic style."

He added: "I wanted to let the feeling of the old model live on, because I thought it didn't need changing to any great extent. The original, in the mould of a 1960s British lightweight sports car, was perfect. However, the new body is more three-dimensional and muscular, with some exciting elements. The rich shapes can be viewed from any angle."

The new body incorporated the Mazda Advanced Impact Distrbution and Absorption System, which helped increase passenger safety in the event of an accident. The front and rear crumple zones effectively absorbed impact energy from both directions. Beefier sills (or rockers) minimized

The final prototype, photographed in the Hiroshima studio. The basic styling was obviously settled on very early in the proceedings, as only detail changes were made on each of the full-size models that followed on from Ken Saward's original drawings.

body distortion in the case of a side impact, aided by twin bars inside the door panels.

At the same time, this enhanced body rigidity provided an excellent basis for the suspension; reinforcement of the suspension's mounting points naturally had a direct effect on handling. After almost 30,000 stress measurements were taken on the all-steel unitary body, it was estimated that overall rigidity had increased by some 38 per cent.

In all, only around 40 per cent

of the new body was carried over from the M1 roadster. Virtually all of the panels were new, including the floorpan, but, due to the limited budget, the original windscreen, windscreen surround, and most of the cowl were retained - this at least meant that the first generation model's hardtop could still be used with the second generation car.

The wings were given a more muscular shape (adding a little to the overall width of the vehicle, even though it went against Kijima's express wish "not to add a single millimetre") with the lines flowing over into the bonnet, while the doors now had a large radius curve at the bottom of the trailing edge (a feature found on the RX-7), and Tanaka's

■Strengthened areas of the New Mazda Roadster's body

The body was again designed with the help of computers. Mazda's Digital Innovation helped strengthen the body in key areas (mainly at each end of the transmission tunnel, in the sills, and at the base of the A-pillars), whilst at the same time keep the weight to a minimum.

楽しさの陰の主役。強くて軽いボディ。ロードスターは、オープン専用に新開発した高剛性・安全ボディ"MAGMA*"。操縦性能を支える高剛性と万一に備える高い安全性を確保しながら、ライトウェイトスポーツの命である軽さを実現している。剛性については、ボディ前後とフロアトンネルの結合部強化、フロン

トピラー・レインフォースメントの大型化と厚みアップ、レインフォースメントの厚みを増したサイドシルとピラーの結合強化などを実施。ボディのねじり剛性をさらにアップし、振動の抑制と、サスペンションを支える骨格としての強さを高めた。

軽量化では、ボディパネルに軽くて強靭な高張力鋼板を多用するとともに、ボンネットフード、シリンダーヘッドカバー、P.P.F.などにアルミ製パーツを採用。より軽量な樹脂パーツも要所に取り入れている。この強くて軽いオープンボディが、ロードスターを思いのままに操る楽しさを基本から支えているのだ。

*MAGMA: Mazda Geometric Motion Absorption
（マツダの全方向整整吸収構造ボディ）

A finished monocoque. The new body-in-white weighed in at just 272kg (598lb).

original door handles were dropped in favour of more modern items finished in body colour.

The sill panels looked heavier than before (as Tom Matano put it, they have "more drama"), merging with the leading edge of the door to give a distinctive styling feature. The crease was deleted between the wheels, but there were still remnants of the M1's centre line where the bumpers joined the body.

The familiar pop-up headlights were deleted in favour of fixed ellipsoid lenses in a bid to save weight at the front. Losing the pop-up lights shed 5.6kg (12lb). This was not only the biggest single saving gained from the weight-cutting operation, it also improved the car's aerodynamics (there was quite a dramatic difference in Cd readings once the old lights were brought up into the raised position, but with fixed lights, this was no longer a problem).

Moving back, the centre edge of the bootlid incorporated a duck-tail lip to improve aerodynamics (as well as the high level rear brake light, the new Mazda badge and number plate lights), while up front, an aluminium bonnet was employed once again, despite the need to save money. The air intake was larger than before, and both bumpers looked less dainty - the styling lines found in the sills continued through to the lower edge of the bumpers.

Interestingly, the rear panel that carries the number plate and badging was now part of the bumper assembly instead of a separate piece. (Or more correctly, two separate pieces from a manufacturing point of view, as the first generation cars for the home market had their own panel which fitted neatly around Japanese registration plates - now all markets had the same specification.)

In addition to the front lights being changed, those at the rear were also modified, but not quite as drastically. The main point of the exercise was to incorporate the rear foglight into the design (for the markets that required one), thus removing the need for a separate item mounted under the bumper.

The manual operation of the hood was kept in order to avoid the weight of electric motors and the complicated mechanism that a power operated hood would require, while the door mirrors were now sharper-looking items - longer and narrower.

Three of the many design proposals put forward for the M2 interior.

Overall dimensions of the new Roadster read as follows: the leading measurements were length 3955mm (155.7in.); width 1680mm (66.1in.); height 1235mm (48.6in.), and wheelbase 2265mm (89.2in.). Ground clearance was 135mm (5.3in.), while the front and rear track were 1405 and 1430mm (55.3 and 56.3in.) respectively, signifying a 10mm (0.4in.) increase in the rear track. The body was therefore slightly shorter, but 5mm (0.2in.) wider; the height and wheelbase were unchanged. With the hood up, the Cd was recorded at 0.36 (an improvement of 0.02 over the original).

The possibility of a coupé was raised during the *Car Graphic* interview with Kijima, to which the disappointing reply was "I don't think so." It was dismissed on the grounds that it destroyed the aim of making a light open car if there was to be a coupé, too, which employs completely different construction methods. One had to take a dedicated approach. Indeed, Takaharu 'Koby' Kobayakawa had stated from the outset that there would never be a third generation RX-7 cabriolet for much the same reasons.

This was a shame, nonetheless, as many had admired the M-Coupé; at the time of its debut in 1996, it was said that, if reaction was favourable - which it was - it might go into production. In reality, it is probably fair to say that Mazda didn't want the possibility of an MX-5 coupé stealing sales from the RX-7, especially given the fact that the sports car market was still shrinking.

Interior

Work on the interior was done solely in Hiroshima, with the main objective being to cut manufacturing costs, whilst at the same time giving the cockpit a feeling of greater quality. To quote the press release handed out at the Tokyo Show: "With almost identical interior dimensions to the first generation, the new Roadster offers comfortably close interior space, enhancing the feeling of oneness between car and driver.

"The design of the T-shaped instrument panel is inherited from the first generation. The centre console wraps around both driver and passenger thanks to the low seat position. All the individual round gauges are gathered in a simple semi-circle cluster. The six-speed manual transmission model features a unique tachometer and speedmeter with needles pointing at the six o'clock start position. The

Once a design was accepted, interior styling bucks were made to check ergonomics and the general 'feel' of the cockpit. Hayashi-san can be seen at the wheel in this picture.

The development of the interior. Like the body, the basic concept was established at quite an early stage, with just detailing to be decided as the design progressed.

steering wheel is a jointly-developed Nardi small-diameter three-spoke type with Supplemental Restraint System (SRS) airbag. The high-back bucket-type seats are superior in holding capability.

"Enlarged storage space in the door pockets and the centre console box provide greater overall storage capacity, and dual cup holders in the rear console box add practicality. The Roadster's exclusive audio system, designed in co-operation with Bose, creates a stereo environment even during open driving. The speakers' thin and lightweight construction also contributes to decreased overall

vehicle weight without sacrificing performance."

The main difference was the more integrated look of the centre console, with the centre vents becoming part of the main fascia. Although the instrument layout was much the same, the odometer was now a digital readout. The 1.6 and 1.8 had different speedos and tachometers on the home market, with the smaller engined model's needles starting from the traditional eight o'clock position, as did all cars destined for export.

Incidentally, speedometers were calibrated to 180kph in Japan (something found on all recent

home market models, from all manufacturers); those for the UK and USA were marked up to 150mph, while cars destined for Continental Europe had 240kph speedos.

Finishing touches
Kijima was of the opinion that although looks were naturally important, it was driving sensations that should be considered the number one priority. Chassis testing was carried out by Masashi Oda on the second batch of mules (completed in mid-1996) and S1 prototypes, with testing as a whole overseen by Takashi Takeshita,

The first S1 prototype to be completed, January 1997. Road testing began almost straight away, with the S1s taking the place of the earlier 'Mechanical Prototypes', or engineering mules.

Vice-Chief of the Experimental Department.

Vehicle development took place all over the world, mainly on mock-ups using the first generation body. It is interesting to note that Oda was at first against the six-speed gearbox in the prototype stages, but, nonetheless, it was eventually perfected.

Although Mazda insisted on one-handed operation of the soft-top, in reality, the material used in the old rear window meant it needed to be unzipped before the lid was dropped to avoid damaging it. The new model's glass rear screen was a vast improvement, as it was now possible to unclip the catches and let the hood fall backwards without worry. Despite the heavier glass screen, the hood as a whole was actually around 1kg (2lb) lighter than its predecessor.

The added strength of the new body made the cockpit brace bar unnecessary, but there was another interesting feature behind the seats - a windblocker (or anti-draft panel), as found on the RX-7 Cabriolet. Kobayakawa-san, its inventor, had requested one for the original MX-5, but Hirai insisted that he wanted passengers to "play with the wind." As a die-hard open car man, Koby, like the author, tends to drop the hood whatever the season (after all, what's the point having a soft-top if you use it like a coupé all year round!), and asked if Hirai had ever played with a winter wind! The answer was no, but Hirai would not be moved, and it wasn't until the second generation model that this simple - but effective - device would be fitted to the little roadster. Mazda's unique "Windblocker is incorporated behind the seats to reduce wind turbulence entering the leg room from behind during open driving. The result, is an improved heater, which enhances comfort during open winter driving."

In its lightest home market form, the new Roadster weighed in at 1000kg (2200lb). This meant a 60kg (132lb) increase compared to the original, but it was only 20kg (44lb) more than the basic 1.8 litre Series II model. Kijima was justifiably proud of this achievement, reiterating that a light package was absolutely crucial.

Testing at the Miyoshi Proving Ground. As well as being put through their paces in Japan, the S1s were also shipped to America and Europe for extensive testing and evaluation.

The pilot build took place in Hiroshima, with these earliest cars once again having the S1 designation; the run was completed in January 1997. Thanks to the use of DPA (Digital Pre-Assembly, which allows the cars to be 'built' on computer before tackling the real thing), very little rectification was needed before the car entered production.

Eager anticipation

By the end of 1996, speculation was rife about the new model. *Complete Car* magazine in the UK noted in September: "Mazda's MX-5 will be in for a facelift by the end of next year, with the now old-fashioned pop-up lights being dropped. The revamp will be subtle … but further ahead Mazda may also consider a more muscular, performance version of the car as an image-booster."

As early as July 1997, several British magazines were carrying details of the new MX-5 after somebody put a Mazda promotional video on the Internet. The new headlight arrangement was obvious from the various spy shots that were published after the leak, but, much to Mazda's dismay, virtually everyone knew the full details of the MX-5's replacement months before the planned launch at the 1997 Tokyo Show.

Although specifications were fairly clear by now, no-one outside

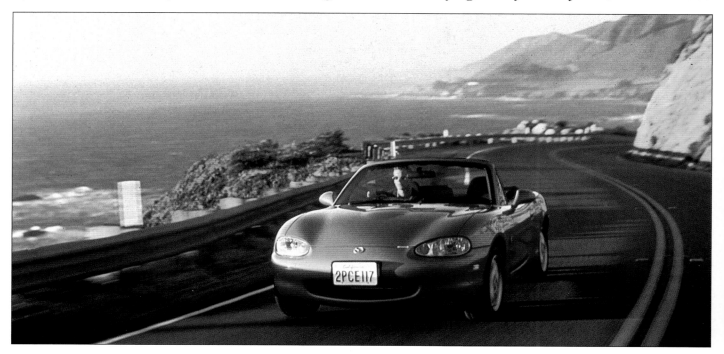

Although only 5mm (0.2in.) wider in reality, the new car looked far wider and lower visually. As Martin Leach (the MD in charge of Product Planning, Design & Programs), said: "It's got more presence." Clinics had been held in both America and Japan, the car's biggest markets.

136

Interior of the new model. Note the 'Windblocker' behind the seats, designed to stop drafts. The hardtop anchorage points on the rear deck were carried over from the previous model.

While the original 1600 looked very basic in the luggage area, the first 1800 had a well-trimmed boot. The second generation model's luggage compartment was also carpeted, but capacity had increased slightly to 144 litres (5.1 cu ft) - an increase of around 15 per cent. However, with the spare wheel and battery moving below the boot floor, the space provided was far more useful.

the company knew what the car was like to drive. It was obvious that Mazda was not going to let the new car fall below the standard set by the first generation model, but it would be reassuring to know for sure.

Writing for *Road & Track* in September 1997, Thos. L. Bryant teased enthusiasts with the following statement: "In the spring, Mazda Motors of America's Vice-President of Public Affairs, Jay Amestoy, suggested that a small group of us should go to Japan to meet with the people designing and engineering the upcoming new Miata ... I am sworn to secrecy, but I will allow as how the new version is sure to please."

The scene was set ...

A rear view of the second generation car. Note the new lighting arrangement (this being a Japanese spec vehicle, it is equipped with twin reversing lights - one in each cluster).

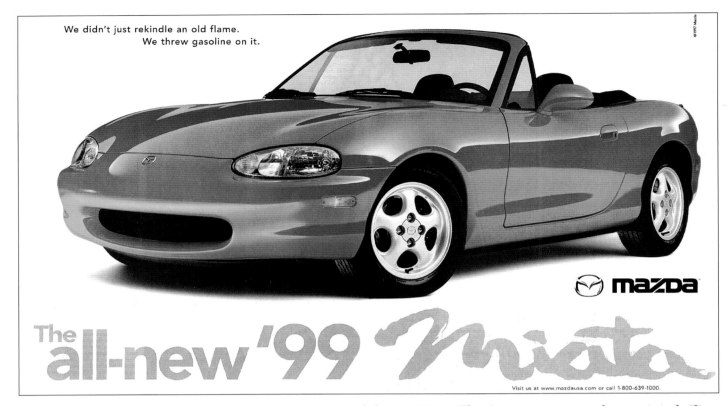

We didn't just rekindle an old flame.
We threw gasoline on it.

©1997 Mazda

The all-new '99 Miata

American advertising showing the all-new 1999 model year Miata. The American press release stated: "It lifts your spirit and renews your soul." The US press launch was held on Big Island, Hawaii.

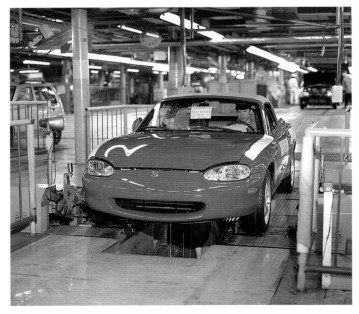

A left-hand drive model fresh from the production line and undergoing a final series of checks.

Production at Hiroshima. Note the new winged Mazda symbol on the nose (it also appeared on the bootlid), said to represent "Mazda spreading its wings as it soars into the future."

138

8

THE NEW CAR TAKES A BOW

Despite various leaks threatening to spoil the build-up, the official launch of the new model at the 32nd Tokyo Show was still a big event for the world's media. The press conference was held on 22 October, three days before the doors at Makuhari Messe opened to the public.

In the highlights booklet handed out at the Tokyo Show, the new Mazda Roadster (the Eunos name had been dropped), was given top billing in the Mazda section:

"The all-new Roadster makes its world debut at the Tokyo Motor Show. This superb car embodies the enduring appeal of authentic lightweight sports cars.

"The new Roadster employs a lightweight, compact and highly-rigid two-seater open body. Its exterior features modern sports car styling carried over from the original Roadster model. Under the hood, Mazda offers a choice of either a 1.8 litre or 1.6 litre engine with enhanced power. These engines

The launch of the second generation Mazda Roadster at the 1997 Tokyo Show. This photograph was taken by the author on the first press day. Note the tiny chin spoiler fitted to the 1.8 litre cars.

Mazda actually had two of the new Roadsters on display at the 1997 Tokyo Show - the gold coloured model on the rotating stand, and this top-of-the-range VS in Grey Green Mica mounted high up in the centre of the display.

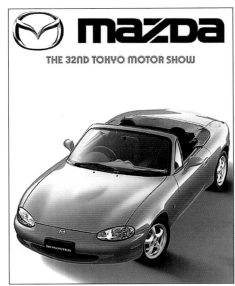

Despite having the MS-X, MV-X and SW-X concept cars at the Tokyo Show, it was the new Roadster that made the cover of Mazda's brochure for the event.

The brochure handed out at the Tokyo Show listed all of the salient points of the new Roadster.

work in harmony with the car's advanced chassis to improve the driving feel, responsive handling and smooth ride.

"The 1.8 litre-engined model comes with a close-ratio six-speed manual transmission. The new Roadster also features the highly-rigid MAGMA safety body."

Mazda had two of the new Roadsters on display - a gold coloured model (a stunning shade that was used extensively in early publicity shots from around the time of the launch) and one finished in a tasteful dark green.

However, apart from the new MX-5s and a solitary RX-7, the theme of the Mazda stand very much reflected the fashion of the time, with MPVs and estate cars dominating. The management couldn't be blamed for this, however, as it was the strongest sector of the market in Japan as the millennium loomed, while sports cars were in danger of becoming a dying breed. Perhaps this was another reason Mazda didn't go too crazy with a brand new design; it was more prudent to stick with a proven winner.

The press release issued at the show (but dated 15 October) read as follows: "Defined as a new vehicle to be marketed in the future, the all-new Mazda Roadster will be exhibited. Since its world debut in

1989, the first generation Mazda Roadster has been [widely] touted as the best two-seater lightweight roadster in the world. The new Roadster inherits virtues of the first generation and balances all the strong points of top-down driving fun with superb sports car performance and incomparable styling."

It also listed the following nine points:

1. The dimensions of the new Mazda Roadster are 3955mm [155.7in.] in overall length, 1680mm [66.1in.] in overall width, 1235mm [48.6in.] in overall height and 2265mm [89.2in.] in wheelbase. Only the overall width is 5mm [0.2in.] greater than its predecessor.

2. The basic layout maintains the front engine, rear-drive layout achieving an ideal front and rear weight distribution. The engine is mounted midship behind the axle [i.e. quite far back in the engine bay].

3. Carrying on the design motif recognizable as the Roadster at a glance, the new Roadster is designed to offer sportier, aggressive and dynamic styling in a three-dimensional form.

4. Either 1.8 litre or 1.6 litre in-line, four-cylinder dohc 16v engines are available. With refinement of the intake and exhaust systems, both engines have improved output and torque, enhanced revving characteristics, and greater acceleration response.

5. The 1.8 litre-engined model features a newly-developed, six-speed manual transmission which optimizes engine speed and acceleration characteristics at high revs.

6. The double-wishbone suspension at the front and rear is further enhanced. Through reviewing the geometry and fine tuning, the driving stability of the new Roadster was refined for more fun driving.

7. By incorporating a glass window with defogger, the view through the rear window was greatly improved. By dropping the zipper around the vinyl rear window, [the hood's] open and close operations were eased, while the overall weight of the soft-top was reduced.

8. The highly rigid and safe body Mazda Advanced Impact Distribution and Absorption System achieves enhanced collision safety (also known as MAGMA or Mazda Geometric Motion Absorption). The well-managed body torsion and vibration as a result of increase in the body rigidity contribute to the superb driving stability of the new Roadster.

9. In addition to the driver's and passenger's SRS (Supplemental Restraint System) airbags, the seatbelts are equipped with an automatic tension function that regulates tension force against a certain level of impact with the occupants.

Of course, Mazda no longer had the convertible market to itself, and more cars were joining the MX-5 and its new competitors all the time. Announced at the 1997 Tokyo Show alongside the new model from Hiroshima, the Toyota MR-S was an indirect replacement for the MR2, designed to compete head-on with the MX-5; although the 1997 vehicle was a concept model, it would go on to star in many fascinating comparison tests with the Mazda Roadster after it went into production. Another debutante at Makuhari Messe that year was the Suzuki C2 - a lightweight open car powered by a 250bhp, 1.6 litre V8. The future definitely looked interesting ...

The home market
As usual, the Japanese market had an extensive line-up of models. The 1.6 litre range included a basic five-speed model, the M Package and Special Package. Both of these latter versions could be bought with a five-speed manual gearbox or four-speed automatic transmission. ABS brakes came as standard with the automatic Roadsters, and were an option on the manual M Package and Special Package cars. All 1.6s came with

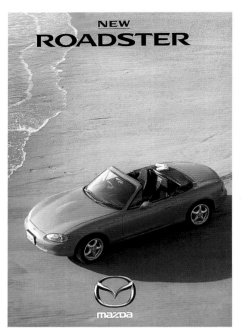

NEW
ROADSTER

The first Japanese brochure for the second generation Roadster. The ubiquitous gold colour (known by different names around the world) was used extensively in build-up publicity and launch material.

Mazda's own four-spoke steering wheel, and the Special Package was equipped with power door mirrors.

As for the 1.8 litre car, this was available in three different specifications - the S, RS and VS. These came with a six-speed manual gearbox, but the four-speed automatic transmission could be specified on the S and VS. An ABS braking system was included in the price on all automatic 1.8 litre cars, and an option on each of the manual models.

All 1.8s came with electrically-adjusted door mirrors and a Nardi three-spoke steering wheel; that on the S and RS was leather-wrapped, while the VS had a wood-rimmed item with matching gearknob and handbrake lever handle. Polished treadplates were standard on the RS and VS, and the latter also came with a CD player straight from the factory.

The Japanese 1600 range, as seen in the first catalogue released for the new model. With a 9.4:1 compression ratio, the 1.6 litre engine produced 125bhp at 6500rpm, and 105lbft of torque at 5000rpm.

The 1800 series for the home market. The first generation 1.6 litre cars carried the NA6CE chassis designation, whereas 1.8 litre models were identified by the NA8C prefix. For the second generation, the smaller engined car carried the NB6C code, whilst 1.8 litre vehicles were identified by the NB8C chassis number.

Incidentally, manual 1.8 litre models had a unique set of gauges featuring red pointer needles instead of white ones.

All cars came with air conditioning and a driver's footrest,

Opposite: A series of four advertisements for the new Roadster. Each describes a notable feature, such as the MAGMA body, six-speed transmission, all-round double-wishbone suspension, and the traditional FR layout.

142

Beautiful publicity shot of the new Roadster, dated January 1998.

This picture of the VS grade was actually used in the first Japanese catalogue.

navigation system could be specified as a cost option on the same three grades.

Five-spoke alloy wheels were standard on the 1.6 litre Special Package and the three 1.8 litre grades, although the sizes were different - 185/60 HR14 tyres mounted on 6J x 14 rims was the norm, but the RS came with lightweight 195/50 VR15 Michelin tyres and 6J x 15 alloys to complement its uprated suspension (including Bilstein dampers and a tower brace bar); the basic 1.6 and M Package had 185/60 tyres on 5.5J x 14 pressed steel wheels. Likewise, a Torsen limited-slip differential came with the same range of vehicles, but only when specified in manual guise.

Overall weights ranged from 1000 to 1060kg (2200 to 2332lb), whilst prices started at 1,819,000 yen for the basic 1.6 litre model, rising to 2,665,000 yen for the top VS models. The sporty RS was slightly cheaper than the equivalent VS model, as the VS had a higher level of trim. Sales started in January 1998 through both Mazda and Anfini dealerships - the Eunos sales channel no longer existed.

Standard exterior colours on the 1.6 litre cars included Classic Red, Highlight Silver Metallic and Chaste White. By opting for the Special Package or M Package, three more options became available: Evolution Orange Mica, Twilight Blue Mica, and Brilliant Black. In all cases, the trim was finished in

and all but the basic grade had power-assisted steering, electric windows, the Windblocker device, and an automatic aerial, although only the VS came with a stereo as standard - a Bose radio/CD unit that could be ordered as an extra on the RS and Special Package. It was the same situation with the remote controlled central locking (standard on the VS, optional on the RS and Special Package), and a

The engine of the 1.8 litre RS grade. With a 9.5:1 compression ratio, the 1.8 litre engine produced 145bhp at 6500rpm, and 120lbft of torque at 5000rpm. Note the brace bar, standard on the RS, and optional on the other models. The RS also came with an uprated suspension package, including Bilstein dampers.

The official body kit offered by Mazda dealers in Japan at the time of the new model's launch.

former Vice-President, had joined Ford in 1973, although his work had brought him close to the Hiroshima marque for the best part of a decade before his new appointment.

The second generation Stateside

The 1998 Detroit Show (which opened on 10 January) saw the official American launch of the second generation Miata (although it had appeared at Los Angeles a week before), tagged as a 1999 model year car - there would be no 1998 models.

Richard Beattie, President of Mazda North America, said: "The weather outside may be cold and dreary, but with the introduction of our new Miata, things are heating up at Mazda. As good as the original Miata was, this new 1999 Miata is better in every single way. We fully expect it to remain the best-selling two-seat roadster on the planet."

The press release stated: "The car that almost single-handedly revived the two-seat open roadster market around the world arrived in Detroit today as Mazda executives unveiled the all-new 1999 Miata at the 1998 North American International Auto Show. The new Miata, which features a more powerful engine, dramatically restyled body, redesigned interior and improved handling, goes on sale in Mazda dealerships early in 1998.

"The new 1999 Mazda Miata

black. Twilight Blue Mica, Brilliant Black and Chaste White could be specified on all 1.8 litre models. The RS and S grades were also available in Evolution Orange Mica (the gold shade that Mazda used in most of its publicity material), Classic Red and Highlight Silver Metallic, while the VS was offered in Grey Green Mica. Again, interior trim was in black, except for the VS which came with tan leather trim and a tan coloured hood.

On the corporate side of things, James E. Miller was announced as Mazda's new President in November 1997, taking the place of Henry Wallace. Miller, the company's

American advertising from early 1998. Note the airdam at the front and the side skirts, meaning that the car used in the picture was fitted with the optional Appearance Package.

The cover from the Detroit Show press release. The matching photograph contained within it had a caption that read: "The 1999 Miata is proof that the sequel can be better than the original. Featuring a dramatically restyled body, improved handling, a glass rear window with defroster and an increase in horsepower to 140, the all-new Miata is ready to continue its reign as the best-selling two-seat roadster in the world." This car features the 15-inch alloys that came as part of the Leather Package.

features a more powerful 140bhp 1.8 litre dohc four-cylinder engine, improved four-wheel double-wishbone suspension, more aggressively styled body and a redesigned interior. The body of the new Miata is more rigid for improved handling, yet it weighs the same as its predecessor. The easy-to-use folding top is even easier to operate and now uses a glass rear window with built-in defroster, a feature not found on several convertibles costing much more.

"The new Mazda Miata may not be on sale yet, but the editors of *Car & Driver* magazine are already

A rear view of the 1999 MX-5 Miata for the American market. Note the optional five-spoke alloy wheels, these being the 14-inch versions, although the 15-inch items looked very similar.

hailing it as one of the '10 Best Cars' in the publication's January 1998 issue. This is nothing new for the Miata - the original car won several awards and accolades before it went on sale as well.

"Since its introduction in 1989, Mazda has sold more than 450,000 Miatas worldwide, with more than half of that total coming in North America. The Miata is the best-selling two-seat roadster in the

The 1.8 litre BP-ZE (RS) engine that powered the US range - the 1.6 unit was not listed in America. Rated at 140bhp in most States, cars destined for California, New York, Massachusetts and Connecticut lost 2bhp because of tighter emissions regulations.

Interior of the standard Miata, showing the Nardi steering wheel supplied as part of the Touring Package (and therefore the Leather, and Popular Equipment Packages) and the Sports Package - the base model had a four-spoke, urethane-covered wheel. Again, however, American cars had to do without the option of a wood-rimmed wheel. Interestingly, the Windblocker was not fitted on standard base models, or those equipped with the Touring Package or Sports Package.

The Leather Package's stylish cockpit. Seat facings were trimmed in tan leather, with the rest finished in a matching vinyl. In America, the passenger airbag could actually be deactivated to allow a child seat to be used.

The Miata where it belongs - on the open road.

world. In addition, the Mazda Miata is a champion on the track, earning several SCCA Class championships."

As with the previous generation car, Mazda's marketing people bombarded journalists with press releases about the new model in a bid to get that extra column inch, but the underlying message was usually the same: "Despite all of the changes to the 1999 Mazda Miata, it remains true to its original concept - a lightweight, affordable, two-seat roadster that delivers the pure enjoyment of wind-in-the-hair driving. It lifts your spirit and renews your soul."

America had only the 1.8 litre car. With a 9.5:1 compression ratio, it was rated at 140bhp at 6500rpm (or 138bhp in California), and had a maximum torque output of 119lbft at 5500rpm (vehicles for California developed 2lbft less, but at a more useful 5000rpm).

The base model had a five-speed manual gearbox, rack-and-pinion steering without power assistance, and 185/60 HR14 tyres mounted on 5.5J x 14 pressed steel wheels. All cars came with dual airbags as standard and - amazingly

- a combined stereo radio/CD player with a digital clock. Basic options included air conditioning, power steering, automatic transmission (not available with the Sports Package), a detachable hard-top, foglights, and bright wheel trim rings. However, there were now no fewer than five option packages to choose from:

Touring Package: This added power-assisted steering, 6J x 14 alloy wheels, power windows and mirrors, and a Nardi three-spoke, leather-trimmed steering wheel. Automatic transmission became an option with this package.

Popular Equipment Package: This included the items in the Touring Package, plus a Torsen lsd (on manual cars), cruise control, power door locks, an upgraded sound system, electric aerial, and the patented Windblocker. ABS brakes became an option if the Bose stereo system was purchased at the same time.

Leather Package: Based on the Popular Equipment Package but with the added bonus of a tan leather interior and tan coloured hood, 195/50 VR15 Michelin Pilot SX GT tyres mounted on 6J x 15 alloy rims, plus the high powered Bose stereo radio/cassette/CD unit with top quality speakers. ABS brakes were optional.

Sports Package: This came with manual cars only, and included a Torsen limited-slip differential, 15-inch alloys with the 195/50 tyres, a three-spoke Nardi leather-wrapped steering wheel, an uprated suspension (including Bilstein shock absorbers), a front strut tower brace, front airdam, and rear spoiler.

Appearance Package: The Appearance Package was not available with the Sports Package, but included a front airdam, side skirts, a rear spoiler, rear mudflaps, and foglights.

Standard colours included White, Brilliant Black, Classic Red, Twilight Blue Mica, Highlight Silver Metallic and Emerald Mica. Trim was in black cloth, or tan leather via the aforementioned package, although the latter was not available with the Sports Package. Prices started at $19,770.

The new car in Europe

The second generation MX-5 made its European debut at the 1998 Geneva Show, held from 5 to 15 March. In his opening statement at the Swiss event, James E. Miller said: "I am delighted to welcome you to the Geneva Motor Show for the first time as President of the Mazda Motor Corporation. Mazda has earned an excellent reputation for superior design and engineering capabilities - a reputation that reflects its attention to form, functionality and advanced

technology, as well as its emphasis on creativity and craftsmanship.

"Today Mazda exhibits automobiles that exemplify our new approach based on this long-standing tradition: the all-new MX-5, the new 626 Station Wagon and the Demio Concept along with the MV-X and SW-X concept cars. The new MX-5 will be marketed in Europe starting in April. The redesign features heightened response and power for truly fun sports car driving, yet retains the feeling of oneness between car and driver that MX-5 users have come to expect and love. We hope that you will feel the strength of our enthusiasm for the future of automobiles through the cars and technology you will see at this show."

The press pack highlighted the following points:

Compact, fun-to-drive package
The optimum product package, balanced for driving pleasure. Mazda made extra efforts to minimize the vehicle weight of the new MX-5. Decreasing both front and rear overhang weight and placing all the mass as close to the vehicle centre as possible, enabled the new MX-5 to achieve excellent yaw inertia moment and ideal weight destribution.

More sporty look and feel
The body is attractive from all angles and retains the MX-5's distinctive design motif. Its sporty look is

One of the pictures that came with the Geneva Show press pack. Although the MX-5 was an important car for enthusiasts, Mazda gave almost as much attention to the 626 and the various concept cars that had made their debut almost five months earlier in Tokyo.

enhanced by lines that stress the wide and low form. Inside, the cockpit is simple and more functional.

Excellent driving pleasure
The new MX-5 offers sharply enhanced driving performance

Below: A confusing photograph of the British 1.6i - confusing because this car is fitted with 14-inch alloys instead of the 15-inch items that are listed as optional in the specifications sheet. The 14-inch wheels would usually be supplied as a £440 option through dealerships, thus allowing owners to keep their original tyres, whereas the move to larger alloys naturally demanded new rubber as well. The 1.6i was launched with a list price of £15,520.

Another shot of the MX-5 in action, but this is a UK specification 1.8iS. Sales started on 25 April in the British Isles.

when compared with the original MX-5, thanks to the powerful 1.8 litre and 1.6 litre in-line four-cylinder dohc 16v engine, and excellent driving stability, made possible by a highly-rigid body and chassis. The five-speed manual transmission further enhances the fun of sports driving.

Superb safety features
The new Mazda MX-5 offers excellent active safety features to help prevent accidents, and outstanding passive safety features to help protect the driver and the passenger in the event of an accident.

Improved functionality
The new MX-5 delivers enhanced practicality with more convenient and comfort-enhancing functions and features. [With new packaging, it offers 42 per cent more luggage space.]

The UK press launch was held on the French Riviera, with the car going on sale to the public from the end of April. Special music, *The Song of the Swift* by John Harle, was played at the dealerships, and tape cassettes of the tune were given as gifts in boxes finished in the same gold colour as seen on the new MX-5.

As the UK press release stated: "The new Mazda MX-5 offers enhanced performance and excellent handling and stability. The 0-62mph [100kph] acceleration time for the 1.6 litre is now just 9.7 seconds, a reduction of 0.9 seconds. The 1.8 litre reaches 0-62mph in 8.0 seconds, down 0.7 seconds from the previous car. Top speed for the 1.6 litre is now 118mph (189kph) - up 9mph, or 14kph - and 127mph (203kph) - up 4mph, or 6kph - for the 1.8 litre.

"The 1.6 litre has had power increased by 20bhp (from 90bhp to 110bhp). The 1.8 litre is up 9bhp (from 131bhp to 140bhp). Output and torque for both engines has been improved through enhancements to the intake and

The 1.8iS was the UK's top model, priced at £18,775. It came with 6J x 15 alloys and a host of extras as standard, but the detachable hard-top was still a pricey option at £1475.

A rear view of the European (lhd) spec MX-5. This picture shows the soft-top fully erected (and therefore the new glass rear window), along with the latest rear light design which eliminated the need for a separate foglight.

exhaust systems, resulting in smooth engine revving from low to high speeds and responsive acceleration."

Indeed, in European trim, with a 9.4:1 compression ratio, the 1.6 litre engine produced 110bhp at 6500rpm, and 99lbft of torque at 5000rpm. On the 1.8, which had a 9.5:1 compression ratio, power was quoted at 140bhp at 6500rpm, while maximum torque output was listed as 119lbft at 4500rpm.

All of the new MX-5s were sold with power steering, an immobilizer, and airbags for both driver and passenger as standard; steel 5.5J x 14 wheels were the norm, fitted with 185/60 HR14 tyres. The 1.8 litre model added electric windows and a Windblocker to the basic specification, while the 1.8iS also came with 195/50 VR15 tyres mounted on 6J x 15 alloys and a number of other more upmarket touches - ABS braking, a Torsen lsd, electrically adjusted door mirrors, power door locks, a stereo radio/cassette with electric

aerial, mudflaps, and stainless treadplates. In addition, a Nardi leather-trimmed steering wheel replaced the urethane-covered item.

In Britain, the 1.6i was listed at £15,520 on the road (almost £1000 more than its predecessor, or about the price of the old 1.8i); the new 1.8i was priced at £16,650, while the 1.8iS was little changed at £18,775. Major options included air conditioning, a detachable hard-top, front foglamps, and a rear spoiler. The Windblocker, alloy wheels, stainless treadplates, and front and rear mudflaps were also made available to upgrade cheaper models.

Standard colours included Classic Red, Classic Black, Racing Silver Metallic, Racing Blue Mica, Racing Green Mica and Racing Bronze Mica, although the metallic and mica shades added £250 to the price of the car. The upholstery was usually in black cloth, but leather could be specified as a £923 option, the colour choices being

black, light grey, anthracite, tan, taupe and mist.

It's interesting to note that automatic transmission was not listed anywhere in Europe. Some European mainland countries, however, such as Italy, got the 15-inch alloy wheels as standard on both the 1.6 and 1.8 litre models, although the ABS braking system, Torsen limited-slip differential, and Nardi steering wheel were reserved for the larger engined car.

Switzerland had two 1.6 litre grades (the 1.6 Youngster and 1.6 SE Youngster), and one 1.8 - the 1.8 Youngster. The basic 1.6 came with steel wheels and a traditional braking system, but the other grades had 15-inch alloys and ABS as standard. Only the 1.8 was fitted with the Torsen lsd, however. Overall weights on European cars ranged from 1015kg (2233lb) for the basic 1.6, to 1047kg (2303lb) for the UK spec 1.8iS.

Mazdaspeed

As Mazda's representative in the

Mazdaspeed's Touring Kit A-Spec for the new Roadster, announced in February 1998, a month after sales of the second generation model started in Japan.

NEW ROADSTER TOURING KIT A-spec.

スポーツカーの
正統なる進化。

新型ロードスター用
「ツーリングキット A-スペック」
新発売！

もう20年以上も世界のサーキットで戦ってきた我々でさえ、新型ロードスターをチューニングすることは、チューナー冥利につきる魅力的な作業といえる。なぜならこの車は、先代が持つライトウェイトスポーツの基本理念をかたくなに踏襲した、まさに「走るため」だけに生まれた純粋な「スポーツカー」そのものであるからだ。この「スポーツカー」を際限なくチューニングすれば、やがて一般公道を走行できない「レーシングカー」になってしまう。が、しかし少しでもそれに近づけたい。そんな想いから「ツーリングキットA-スペック」は誕生した。開発にはもちろんレーシングカーと同様の手法を踏んでいる。綿密な風洞実験、度重なる走行テスト、膨大なデータ解析等々…。全身にレーシングカー譲りの機能パーツをまとったこの車のステアリングを握った瞬間から、スポーツカーの正統なる進化を体感できるはずだ。

※写真の車のステッカーは撮影用です。
商品には含まれておりません。

MAZDASPEED

field of motorsport and the factory's outlet for works tuning parts, it's not surprising that Mazdaspeed was the first company to offer aerodynamic body kits and tuning components. In a news release, the Touring Kit A-Spec was announced as follows: "Mazdaspeed Co. Ltd is proud to announce that the Touring Kit A-Spec for the new Roadster (NB8C/NB6C) is now under development and will be available through its Sport Factory, other nationwide Mazda group dealers and retailers from 26 February 1998.

"The development of the Touring Kit A-Spec has been made on the orthodox and evolutionary concept focusing on the aerodynamic and suspension parts to withdraw maximum onroad potential. A special feature of the tuning parts is the overall three-dimensional body design with which wind tunnel tests showed a positive improvement to the Cd (the air resistance factor) and Cl (the lift factor) readings. In addition, the front spoiler is that of the first generation Air Scoop design reducing air resistance. Furthermore, the headlight finisher has been designed to provide a smooth look with a strong outline definition. Moreover, the three-dimensional shaped side skirt allows the airflow to channel smoothly by the body side. All other aero-parts, namely the rear wing and rear skirt, have undergone wind tunnel tests to find their optimum setting to increase the aerodynamic effect.

"Optional parts designed for the new Roadster (MX-5) include a newly-designed air filter. This adopts three special layered Welten Sponges which in tests showed a suction restriction of 20 per cent, contributing to better fuel economy and accelerator response. Secondly, [for the 1.8 litre car, there is a] limited-slip differential which has been designed for better traction for both wheels, enabling controlled and effective cornering.

"An additional item [for the 1.8 litre model] is the asbestos-free brake set designed for durability and controllability. The clutch set has been designed to transmit high power from the engine to the drivetrain. Furthermore, a lighter flywheel is available, enabling a quick engine response without engine stall or difficult clutch operation. A shaving process of the chrome-molybdenum and the ion-nitrogen treatment has been carried out on the flywheel surface, making this product a sufficiently hard and durable item.

"Moreover, suspension parts, sports sound muffler, exhaust manifold, roll bar, sports driving meters [white-faced gauges], high volt silicone leads, and the brake line set are presently undergoing development and will be available from April.

"Among the selections of Touring kit devised for public roads is the Touring Kit A-Spec, of which, parts exclusively for competition use are called the Sports Kit. Each part can be purchased separately to tailor the needs and budget of the buyer."

Prices ranged from 35,000 yen for the headlight finishers, up to 58,000 yen for a rear spoiler or the side skirts. The body kit was completed by the front spoiler and rear skirt, each priced at 48,000 yen. Mazdaspeed seats ranged from 64,000 to 88,000 yen apiece.

Mechanical components for the 1.8 litre car included the limited-slip differential at 75,000 yen, and the front pad set at 15,000 yen (2000 yen more than for the rear set). For both power units, 48,000 yen would buy the lightened flywheel, while the clutch set was 54,000 yen on the 1.8, or 52,000 on the 1.6 litre.

Initial press reaction

In America, *Motor Trend* was very quick to cover the new model, claiming that "although the second generation of this petite two-seater rolls onto the scene next spring with a new look and new level of sophistication, remaining fully intact are all the wonderful traits that made the original car fun to drive and easy to own." This view was echoed in *Road & Track*, the sub-heading of its April 1998 test reading: "The same basic formula taken to new heights."

Thos. L. Bryant introduced the car to Australian readers in *Wheels* magazine, and had this to say: "The tail of the MX-5 prototype wiggled just a little as I went through a series of esses at the Miyoshi Proving Ground. The signal from the car was polite but firm: 'You're going too fast for these conditions.' As I eased off and the all-new MX-5 settled itself, a grin spread across my face. I've loved the MX-5 since it was introduced in 1989, but this new one is markedly improved."

Writing for the popular British *Top Gear* magazine in February 1998, Yasushi Ishiwatari noted: "Though it's not exactly a quantum leap in styling from the old MX-5, there's more to be enthusiastic about than you'd think; it really does feel more like a new car than anyone would imagine from looking at it ... It hasn't lost any of the charm of its predecessor. The good points have been further improved, and they've fixed many of the niggly and irritating problems."

The same journal carried out a comparison test between the MX-5 1.8iS, MGF and Fiat Barchetta. Although it felt the new car was not as much fun as the original, and had lost some of its character along the way, the Mazda still came out on top.

In a similar test, *Car* thought it was an obvious decision in favour of the car from Hiroshima: "Compared with the Mazda, the Barchetta is too much the fashion model and not enough the mean mover, while the MGF is the victim of a purge against its dynamic purity. It's also too expensive. That's an accusation you can't level at the lovable Barchetta, but the Mazda has to be worth the extra outlay for its driving entertainment. Or you can have an MX-5 1.6 for Barchetta money - and there's also the question of whether you could live with the Fiat's compulsory left-hand drive layout.

"Whenever we've tested 'affordable' sports cars recently, the result has never been clear-cut. This time, with just a slight confusion in the styling plot, it's simple. Mazda's new MX-5 does all that a sports car should. It's a cracker."

Autocar (which added BMW's Z3, launched in time for the 1997 season, to the equation) was also wooed by the appeal of the MX-5. In its verdict on the new 1.8 litre MX-5, *Autocar* said in another article: "[It has a] much improved chassis [and] better quality interior materials make the cabin more classy. Mazda's jewel finely polished."

As you will have gathered, almost all of the early road tests were complimentary, and Mazda was often praised for not making changes for the sake of it. The Japanese *Motor Magazine* seemed to sum up the mood perfectly: "The new car is the next level up from the first generation Eunos Roadster. The looks have changed, but the soul remains the same."

After an uncertain start, the original MX-5 went on to take the world by storm. If initial reactions were anything to go by, the future looked set to be every bit as good as the past had been for Mazda's LWS …

9

THE LEGEND CONTINUES

Following a successful launch, the Mazda team now had the difficult task of selling the second generation model. Sports cars were falling from favour with the young and trendy - they were not as fashionable as RVs and SUVs, and insurance premiums on sporty two-door machines had escalated to such an extent that many potential buyers were put off the idea upon discovering how much it would cost to insure the vehicle. Yet more and more manufacturers were entering the LWS arena all the time.

At the 1995 Tokyo Show, Toyota exhibited the MRJ, which was later developed into the MR-S concept of 1997. Although slow to join the LWS class, Toyota's intentions were clear. The MR-S (also known as the MR2 Roadster and MR2 Spyder) duly went on sale at the end of 1999 on the home market, with export sales beginning in April 2000. Another debutante at the 1995 Tokyo Show was the Honda SSM, which later became the superb S2000 production model of 1999 vintage. Mitsubishi also joined the open sports car fold with its Eclipse Spyder (recently heavily revised for the 2001 model year), and there were even rumours of Isuzu building a two-seater, only to be quashed when the company announced its withdrawal from all but the RV and commercial vehicle arena.

On the European front, Audi showed its TT Coupé at the 1995 Frankfurt Show, and followed it up with a Roadster version for the Japanese event. The TT Roadster would also go into production, joining the likes of the MGF, Fiat Barchetta, Alfa Romeo Spider, BMW Z3, the Lotus Elise and Caterham 21 (both of these Brits were announced at the 1995 Earls Court Show, but deliveries would not start until late 1996), and the Mercedes-Benz SLK (eventually launched in time for the 1997 model year after a protracted arrival) for a bite of the open sports car market. There was also the Porsche Boxster, though it's fair to say that price probably elevated it to a slightly different level.

From America, perhaps only the well established Ford Mustang and Chevrolet Camaro convertibles could be classed as true competitors. However, there was no doubt that the MX-5 had a great deal of new competition to contend with in a shrinking market ...

The 1999 season in Japan

There was little change in the home market line-up for 1999; even the catalogue was the same as that for the previous season. However, the 1.6 litre five-speed basic model was now priced at 1,770,000 yen (although deleting the standard air conditioning brought it down to 1,594,000 yen), the M Package was listed at 1,860,000 yen (or 2,003,000 yen with automatic transmission), while the Special Package was 1,960,000 yen in manual guise, or 98,000 yen more

Advertising from the Auto Exe concern of Tokyo, and featuring the new Roadster. The gentleman at the top of the page is Japan's very own "Mr Le Mans" - Yojiro Terada. The founder of Auto Exe, Terada's links with the Mazda marque extend over three decades.

The 1999 MY Miata fitted with the Leather and Appearance Packages. A total of 25,332 MX-5s had been shipped to North America in 1998 (just under 1300 of which went to Canada), although the figure dropped to 16,763 units the following year (15,591 for the USA; 1172 for Canada).

if the buyer wanted an automatic gearbox.

In the 1.8 litre line-up, the entry level S grade cost 2,185,000 yen with a six-speed manual transmission, or 2,233,000 yen with an automatic. The manual only RS was listed at 2,295,000 yen, whilst the top-of-the-range VS came in at 2,395,000 yen, or 2,443,000 yen as an automatic. All of these prices were held until the start of the 2000 model year.

America's 1999 model year proper

Although the second generation was known as a 1999 model from the time of its launch, the 1999 model year proper was announced in September 1998. Naturally, changes were few - even the $19,770 sticker price was carried over.

Essentially, the option packages were much the same, too. For the 1999 season, the Touring Package was priced at $1100, the Popular Equipment Package was $2330 (or $1940 with automatic models, as the Torsen lsd was not supplied), the Leather Package was $3975 (again, it was $390 cheaper on automatic cars because of the lack of a limited-slip differential),

while the Sports Package was $1900.

One of the few changes made was in the Appearance Package, which now came in two parts. The front airdam, side skirts and rear mudguards were batched together at $595 (code 1AP), while the full set - everything in 1AP, plus a rear spoiler and foglights - came in at $995. Not surprisingly, this was given the 2AP moniker. In addition, there was a Power Steering Package which included PAS and wheel trim rings only.

Individual options included air conditioning ($900), power-assisted steering ($300), automatic transmission ($850), ABS brakes ($550 when combined with certain packages), a detachable hard-top ($1500), foglights ($250), front and rear mudguards ($125), the Bose stereo upgrade ($550), a cassette

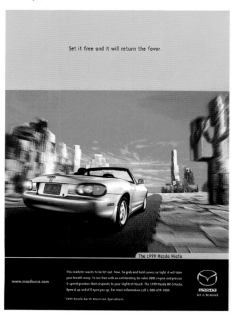

American advertising of spring 1999.

Cover from the Mazda UK brochure for the 1999 model year range. It featured the MX-5 Sport - a new variant, taking the British line-up to four MX-5 models.

The new Mazda 1999 model range

Mazda MX-5

Some of the accessories offered by Mazda UK for the 1999 season. Note that all of the components which came together to make the MX-5 Sport were available as separate dealer options.

You'll be amazed at a Mazda MAZDA

Accessories

Rear Spoiler, Side Sill Set, Rear Mud Flap Set

Detachable Hard Top and Stainless Steel Door Edge Protector Set

Scuff Plate Set

Front Air Dam Skirt and Fog Lamp Set

Wood Trim Kit, Gear Knob and Parking Brake Grip

Rear Wing Spoiler

Radio Cassette - CD Autochanger Compatible

Radio - Single CD - CD Changer Compatible

6 Disc Autochanger

Full Tonneau Cover

Luggage Carrier

14" Image Alloy Wheels

14" Stealth Alloy Wheels

15" Reflex Alloy Wheels

15" Gemini Alloy Wheels

player ($250), wheel trim rings ($50), and floormats at $80; the patented Windblocker was available with the Touring or Sports Package for an extra $150.

European update

In Britain, prices and options on the three original MX-5 grades were carried over for the 1999 model year, so the 1.6i was listed at £15,520, the 1.8i was £16,650, and 1.8iS was £18,775. At the end of 1998, however, these were joined by a new model - the MX-5 Sport.

The MX-5 Sport was based on the 1.8iS, but had a number of extras as standard. It came with air conditioning, a detachable hard-top finished in body colour, leather trim (all previously expensive options), along with the body styling kit (including a lowered front airdam with foglights, side skirts, rear mudflaps and a rear spoiler) and wood trim kit that were usually offered as accessories.

Indeed, Mazda UK had an extensive list of dealer options. As well as the aforementioned items (the wood trim kit consisted of a

Stunning publicity shot of the 10th Anniversary model in home market guise.

The 10th Anniversary car had black leather seats with blue suede-like inserts, and a steering wheel and gearlever to match. It came with red needles on the gauges, like all six-speed models in Japan since the launch of the second generation. Of course, for the Americans and Europeans, this was something new, as the limited edition vehicle marked the debut of the six-speed gearbox in those markets. Note also the carbonfibre-style console trim.

console finishing piece, gearknob and handbrake grip, incidentally), dealerships were able to offer various alloy wheel designs, a radio/cassette or radio with a built-in, single-play CD, a CD autochanger, stainless treadplates, door edge protectors, a tonneau cover, and a rear deck luggage rack. Incidentally, during the 1998 calendar year, Mazda sold a total of 6307 MX-5s in the British Isles, while sales for the rest of Europe amounted to around 15,000 units for the same period.

The 10th Anniversary model

Just in time for the 1999 season, the 1.8 litre Roadster 10th Anniversary model was launched. The equipment specification was basically the same for all markets around the world, with 7500 being produced in total. Japan was allocated 500 of these, at a price of 2,483,000 yen. To put that into perspective, the new RX-7 range started at 2,898,000 yen at the time.

Features included a six-speed manual transmission, polished 15-inch alloys, an uprated suspension with Bilstein shock absorbers (to Japanese RS specifications), air conditioning, dual airbags, half-leather, two-tone trim (with a matching steering wheel and gearknob), a Bose CD sound system surrounded by a carbonfibre-style console trim, chrome rings around the gauges, central locking, unique treadplates and floormats, a blue

hood, and a striking Innocent Blue Mica paint finish; each came with a certificate of authenticity, special badging (which carried the car's number) and a commemorative ignition key.

Of the 7500 produced, 3700 were destined for Europe, and Britain received 600 of them, priced at £21,100 apiece. Like the

Japanese market model, it featured Innocent Blue Mica coachwork, a two-tone black and blue interior, a blue soft-top and hood cover, and the six-speed gearbox - the first time the latter had been offered outside Japan; the UK model also came with ABS brakes.

Top Gear looked at the limited edition vehicle in its May 1999

A British brochure for the 10th Anniversary limited edition.

This is the 10th Anniversary model that Top Gear *tested. The magazine was full of praise for this latest variation, but only 600 of them were available in Britain (sales starting from 3 April). Note the tiny badge on the trailing edge of the front wing - it stated the car's limited edition number, and always appeared on the driver's side.*

The 500,000th MX-5, pictured in the Mazda Museum. Built for the American market, it was finished in Evolution Orange Mica, a colour that wasn't officially available in the States until the 2000 model year.

issue. Tom Stewart said: "The standard MX-5 already pretty much sets the standard for pin-sharp, balanced handling, but subtle chassis improvements on this model further improve the car's already accurate steering and superb cornering prowess. The firmer Bilsteins haven't eradicated the MX-5's slight skittishness over the bumps when pushed, but the car's still a hoot on a twisty road and the new six-speed 'box makes a big contribution. Use it properly and the motor will never be caught off guard."

America received 3150 of these special six-speed vehicles (where the colour was known as Sapphire Blue), and Australia took the remaining 150. Whereas home market sales began at the beginning of January 1999, export deliveries started during the spring. As in Japan, buyers were treated to a pair of blue-faced wristwatches.

Incidentally, on 8 February 1999, the 500,00th car was built - a US specification model finished in Evolution Orange Mica with a leather interior. This was an important landmark in the MX-5's history, prompting a special ceremony at the Ujina factory.

The home market & the NR Limited

There was very little change for the 2000 model year in Japan, although prices increased slightly - by the princely sum of 20,000 yen on all grades - from 1 October 1999. It was hardly a figure to worry about, and perhaps gave as good an indication as any of how competitive this sector of the market had become.

During December 1999, Mazda announced the NR Limited. Based on the manual 1.8 litre S grade, it featured Art Vin Red Mica bodywork, a parchment coloured leather interior with matching beige hood, polished 15-inch alloy wheels (they were the familiar five-spoke 6J x 15 rims, but buffed to look like those on the 10th Anniversary model), a front tower brace in body colour, and a few items borrowed from the VS, including the Bose stereo radio/CD unit, wood-rimmed Nardi steering wheel (plus the wooden gearknob and handbrake trim, all in a slightly darker material

This was the only Roadster on display at the 1999 Tokyo Show. It was joined by an RX-7 finished in the same colour, but it was the RX-EVOLV concept car that received most of the crowd's attention. This rotary-engined machine was later developed into the RX-8.

Japan's elegant NR Limited. A similar six-speed model was duly launched in Europe and the States, although all had subtle differences.

Interior of the NR Limited. Note the white faces on the gauges and the darker than usual wood on the steering wheel, gearknob and handbrake grip. All 500 cars had a six-speed transmission, as an automatic was not offered.

than usual), stainless treadplates, and remote central locking. A unique feature was the meter panel, which incorporated white-faced gauges with chrome finishing rings - definitely a glimpse into the future - and there was also fake wood trim on the centre console.

Limited to just 500 examples, the NR Limited was priced at 2,516,000 yen, or 2,566,000 yen with floormats and other necessities. Sales started from 18 January, and officially, no options were offered with the vehicle.

Car Graphic compared the sporty 1800RS with the Toyota MR-S in its January 2000 issue. It declared that the Toyota was great fun and dynamically hard to fault. However, as a long-term prospect, it would plump for the Mazda - no less a sports car, but with a distinct advantage in the practicality stakes. It was also felt to be the more attractive of the two, although, in all fairness, the author has noticed that an awful lot depends on the coachwork colour.

Y2K in America

The 2000 model year saw an extensive reshuffle in the Miata line. The base model continued, acquiring alloy wheels shod with 185/60 HR14 rubber, power-assisted steering, the exclusive three-spoke, leather-trimmed Nardi steering wheel, electrically adjusted door mirrors, power windows and an automatic aerial along the way, but it was now joined by an 'LS' grade.

The LS came with five-spoke

160

Cover from the American brochure for the 2000 model year Miata.

15-inch alloys, slightly wider, VR-rated tyres, a Torsen limited-slip differential, cruise control, the 200w Bose stereo system (with a cassette deck added as well), a tan leather interior and tan coloured soft-top, the Windblocker device, power door locks, and floormats. ABS brakes were available as an option on this model.

Naturally, with the higher standard specifications, increases in both weight and price could be expected - and there were. The base model was now 15kg (33lb) heavier at 1060kg (2332lb) and $21,245, while the new LS grade was 1082kg (2381lb) and $23,995.

In line with the revisions, the options were also changed. The base model could be upgraded via the Convenience Package (with cruise control, central locking, the Windblocker, and two additional door-mounted speakers) for $795, or with the $995 Suspension Package - but not both. The Suspension Package came with an uprated suspension, a front strut brace, Torsen lsd, and 15-inch alloy wheels. It was also available on the LS, but with the limited-slip differential and larger alloys already part of the standard specification, it was only $495 on that vehicle.

The 1AP Appearance Package continued unchanged, but the 2AP

A series of pages from the US catalogue, printed in September 1999.

option was deleted from the lists. Instead, the rear spoiler and foglights were priced individually, at $295 and $250 respectively. Other options included air conditioning ($900), automatic transmission ($900), ABS brakes ($550), a hard-top ($1500), mudguards ($125) and, for the base model, a Torsen lsd ($395), cassette deck ($250), the Windblocker ($150), and floormats, quoted at $80.

Dealers were also able to

The 2000 Miata Special Edition.

provide such goodies as a front mask (or 'bra', as it is affectionately known in the States), a tonneau cover, treadplates, a wooden dash kit, wooden gearknob, a chrome rear deck rack, and a purpose-made car cover.

In addition, at last, the signature gold bodywork colour - seen everywhere at the time of the second generation model's launch - was made available in the States, known in this market as Evolution Orange Mica. The other six coachwork colours continued unchanged, with black cloth for the interior on the base car, and tan leather for the LS. The hood was the same shade as the interior trim in all cases.

Peter Nunn compared a Miata LS with the new Toyota MR2 Spyder for *Automobile* magazine and concluded: "The Toyota puts up a good fight and is the value winner here. It's the more eco-friendly roadster, one that's strong on refinement, quality, and the ability to cover ground effortlessly. It's new and it's different, but the design is peculiar and space utilization is poor. As it has been since day one, the Miata is something special - to look at, to sit in, to drive, and to own. After two days of hard driving, the decision between the new Toyota and the Mazda was an easy one to make. The Miata is still magic."

At *Car & Driver*, too, the Miata won the battle, although only just on this occasion. Described as "the

Japanese roadster with more soul than James Brown," it was the car's styling and distinct advantage in the practicality stakes that handed the victory to the Mazda.

In all fairness, though, when *Road & Track* brought the two Japanese competitors together, it was a different story: Dennis Simanaitis (a long-term Miata owner) went for the MR2, while Douglas Kott voted for the Hiroshima machine. Both lapped

the Willow Springs race track within a fraction of a second of its rival, and each covered the standing-quarter in similar times (the Mazda in 16.1 seconds, the Toyota in 15.6). They went through the handling tests evenly matched, but the MR2 shone in the braking department. Ultimately, the Toyota won the day on a clear cut points decision, but it was noted: "Both the Miata and MR2 deserve to sell like hotcakes."

From the author's personal

experience of the two cars, he would have to agree with that closing statement. After a test drive, one can quickly establish that both are dynamically superb, and both are a lot of fun. In this case, a sale depends not so much on which car is 'better', but on which set of plus and minus points that come with such different designs are the most critical to the buyer.

The British 2000 model year

Prices were increased slightly for the 2000 season, meaning that the 1.6i was listed at £15,685, the 1.8i was £16,815, and the 1.8iS £18,790. In addition to the standard line-up, Mazda UK brought back the SE model, announced in mid-September 1999.

The SE (or MX-5 Special Edition to give it its proper title) was limited to 500 units, priced at £18,495 apiece. The 1.8 litre model came with Racing Green coachwork, a tan leather interior and matching hood, 15-inch alloys, power-assisted steering with a Nardi wood-rimmed wheel (complemented by a wooden gearknob and centre console trim), and electric windows.

As a matter of interest, Mazda UK sold 6411 MX-5s during the 1999 calendar year - 104 more than the previous annual total.

Including those destined for sale in Britain, no fewer than 23,255 vehicles were exported to Europe that year.

Corporate news

The start of 1999 saw a massive shift in exchange rates around the world. The introduction of the ECU in Europe led to the pound weakening against the yen, as Japan threw its support behind the new currency. From a peak of 240 yen to £1 in the autumn of 1998, the rate settled back to around 200 before moving quickly to 185 yen to £1 in the opening days of the new year.

However, despite the unfavourable rates, by 1999, after six fiscal years of recording an operational loss, Mazda was once

マーク・フィールズ
Mark Fields

Mark Fields - Mazda's new President - seen here with an RX-8 styling model.

The Miata Mono-Posto Concept that made its debut at the 2000 Los Angeles Show.

Finished in a striking Red Pearl Mica, the Mono-Posto Concept certainly attracted attention. The engine was modified to produce 190bhp at 6100rpm, with maximum torque quoted as 243lbft at 4100rpm. It was estimated that 0-60 could be covered in around six seconds!

again profitable. Good results in Europe had a lot to do with this turnaround in fortunes: figures released for January-June 1999 revealed MX-5 sales of 13,448 units - up 70 per cent on the same period in 1998.

December 1999 saw another change at the top, with Mark Fields taking over the reins from James Miller as Mazda's President. Born in 1961, Fields joined Ford in 1989, and quickly moved up the ranks. A proper car enthusiast, he first became attached to the Mazda marque in 1998. In an enlightening interview for the RJC, Fields revealed his plans to reduce the time involved between a design freeze and a new model entering production (which bodes well for some of Mazda's interesting prototypes unveiled recently), and his desire to allow the company to move in a uniquely Mazda direction - to encourage the engineers, designers and management to let Mazda's spirit and flair show in its products, rather than try and follow others in the chase for mainstream sales. It's a refreshing viewpoint, and one that the author supports wholeheartedly.

The Miata Mono-Posto

We'd seen the Club Racer, the M-Speedster and the M-Coupé based on the first generation model, but few were prepared for the Miata Mono-Posto Concept that appeared at the 2000 Los Angeles Show, although those attending the 1999

SEMA Show for aftermarket tuning had already been given a sneak preview.

Inspired by the legendary road racers of the 1950s, Tom Matano stated: "It has been designed for someone who prefers to be alone with the road, focused purely on driving." With only one seat (the meaning of *monoposto*), the driver didn't have much choice but to be alone! This was a pure driving machine: with a 190bhp turbocharged engine (the extra power and torque - all 243lbft of it - coming courtesy of HKS, the tuning specialist), wide, 18-inch wheels and tyres, and uprated braking and suspension, it was

much more than just a styling exercise.

To match the sporting exterior, the cockpit - perhaps the perfect word in this case - was also heavily modified, with a Sparco racing seat, Momo F1-style steering wheel and new instruments providing the finishing touches.

A few months later, the Americans were treated to another special, but this time one they could buy - the 2000 Miata Special Edition. Finished in Mahogany Mica with a parchment coloured leather interior and soft-top, this was basically the US equivalent to the NR Limited. The second Miata to reach American shores with the six-speed transmission (the first had been the 10th Anniversary model), only 3000 were built, priced at $25,055 apiece. In addition to the six-speed gearbox, it came with a Torsen limited-slip differential, polished five-spoke alloy wheels, the Appearance Package, foglights, a Nardi wood-rimmed steering wheel (with a matching gearknob and handbrake handle), white-faced gauges with chrome trim rings, and a top-of-the-range Bose stereo system incorporating a CD player, radio and cassette deck.

British Specials

March 2000 saw the launch of the £19,200 MX-5 Icon. This was basically the same model as Japan's NR Limited and America's Special Edition. As such, it came with a six-speed gearbox, unique Art Vin

The MX-5 Icon was the UK equivalent to the home market NR Limited.

The 1.6 litre MX-5 California, launched in May 2000. Like Britain's 1995 California Limited Edition, it had Sunburst Yellow paintwork, a black interior, and non-standard five-spoke alloys.

Conran and the MX-5 limited edition that carried his name.

A press photograph of the MX-5 Jasper Conran Platinum. The Platinum title derives from the name of the car's unique paint. With this in mind, the Classic Black title needs no explanation. Only 100 were finished in this silver colour, with 400 in black.

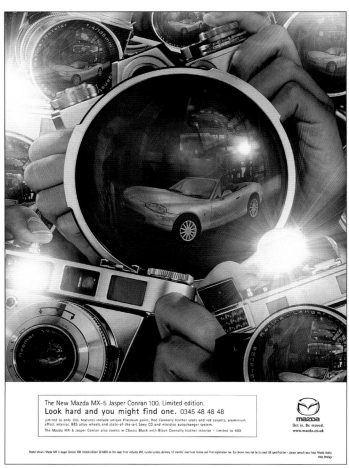

The New Mazda MX-5 Jasper Conran 100. Limited edition.
Look hard and you might find one. 0345 48 48 48
Limited to only 100, features include unique Platinum paint, Red Connolly leather seats and red carpets, aluminium effect interior, BBS alloy wheels and state-of-the-art Sony CD and minidisc autochanger system.
The Mazda MX-5 Jasper Conran also comes in Classic Black with Black Connolly leather interior – limited to 400.

Get in. Be moved.
www.mazda.co.uk

Tasteful advertising for the Jasper Conran model.

The MX-5 Isola - yet another limited edition from the UK. It came with a hard-top as part of the package, which is an ideal accessory for coping with British winters. Weighing in at 22kg (48lb), however, it really takes two people to put it on or remove it.

Red Mica paintwork, an oatmeal coloured leather interior and matching hood, polished 15-inch alloys, white gauges with chrome trim rings, a wood-rimmed Nardi steering wheel and gearknob, plus the standard features one would expect to find on the 1.8iS.

Mazda UK's Managing Director, Tim Tozer, said: "Mazda will only sell 750 Mazda MX-5 Icon models, so owners can add exclusivity to the long list of standard equipment and all the hallmarks of this super sports car. It oozes charm and style, it's fun to drive, and I'm delighted to say that it has already caught the eye of many buyers."

In May, the popular yellow coachwork colour made a welcome return on the MX-5 California. Based on the 1.6 litre model, it featured Sunburst Yellow paint with a black interior, special five-spoke alloy wheels, and a CD player. Only 500 were produced, selling at just £16,000 each - the same as the revised price for the standard 1.6i. By this time, the 1.8i was £17,200, while 1.8iS was quoted as £19,200.

A month later, the MX-5 Jasper Conran made its debut. In reality, this wasn't one limited edition, but two - the 100-off Jasper Conran Platinum and the 400-off Jasper Conran Classic Black. Conran, the famous designer, had the 1.8iS to work on, and gave it a highly distinctive interior. The Platinum version had a unique silver coachwork colour.

The Jasper Conran Platinum carried a red Connolly leather interior (which extended to the door panels and the hood cover) with red carpets - even the boot was trimmed in the same carpet, which played host to a custom-made luggage set on the £24,000 model. Other interior features included an aluminium and leather steering wheel, and aluminium finishes on the centre console, air vents, gearknob, handbrake grip and door pulls.

The Classic Black variant was trimmed in black Connolly hide with black carpets - plus the same unique aluminium pieces - but this £21,000 version lacked the luggage.

The facelifted MX-5, easily distinguished by its new headlights, air intake, and the apertures to each side of it (sometimes used as foglight housings). The latest headlamps on the NB2 are said to be some 20 per cent brighter than those of the original second generation model. Low beam performance is almost as good as main beam with standard halogen lights. Note also the 16-inch wheels and tyres. This is a left-hand drive version for Continental Europe, incidentally.

Both, however, came with a CD/MD stereo system, and 15-inch 12-spoke alloy wheels sourced from the BBS concern.

On 26 July 2000, yet another limited edition model was launched - the MX-5 Isola. This was a 1.6 litre model in Classic Red, but with the added bonus of a body coloured hard-top and five-spoke alloy wheels thrown in for the same price as the standard 1.6i. Only 500 were made available.

Interestingly, despite this flurry of limited edition models, Mazda UK's MX-5 sales fell to 5199 for the year 2000. Although this represented a drop of more than 1200 units on the previous record-breaking season, it should be borne in mind that sales in Britain during the early 1990s were hovering around 20 per cent of this figure. Including those sold in the UK, a total of 19,583 MX-5s were exported to Europe that year.

Major changes for the Roadster

In May 2000, the MX-5 was officially recognised in the *Guinness Book of Records* with 'The World's Largest Production of Lightweight Open Two-Seater Sports Car'. However, Mazda was not prepared to rest on its laurels and, on 18 July that year, the Hiroshima concern announced a major facelift for the Roadster.

The press release read: "Here's good news for lovers of lightweight open two-seater sports cars. The best just got better. Mazda Motor Corporation's new Roadster, just introduced at Mazda Anfini and other selected Mazda dealers throughout Japan, has a powerful new 1.8 litre engine, increased body rigidity, and a number of exterior and interior enhancements.

"Since the launch of the original Roadster in September 1989, Mazda's engineers have continued to embrace the 'Oneness Between Car And Driver' philosophy for the model, aiming at providing drivers with a refreshing feel of open car driving and distinctive styling. Generating a new market for lightweight, open two-seat sports cars, Mazda has sold over 565,000 units of the Roadster worldwide since 1989. The Roadster was recognized recently as the world's top-selling two-seater sports car by *Guinness World Records* .

"Incorporating a series of significant improvements into the engine, body and suspension system, the new Roadster achieves 'Oneness Between Car And Driver' at an even higher level. Monthly sales volume in Japan is expected to be approximately 500 units."

The release went on to describe the salient points:

New dynamic styling for a sporty, high-grade look
Mazda has revamped the exterior and interior to reflect the company's design theme, 'Contrast In Harmony', resulting in an even

sportier and more forceful look.

The front air intake opening incorporates the 'five-point grille' for the distinctive Mazda family appearance. Slimmer headlamps create a sharp and stylish impression.

The headlamps consist of multi-reflector-type high beam lamps and projector-type low beam lamps. Additionally, the rear combination lamps incorporate a new design that give the turn-flasher compartment a transparent look.

Instrument panel gauges incorporate a white coloured meter panel, a shiny metal frame and an amber illuminated lamp. The re-designed door trims lend a sporty and sophisticated feel.

The RS model, designed for better handling performance, features a black interior. The [new] RS-II model features a two-toned interior colour: black and red.

Driving pleasure that gives the feeling of 'Oneness Between Car And Driver'
The Roadster delivers driving pleasure that gives the feel of Oneness Between Car And Driver, which is known as Mazda's 'Dynamic DNA', a development theme common among Mazda's products. The Roadster conveys precise steering and handling, responsive and linear braking, composed and confident ride, and linear and lively performance.

The new Roadster also incorporates improvements to its engine, body and suspension and, as the symbol of the Mazda brand, delivers further improved driving pleasure.

Improved engine performance
The 1.8 litre engine now incorporates the S-VT mechanism that optimizes the open/close timing of the intake valves from low to high rpm ranges. Additionally, the improved intake/exhaust system provides smoother accelerating performance up to the high rpm range and attains a sporty and pleasant engine sound. [Maximum power has been increased to 160bhp at 7000rpm, with torque output enhanced to 125lbft at 5500rpm.]

More rigid body, improved suspension & newly-adopted tyres
Components that contribute to body rigidity, such as the body frame and crossmembers, have undergone painstaking improvements. The more rigid body results in more solid handling, a smoother ride, and an overall higher quality driving experience.

The RS and RS-II models, which were designed with an emphasis on power and acceleration, are now equipped with 205/45 R16 tyres and lightweight 16-inch aluminium wheels with flat flanges.

The body of the RS and RS-II models incorporates reinforcements such as newly-added truss members for substantially increased rigidity.

The RS and RS-II models are equipped with a new type of damper

The latest 1.8 litre BP-VE (RS) engine. The S-VT mechanism featured continuous phase variable valve timing to enhance response throughout the rev range. The phase of the intake valve timing to the crank angle is changed continuously in relation to hydraulic pressure by a pen-type actuator, controlled by a computer that calculates the timing. The S-VT system inhibits air intake countercurrents during high load, low rotation periods by closing the intake valve early, to improve low speed torque by increasing charging effiency. Conversely, in high load, high speed situations, the intake valve is closed later, improving output by taking maximum advantage of the inertia of the air being taken in. In medium load operation, the intake valve opens early to expand valve overlap, increasing exhaust gas diffusion and decreasing pumping loss.

manufactured by Bilstein that has additional valves for controlling the rebound side only. This is the first time these dampers, which contribute to improved driving dynamics, have been offered in Japan.

Enhanced brakes
Enlarged brake components provide improved braking performance with a more responsive feel. Models equipped with 16-inch tyres have larger brake discs, and the brakes on models equipped with 14- or 15-inch tyres have oversized master cylinders and boosters.

For more precise braking, a four-wheel, ABS-enhanced, electronically-controlled braking force distribution (EBD) system, which automatically optimizes the distribution of braking force to match the front and rear load when the brakes are applied, is now available either standard or optional, depending on the model.

Improved seat structure
The seats have been enhanced to provide better support for the shoulder, lumbar, and side areas. This provides drivers with driving pleasure that gives the feel of oneness between car and driver.

More convenience in day-to-day driving
To ensure that the new sports car is enjoyable to drive on a daily basis, the Roadster features an innovative upgradeable audio

The 1.6 litre unit continued in a number of markets around the world, but it was not given the benefit of the S-VT mechanism.

system and a re-designed centre console.

The audio system contains separable audio components. This makes it easy to add more functions in the future, such as a CD changer or an MD player. This audio system configuration shows a new concept that the user can add to the audio system new components including the advanced audio appliance that supports the digital music distribution systems. This Mazda-original audio system provides a new level of post-purchase extensibility.

The size of the centre console box has been increased to acommodate up to six Cds.

The shape and location of the cupholders and ashtray have been modified to make them easier to use. It is also possible to remove the ashtray and use the resulting space as a storage compartment for small objects or another cupholder.

A keyless entry system, including a trunk-lid opener, is available as standard or as an option on certain models. This makes the trunk, which is large enough to accommodate two golf bags, even more convenient.

Enhanced safety

Standard equipment on all models now includes seatbelts with pretensioners and load limiters, as well as the previously offered Supplemental Restraint System (SRS) airbags on the driver and

The facelifted interior, with its new gauges, steering wheel design (the three-spoke Nardi wheel was also subtly revised, with the Mazda badge finding its way onto the centre boss), seats, and storage arrangements. This is an automatic 1600M for the Japanese market.

The door trim and furniture was also changed as part of the 'NB2' facelift. This is a home market VS model, so features tan panels instead of the more common black items.

passenger sides.

A few things deserve further explanation, such as the changes to the 1.8 litre twin-cam engine and the body structure, wheel types

and sizes (plus the tyres fitted to them), uprated braking systems, and the new gauges.

The 1.8 litre power unit - given the BP-VE (RS) code - received a number of modifications, including

Revisions to the tail-end were more subtle than those at the front of the car, although the new rear combination lights were easy to spot. Again, this is a Japanese-spec vehicle (a 1.6 litre SP), but the same basic design was adopted for all markets. The script on the 'Roadster' badge remained in black, as it had since the launch of the second generation model.

adoption of S-VT (Sequential Valve Timing), a hike in the compression ratio (via new pistons), and subtle refinements in the ignition, intake and exhaust systems. For the home market, power increased to 160bhp at 7000rpm, with maximum torque quoted as 125lbft at 5500rpm.

Buyers in most countries could now specify a six-speed gearbox with the 1.8 litre car. Ratios in Japan were carried over on all transmissions, as were those for the five-speed models destined for US and European markets. Six-speed cars inherited Japan's internal ratios, but the 3.91:1 final-drive was only used in America - European specifications listed a 3.64:1 ratio.

Incidentally, all markets had the same cogs in the automatic transmission (2.450 on first, 1.450 on second, a direct third, and 0.730 on top), with a 4.10 final-drive on the 1.8, or 4.30 on 1.6 litre vehicles.

The body was significantly stronger than before. To quote a different press release: "Additional reinforcements have been made to the body throughout the vehicle. The front and rear inner side sills have a larger cross-section and are made from a thicker plate, the rear floor frame is thicker, and the tunnel gussets have been changed from a short-skirt to a deep-skirt type. These enhancements improved bending rigidity by 13 per cent and

torsional rigidity by 6 per cent compared to the 10th Anniversary version, which was the top performance model in the series.

"Exclusive body reinforcements have been added for the 1.8 litre Sport model [the UK equivalent to Japan's RS grade]. The new front suspension tower bar has been reinforced at the head of the suspension tower, the tower bar strengthened, and a tower bar mount adopted. In addition, corner gussets have been added to the rear bulkhead, as well as a trans-member under the floor and a tunnel member behind it, and two rear cross bars added to the rear performance bar. Through these improvements, bending rigidity is 16 per cent greater than the 10th Anniversary version, while torsional rigidity is improved by 22 per cent."

Satoru Akana was in charge of the latest styling updates, introduced purely to freshen up the car's appearance in a bid to revive falling sales in Japan, and to make it more appealing to male buyers. Knowing of his love for the original MX-5, the author asked Tom Matano what he thought of the design. He replied: "The lines have simply got more muscular as engine power has increased. It's a perfect piece of evolution."

Regarding the wheels, steel rims were now something of a rarity, but some markets still received

them on the cheapest grade. With a 5.5J width, they came fitted with 185/60 HR14 rubber; the 14-inch five-spoke alloys (6J rim width) were shod with the same tyres.

The 15-inch alloys were also carried over (6J x 15, with a similar five-spoke design to the 14-inch items), and these came with 195/50-section VR-rated tyres. A new five-spoke alloy wheel with a sharper appearance was introduced to give a 6.5J x 16 option, and this rim was fitted with 205/45 WR16 tyres.

As for the brakes, cars fitted with 16-inch wheels and tyres inherited a larger set of discs - 270mm (10.6in.) up front, with 276mm (10.9in.) diameter items at the rear. However, the discs continued to be ventilated at the front only, and, whilst ABS was standard in some markets, it was an option in others.

Moving inside the car, perhaps the biggest change was the adoption of white-faced gauges in the meter panel, complete with chrome trim rings around the speedo and tachometer. Mazdaspeed had offered these for some time, and they were a key feature on the NR Limited (and its numerous offspring offered in export markets). White in the daytime with black calibrations, at night they appeared black with amber and red markings - attractive, but, more importantly, very effective in service.

Other less obvious interior modifications included a new

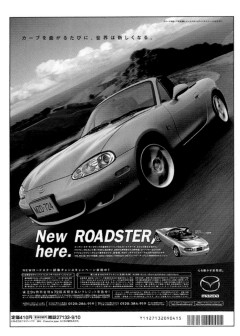

Japanese advertising for the facelifted Roadster, dating from the time of launch.

The author bought this six-speed VS model in Supreme Blue Mica on the first day of sales. Being a VS, it has tan leather trim and a matching hood. It corresponds exactly to original catalogue specifications, and this was its first outing after delivery.

storage arrangement in the transmission tunnel area, modified door trim panels, a revised steering wheel design (for both three- and four-spoke items), and new seats incorporating a taller, integral headrest.

The home market

Following the latest revisions to the vehicle, the grades were reshuffled. The 1.6 litre engine still developed 125bhp at 6500rpm, along with 105lbft of torque at 5000rpm. It was available with either a five-speed manual or four-speed automatic gearbox (the latter coming with ABS brakes as standard), but with the basic model gone, the M became the entry-level Roadster.

Priced at 1,839,000 yen (or 1,982,000 yen in automatic guise), the 1600M had power-assisted steering, 14-inch alloy wheels, air conditioning, power door mirrors and windows, and an electric aerial included in the price. The SP was the only other 1.6 litre car, and that

came in at 1,990,000 or 2,040,000 yen for the five-speed manual and the automatic respectively. The extra money gave the buyer a Torsen limited-slip differential (manual vehicles only), ABS brakes, a Nardi steering wheel, the Windblocker, and remote control central locking.

The 1.8 litre range was more extensive. The 1800S was roughly the same as the 1600SP, although ABS brakes were standard on the automatic model only. The Windblocker and remote locking became optional, although additional features included a leather-wrapped gearknob, and an AM/FM stereo radio with two speakers.

The RS had 16-inch wheels

The interior of the VS. All cars now had white gauge faces with red pointers, but again, the needles on six-speed manual models started at the six o'clock position, whilst those on other vehicles started at the eight o'clock position; the calibrations were also different. Note the latest steering wheel design, seen here with a wooden rim (standard on the VS grade). The leather-wrapped wheel looked similar, apart from the obvious difference in materials, although that for the RS-II followed the same two-tone pattern as that established on the 10th Anniversary model.

Pages from the Japanese catalogue covering the 1.6 litre models and the 1800S.

An interesting catalogue shot that perfectly illustrates the sculptured curves of the MX-5. The light blue shade (Crystal Blue Metallic) used in most of the publicity material for the new model won the Japan Fashion Colour Association's '2001 Auto Colour Award'.

Section of the Japanese brochure devoted to the RS and the new RS-II grade, with its striking interior. Note the Bilstein dampers, additional body reinforcements, the 16-inch wheels and tyres, and the uprated braking system. The car on the right is an RS, as the RS-II was not available in either of the blue shades on offer.

and tyres, a limited-slip differential, uprated suspension with front strut bar and Bilstein dampers, a Nardi leather steering wheel and gearknob, stainless treadplates, an AM/FM radio and rear mudguards, while the RS-II came with a similar

specification but red cloth seats, and the Nardi wheel had a two-tone finish. In addition, the remote control locking, Bose sound system and Windblocker were standard.

The VS was the "luxury" model, with 14-inch five-spoke alloys, a

Torsen lsd, tan leather trim with matching hood and hood cover, a Nardi wood-rimmed steering wheel, a wooden gearknob and handbrake grip, the Windblocker, stainless scuff plates, power door locks with remote control (plus chromed

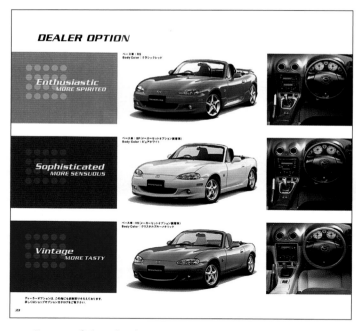

Some of the dealer options available in Japan during the 2000/2001 season.

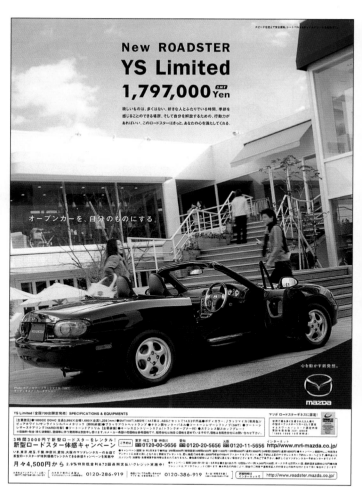

Advertising for the YS Limited, launched in Japan during December 2000. Only 700 were made available, although there were three exterior body colour choices. This car is finished in Black Mica, a shade unique to this model.

interior release handles), and the Bose radio/CD player.

As for prices, the six-speed S was listed at 2,178,000 yen (or 2,226,000 yen with the four-speed ECT), while the manual only RS was 2,328,000 yen; the new RS-II, with its striking red and black interior (also available with the six-speed gearbox only) was priced at 2,437,000 yen, and the leather-trimmed VS was 2,390,000 yen, and 48,000 yen more if specified with automatic transmission.

Paintwork choices included Crystal Blue Metallic, Sunlight Silver Metallic, Classic Red, Supreme Blue Mica, Pure White and Brilliant Black. The RS-II was not available in the two blue shades, and the VS had to do without the red and silver options, but gained a unique Grace Green Mica colour.

The YS Limited (the YS standing for Youthful & Sports) was officially announced on the 22 December 2000, although RCOJ members were given a sneak preview at the club's Christmas party. Based on the 1600M, it was aimed at younger buyers, mainly because of attractive pricing, but also due to its unique interior.

While the body could be finished in Black Mica (a special paintwork colour, only available on the YS Limited), Pure White or Sunlight Silver Metallic, the interior was finished in black with a number of titanium accents. A two-tone black and titanium finish was adopted on the Nardi steering wheel and gearknob, the centre console panel and door trim featured titanium-style inserts, and there was even titanium coloured stitching on the seats.

Other items included blackout headlamps (the bezel portion of the headlights was black-coated), stainless treadplates, and remote control central locking. Only 700 were made available, priced at 1,797,000 yen for the basic five-speed model (1,828,000 yen with a radio), or 1,940,000 yen for the automatic version.

The new model in Europe

The changes announced in Japan during the summer of 2000 were eventually introduced in European markets the following spring. All of the exterior and interior enhancements were adopted, along with the structural and mechanical

174

improvements. The six-speed gearbox was now part of the standard specification (at least on the 1.8i Sport model), and an automatic transmission - available from August 2001 - was also listed in a bid to try and extend the car's appeal.

With a 10.0:1 compression ratio, the 1.8 litre engine produced 146bhp at 7000rpm in European trim, along with 124lbft of torque. This was enough to endow the vehicle with a 0-60 time of around 8.5 seconds, and a top speed approaching 130mph (208kph) - the five- and six-speed models were very similar. Automatic versions came with 139bhp at 6500rpm, incidentally, which combined to give an 11 second 0-60 increment, and a maximum of 119mph (190kph).

The 1.6 litre power unit had a 9.4:1 c/r, giving 110bhp at 6500rpm, and 99lbft of torque. Linked to a five-speed gearbox (an automatic transmission was not available with the smaller engine), the official 0-60 figure was 9.7 seconds, whilst top speed was almost identical to that of the automatic 1.8 litre car.

In Britain, Europe's largest market, four grades were available: the 1.6i, priced at £14,995 on the road, the 1.8i (£15,995), the 1.8i Auto (at £16,995) and the 1.8i Sport, which had a sticker price of £17,995.

The basic 1.6 litre model (which weighed in at 1035kg, or 2277lb) had steel wheels shod with 185/60

The new model as it appeared in Europe. This is actually a German registered car with the latest 16-inch wheels and tyres.

Tail of the same vehicle. Note the new rear combination light design. Lighting was quite different for the main markets (America, Europe and Japan): US cars had no rear foglight, so the inner sections on the combination lamp were clear on both sides, like those for the home market. All had orange front side markers, but the rears were red on American- and Japanese-spec vehicles, and orange on cars destined for Europe. Another difference concerned the side repeater lights (situated between the front wheelarch and the door), which were not fitted on US cars, but standard on European and Japanese models.

HR14 tyres, engine speed-sensing power steering, cloth trim, power windows, a stereo radio/cassette with two speakers, dual airbags,

Interior of the European MX-5 in left-hand drive guise. The white gauge faces and revised steering wheel (with the Mazda corporate symbol in the centre, and the Nardi badge moving from that position to the lower part of the wheel) can be clearly seen in this picture.

suspension was available as an option on this 1100kg (2420lb) model, as was a cassette player.

Coachwork colours for Europe included Brilliant Black, Racing Green Mica, Supreme Blue Mica, Eternal Red, Crystal Blue Metallic and Sunlight Silver Metallic, incidentally. Trim was either available in black cloth, or black leather.

News fom the Antipodes

Sales in Australia were at last picking up. After a disastrous 1997 season, in which only 118 MX-5s were imported, 1586 examples made the journey from Japan in 1998. In 1999, this figure dropped to 1263, and again to 1106 in 2000, but it was a very different story to that of three years earlier.

Another view of the German car, this time with hood erected. The styling changes, especially when combined with the bigger wheels and tyres, gave the MX-5 a far more aggressive look.

remote fuel door and bootlid releases, and an alarm/immobilizer.

The manual 1.8 litre car weighed 30kg (66lb) more in its cheapest form, but only the heavier engine and a Windblocker accounted for the difference. The 1.8i Auto had the same basic specification as the five-speed model, although the automatic transmission added a further 15kg (33lb) to the vehicle's kerb weight.

The six-speed 1.8i Sport added 16-inch alloy wheels shod with 205/

45 rubber, ABS brakes (with the larger diameter discs), a limited-slip differential, front foglights (those at the rear were standard on all cars to comply with the law), black leather trim (including on the Nardi steering wheel and gearknob), seat warmers, remote control central locking, chromed inner door handles, stainless treadplates, electrically-adjusted and heated door mirrors, a modular radio/CD unit with four speakers and an electric aerial, and rear mudguards. The uprated RS-type

For 2001, the Australians had two basic models to choose from - one with a hard-top and one without. They did, however, get a very high specification vehicle as standard. Powered by the latest 155bhp version of the 1.8 litre engine, it came with a six-speed gearbox (final-drive ratio 3.64:1), 6.5J x 16 five-spoke alloys shod with wide 205/45 rubber, power-assisted steering, ABS brakes, Bilstein dampers, a front tower bar, foglights, the elegant Nardi leather-wrapped steering wheel and matching gearknob, power windows and door mirrors, remote control central locking, a four-speaker radio/CD player, the Windblocker device, and an engine immobilizer.

Cover from the US brochure for the 2001 model year Mazda range. Note the white faces on the instruments, which were soon joined by some red faces in the camp - a blunder in the specifications (namely an engine with "155bhp") was to cause some embarrassment.

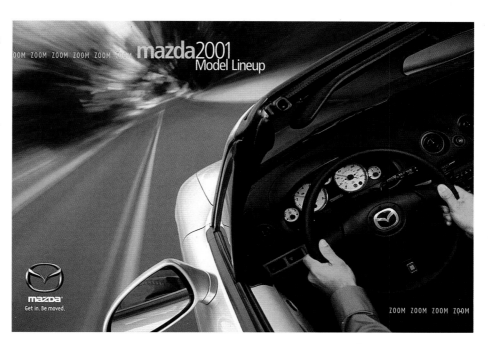

Writing for *Wheels* magazine, Peter McKay noticed a tendency for the suspension to bottom out, and also stated: "In any case, the ride is not pleasant as it judders and bangs and leaps over the bumps." However, in most other areas, he was quite complementary about the car, and, after comparing it with the MR2 Spyder, observed: "Chasing the rival MX-5 broader demographic, Toyota has expressed higher volume aspirations for the MR2 Spyder (with younger buyers and more females), built on reduced price and easy-to-drive sequential shift.

"But it won't grab those people seeking an affordable, traditional sports car. The MX-5 has that parcel tidily wrapped up. The Mazda's classical looks, cult status and excellent retained values - along with its acclaimed dynamics - give it the nod.

"The MR2 Spyder is better than the MX-5 in some ways, but lacks the lineage - and the right gearbox - to make it a winner here. Then again, I'm not a PlayStation regular or Gen Xer …"

Launched with a tag of $41,190, by summer 2001, the standard six-speed model was priced at $43,485, with the hard-top version coming in at $3000 more. Although the hard-top could be bought separately, there was only actually one real option - air conditioning, priced at $1950. In addition, for those not happy with the factory engine, Mazda Australia's

motorsport section prepared a Turbo 'SP' version which developed a healthy 190bhp.

Standard colours for Australia included Classic Red, Grace Green, Supreme Blue (a dark shade), Sunlight Silver, Polar White, Brilliant Black, and Crystal Blue Metallic. The hood and cloth interior trim were available in black only.

The US market

For the 2001 model year (announced in September 2000), the American line-up was revised once again to bring it in line with the Japanese market's cars. Apart from the exterior and interior changes, more power was promised (155bhp was quoted in early catalogues and publicity material), and the six-speed gearbox made a welcome appearance as a cost option.

The base model, with black cloth trim, inherited the 15-inch wheels and tyres, Windblocker and floormats from the previous season's LS, but also gained air conditioning, an anti-theft system (with engine immobiliser), and foglights. Surprisingly, however, the price went down to $21,180,

meaning it was $65 cheaper than the previous year's car, despite the additional standard equipment.

The LS, now $23,930, had these new features to augment those already found on the top model, plus the new five-spoke 16-inch wheels shod with ultra-low profile 205/45 tyres, remote control locking, a front strut brace, and what used to be the 1AP Appearance Package - no longer listed as an option. Incidentally, all cars with 16-inch rims acquired the uprated braking system described earlier.

The base model could be upgraded via the Convenience Package (given the CV1 code, it came with remote keyless entry system, power door locks, cruise control, and door-mounted tweeter speakers), priced at $795. The Suspension Package came with an uprated suspension with Bilstein shock absorbers, a front tower bar, Torsen lsd, 16-inch wheels and tyres, and larger brakes. Listed at $1025, the suspension pieces were also available on the LS grade for a very reasonable $395.

Interestingly, Patrick Bedard at *Car & Driver* stated: "The Suspension Package, and

Engine bay of the American Miata LS grade, photographed by Ken Hoyle at the 2000 San Francisco Show, held in November that year. Note the new strut brace design, the same as that used on the home market's RS models. (Courtesy Ken Hoyle)

particularly its grippy tyres, give the Miata a quick-steering, glued-to-the-road feel. Grip matched that of the last test Miata (also 'Packaged') at 0.88g. A good number. But zesty little drop-tops are less about heroic cornering numbers and more about jaunty drifts at recreational speeds. The sticky 16-inch tyres are stingy with their drift angles, even when you blur the scenery. And the Bilsteins hammer over frost-heaved roads. If you're thinking of autocrosses, choose the Suspension Package without hesitation, but for fun and frolic according to the original sports car formula, we strongly prefer the base car."

Other options remained pretty much unchanged, with the obvious exception of those items adopted as part of the standard specification for 2001, although the cassette player was now $150 for all cars (it was previously more expensive on the base vehicle but standard on the LS). There was one interesting addition, though - the option of the six-speed manual gearbox for the LS grade, priced at $650.

Americans had some interesting accessories to choose from: a CD autochanger, front

Two double-page spreads from a US brochure put together to advertise the 2001 model year Miata. Note the chrome door handles on the LS grade - a feature added for the 2001 season.

178

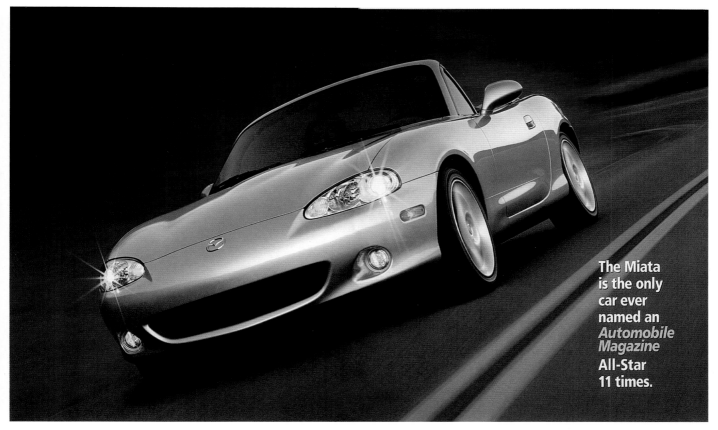

The Miata
is the only
car ever
named an
*Automobile
Magazine*
All-Star
11 times.

The 2001 model year Miata LS.

mask, a tonneau cover, treadplates, a wooden dash kit, wooden gearknob, wooden handbrake grip, chrome deck rack, a racing-style fuel filler, front and rear mudguards, a car cover, and even an engine block heater for those living in cold climates.

The colour and trim chart was slightly different to that of the previous season, incidentally, with White being replaced by Pure White, Highlight Silver Metallic being superceded by Sunlight Silver Metallic, and Twilight Blue Mica giving way to Midnight Blue Mica. By far the biggest change was the loss of Evolution Orange Mica in favour of Crystal Blue Metallic. Trim was still available in either black cloth or tan leather for all of the coachwork hues.

The conclusion at the bottom of the *Car & Driver* test read: "The

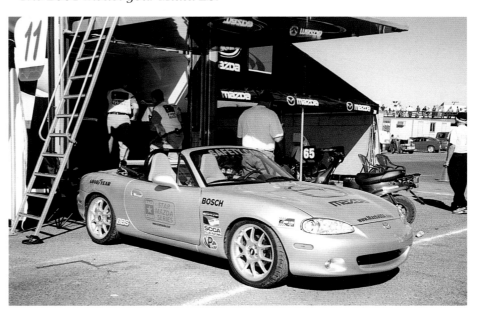

The MX-5 has continued to entertain race-goers all over the world. This Miata was being used as a Safety Car during a summer 2001 meeting at Sears Point in California. (Courtesy Ken Hoyle)

179

Miata is better than ever." And most people agreed. As Ann Job of the *San Jose Mercury News* observed: "The new roadster just keeps getting better … In a slalom, back-to-back test drives of last year's Miata and this year's LS with Suspension Package showed how much more taut and confidence-inspiring this 2001 model is. As you'd expect, I made better time in the new car, too."

At *Motor Trend* , following a comparison test between the standard Miata and an MR2 Spyder, it was noted: "The Miata and MR2 Spyder are the types of cars real enthusiasts spend their weekends driving around in - just because … The driving sophisticate will get more out of the MR2 Spyder, but the Miata wins in the giggle department."

However, there was an embarrassing moment for Mazda in the States when it was found that the boost in horsepower was nowhere near as large as that advertised - in Japan, yes, but America, no. With a 10.0:1 compression ratio, the power stated in US brochures was quickly revised to 142bhp at 7000rpm, with maximum torque put at 125lbft at 5000rpm.

This makes Patrick Bedard's comments, made at the start of the year, all the more interesting: "Zero to 60 clocked in at 8.1 seconds [with the five-speed car], a half-second behind the old model in the July 2000 issue. A second 2001,

with the optional six-speed, hit 60 in 7.9 seconds, still not up to past zip. Both new cars were hampered by green engines and a modest weight increase from reinforcements added to stiffen the body, but it's apparent that 12 or 13 of the promised 15 extra horses weren't answering roll call."

Meanwhile, to avoid possible legal problems, the company contacted its clients and offered to buy back all of the early 2001 models (around 3500 cars) should the owner feel disgruntled after hearing the news. If the owner decided to keep the vehicle, as an apology, they were offered free servicing for the rest of the warranty period. In the end, this potentially damaging mistake was turned into a public relations triumph.

A total of 19,369 Miatas were shipped to the States in 2000, with a further 1349 making their way to Canada.

The present & the future

The Web-Tuned Factory - a way of ordering a custom-built Roadster via the Internet - was launched in February 2001. Customers could access a massive amount of information, delete or add items to get the exact specification they wanted, and even arrange trade-ins and credit in the comfort of their own home. The Web-Tuned Roadster had a total of 4160 combinations to choose from, including Sunburst Yellow coachwork (albeit limited to 450

people) and Sony stereo equipment. For the time being at least, this service was only available for clients living in Japan.

A catalogue issued in spring 2001 confirmed that specifications and colour schemes had been carried over on the standard range. In fact, apart from a new cover picture and an updated line in the keyless central locking specification, it was the same brochure as the one dated July 2000. Prices were carried over, and the 'Shop Options' booklet was also pretty much the same as the original one.

At the 2001 Tokyo Auto Salon, the Mazdaspeed stand featured the 'MPS' Roadster (that particular story is covered later on); a few months later, in May, there was the introduction of another tuned MX-5 - the RS-based limited edition Mazdaspeed Roadster.

Restricted to just 200 units, it featured Starry Blue Mica coachwork, a colour-coded aerodynamic body kit and light trim, gold-painted, 16-inch alloy wheels, a new exhaust system (both to improve efficiency and provide a sporting exhaust note), adjustable dampers (with four settings), uprated engine and differential mounting rubbers, a four-speaker Kenwood stereo, and a number of sporty touches for the interior, such as a carbonfibre-style centre console trim piece, blue coloured gauge trim rings and blue stitching on the seats, steering wheel,

Brochure showing the Aero Package offered by Japanese dealers for the 2001 season. Television commercials from the time showed a plastic model kit box with a standard Roadster on the lid, which opened to reveal movie footage of a real vehicle being driven by an attractive young lady.

gearknob and gearlever gaiter. This special Mazdaspeed vehicle sold for 2,548,000 yen.

After making its debut at the 2001 Chicago Show, the Americans eventually received the Miata Special Edition during the spring. Featuring British Racing Green

The options available on the Web-Tuned Roadster in more detail.

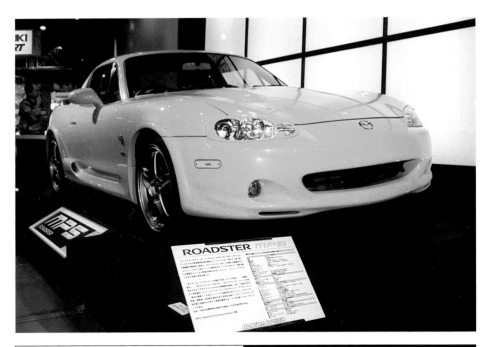

The Mazdaspeed MPS Roadster at the 2001 Tokyo Auto Salon. The 200bhp car was developed under Mazda stalwart, Hirotaka Tachibana, and featured a number of interesting modifications, such as aluminium brake discs, adjustable suspension, and a central exhaust.

より深化した領域へ。

MEET THE POTENTIAL

MAZDASPEED ROADSTER 限定生産200台。

ロードスターのドライビングプレジャーをよりダイナミックに研ぎ澄ますために。スポーツを知り尽くしたマツダスピードのノウハウを惜しみなく注いで、いまMAZDASPEED ROADSTERが生まれた。人馬一体の楽しさをさらに磨き上げたその走りは、マツダのDNAに潜む走りのポテンシャルの高さを証明するものに他ならない。

May 2001 saw the introduction of the limited edition Mazdaspeed Roadster. Only 200 units were made available.

paintwork, the $26,195 SE (limited to 3000 units) came with the familiar 16-inch alloy wheels but with a polished finish, a tan leather interior with matching hood, a Nardi wood-rimmed steering wheel (a real rarity in the States), wood trim on the six-speed transmission's gearknob and handbrake grip, a wood-look centre console panel, stainless treadplates, a polished aluminium fuel filler cover, and special badging and floormats. Incidentally, by this time, the base model had gone up to $21,660, while the leather-trimmed LS was $24,410.

There has been little sign of the MX-5 losing any of its popularity, as Mazda has been very careful not to lose sight of the original LWS concept, whilst still keeping the vehicle contemporary - Kijima-san is adamant that this element, the car's very spirit, will never change.

However, forthcoming noise regulations are of great concern; while the automatic versions will comply with little problem, something will have to be done to quieten the manual cars. Current indications point towards the third generation model arriving in 2004. Already, the company is asking RCOJ members for their thoughts on what they would like to see changed and, just as importantly, what they don't want changed. For the record, the author requested the option of a semi-automatic transmission of some sort: I prefer a manual gearbox, but my wife is a two-pedal driver. With a sequential gearbox, we could both enjoy the car ...

The 2001 Tokyo Show
One month before the Tokyo Show, in September 2001, Mazda announced its intentions to run a one-make series in Japan for Roadster owners. Starting in May 2002, it was to be contested over four rounds by 1.6 litre 'NR-A' cars, which could also be registered for road use.

instincts

Perfect handling comes naturally.

this is a roadster with perfect balance.

1 3 5

2 4 6 R

Rain or shine, the Mazda MX-5's handling is legendary. We can thank its double-wishbone suspension for that, but now there's also a hugely stiffer chassis for this fine suspension to push against. Link this set-up with classic roadster 50:50 weight distribution and you have a recipe for natural agility and bend-straightening handling. The Mazda MX-5's renowned road holding is boosted by larger tyres on the Sport model for extra grip. For looks as well as grip, clip on the stylish hardtop (optional) for winter snugness.

Superb handling, whichever way you look at it. Coupled with an ultra-stiff chassis, the Mazda MX-5 features classic double-wishbone suspension all round.

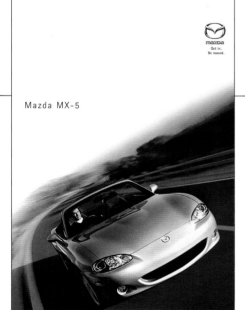

Mazda MX-5

The cover (left) and a double-page spread from the UK catalogue of May 2001. The car featured in the action photography is a 1.8i Sport model, which had the strut tower bar shown in the ghosted drawing. As European specifications were firmed up, it was noted that all models now came fitted with ABS brakes (incorporating the EBD system) as standard, although there was no change in vehicle pricing.

Modifications for the NR-A model included an uprated suspension with Bilstein shock absorbers, 15-inch wheels and tyres, larger brakes, increased cooling efficiency (through a larger radiator capacity), reinforced engine and differential mountings, performance rods and other components to stiffen the bodyshell, a limited-slip differential, special seats, and a Nardi steering wheel. For racing, the owner is required to order the Mazdaspeed roll cage, four-point harnesses, and front and rear towing hooks.

The 35th Tokyo Show saw the debut of the production RX-8 and the elegant Atenza saloon, but there was another MPS (Mazda Performance Series) Roadster. The first one had been shown at the Tokyo Auto Salon earlier in the year, and it gave a good idea of what was to come. It was one of two prototypes built to explore the viability of more powerful variants, whilst a third had been produced by Ford in Dearborn, featuring a 210bhp three-litre V6.

This latest MPS car featured a 1.9 litre four (which produced 197bhp at 7000rpm, and 145lbft of

Advertising for the Tsukuba 4-hour Endurance Race - an annual event for Roadster enthusiasts. It is hoped to introduce the race to American shores in the future.

torque at 6000rpm) linked to a six-speed manual transmission. The heavily modified body sat on 17-inch wheels and tyres, while the interior featured a black metallic dashboard and a mix of black buckskin and Alcantara fabric for the seating. Sources close to the project stated that, with any luck, the MPS series would reach Mazda showrooms in the spring, but there was still no sign of it at the time of writing.

Meanwhile, the Americans had already announced the 2002 model year changes in September - basically, there was nothing major outlined for the Miata, although

The NR-A pictured at Tokyo Disneyland, the venue for the press preview of Mazda's Tokyo Show exhibits. At this event an official announcement was made that the rotary engined RX-8 would go into production.

the aerodynamic body kit reverted to the options list, with two Appearance Packages (AP1 had a large front airdam, side skirts and rear mudguards, whilst AP2 had

Two views of the MPS version of the Roadster unveiled to the public in autumn 2001. It is hoped that this stunning, high performance model can be seen in Mazda showrooms in the very near future.

smaller skirts and mudguards). Otherwise, all the leading features remained the same, with prices starting at $21,280 (plus delivery charges) for the base model. Coachwork colours included Pure

At the 2002 Tokyo Auto Salon the Mazda organisation pulled out all the stops. This special brochure, produced by Car Top, gives a good idea of the key exhibits on the company stand. From the top: the Mazdaspeed version of the new Atenza, the RX-7 R-Spec (winner of the 2001-2002 RJC 'Special Award'), Roadster NR-A, Mazdaspeed Roadster MPS, the Cosmo 21 and the RS Coupé.

White, Brilliant Black, Classic Red, Midnight Blue Mica, Sunlight Silver Metallic, Emerald Mica, and Crystal Blue Metallic.

In Britain, all cars gained ABS brakes and power door locks for the 2002 season. However, in a bid to make the MX-5 more competitive, while the 1.6i remained at £14,995 on the road, the list prices of 1.8 litre cars were reduced by £500. The 1.8i was now £15,495, with the top-of-the-range 1.8i Sport priced at £17,495.

Stop Press

Just before this second edition was finalised, more special cars were launched in Japan. The 1600SP-based MV Limited, announced in December 2001, featured attractive Titanium Grey Metallic paintwork, maroon leather interior (with matching hood cover), new five-spoke, 15-inch alloys, a two-tone Nardi steering wheel, a leather gearknob, aluminium coloured air vents, centre panel and shaft plate, and stainless treadplates; manual cars also came with aluminium pedals. Restricted to just 300 units, it was priced at 2,098,000 yen in five-speed guise, or 2,148,000 yen with automatic transmission.

A sister car was duly launched in the UK during the spring, known as the Phoenix MX-5 SE. Featuring the same Sienna Brown (maroon) seats and Titanium Grey paintwork (although Black was also available in Britain), 15-inch alloys and interior modifications, it was limited

速さを楽しむ正統派スポーツセオリー

編集：(株)交通タイムス社 CARTOP編集部
発行：(株)アルテークス
〒164-0012 東京都中野区本町1-13-13
Tel.03-3372-8585 Fax.03-3372-8585
HP：www.artex.co.jp ℡：info@artex.co.jp

CARトップ

POWERFUL CAR MAGAZINE

Atenza A-spec.×RX-7 R-spec.×ROADSTER NR-A×ROADSTER MPS clubman×Cosmo21×RS Coupe

マツダDNAに昂る

TOKYO AUTO SALON 特集

to 1500 units and priced at £15,995 in 1.6 litre guise, or £16,595 for the 1.8 (the metallic paint was classed as a £150 option).

Mazda had a massive stand at the 2002 Tokyo Auto Salon, which saw the debut of several important concept vehicles, including a Roadster-based (though rotary powered) Cosmo replica, the RS Coupé, and a silver Roadster MPS with Mazdaspeed badging. The Cosmo 21 and RS Coupé were developed by Mazda's so-called M'zIF subsidiary (under the watchful eye of Shigenori Fukuda), and built by Mazda Sangyo. The RS Coupé is, perhaps, the most interesting of the two, as it stands more chance of being seen in the showrooms. Speaking to the author, Fukuda-san said it was designed to "encompass styling cues from the entire Ford family." The front does hint strongly at the RX-8, the tail is definitely Aston Martin-like, and there are shades of Jaguar in there, too.

The Mazdaspeed Roadster MPS featured an open body, strengthened by a roll-over cage, a substantial front strut bar, and the same underbody bracing as that on the Tokyo Show coupé. With a 185bhp version of the 1.8 litre four linked to a six-speed gearbox, it had the performance to back up its aggressive looks; a sporty, purposeful interior, deep airdam, separate headlights, flared wheelarches, various cut-outs in the panels, a rear spoiler, 7J x 17 OZ alloys shod with 215/40 rubber, and twin exhaust pipes (a Tachibana trademark) exiting from the centre of the rear valance.

Mention should be made of the beautifully prepared engine bay, with its carbonfibre-type air filter housing and radiator granish, a black crackle finish on the cam cover, and polished exhausts - a true piece of automotive sculpture. Maximum power was produced at 7000rpm, incidentally, with 133lbft of peak torque coming in at 6000rpm.

APPENDIX

Production figures

The figures below are taken from official Mazda records. The table shows production figures and the number of cars exported in each year; running totals for both have been added in. Given the short production life of the model, the state of the world economy, and sports car sales in general, these figures are very impressive.

Year	Production	Cumulative Totals	Exports	Cumulative Exports
1988	12	12	0	0
1989	45,266	45,278	34,021	34,021
1990	95,640	140,918	67,400	101,421
1991	63,434	204,352	40,729	142,150
1992	52,712	257,064	34,096	176,246
1993	44,743	301,807	27,909	204,155
1994	39,623	341,430	29,079	233,234
1995	31,886	373,316	27,648	260,882
1996	33,610	406,926	29,231	290,113
1997	27,037	433,963	22,856	312,969
1998	58,682	492,645	48,352	361,321
1999	44,851	537,496	41,380	402,701
2000	47,496	584,992	41,674	444,375

Also from Veloce Publishing -

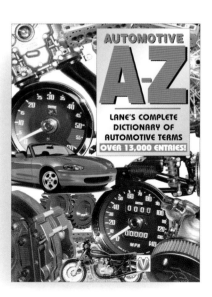

For more information on these or any of our titles, visit our website:

www.veloce.co.uk

or call 0044 (0)1305 260068

for a free catalogue.

INDEX

The Mazda Motor Corporation, its subsidiaries and products are mentioned throughout the book.